# Dialect Matters

Based on Peter Trudgill's weekly column in the *Eastern Daily Press* newspaper, this book has two overall messages. The first is that language is a fascinating and enjoyable phenomenon, which not enough people know enough about. The second is that we should not discriminate negatively against individuals and groups because of their accent, dialect or ~nguage. ~ prejudice, known as "linguicism", is more public ted than racism and sexism, as is "prescriptivism t anguage or language variety as "better" than an~ ing and accessible style, Trudgill's columns support ~. of ordinary people. Exploring topics such as nonstandard versus standard dialects; vernacular (every-day) language as opposed to purist and politically correct language; informal vocabulary as opposed to business-school jargon; and minority versus majority languages, they will appeal to a wide audience. Each article is also accompanied by notes designed for students and those who are unfamiliar with the East Anglian setting.

PETER TRUDGILL is a theoretical dialectologist and sociolinguist, who has held professorships at the Universities of Reading, Essex, Lausanne and Fribourg. He is currently Professor of Sociolinguistics at the University of Agder, Kristiansand, Norway, and Honorary Professor of Sociolinguistics at the University of East Anglia, Norwich, England. He is a Fellow of the British Academy, and has been awarded honorary doctorates by the University of Uppsala, Sweden, the University of East Anglia and La Trobe University, Melbourne, Australia. He has authored and edited more than forty books, including *Sociolinguistics: An Introduction*, *Dialects in Contact*, *New-dialect Formation: The Inevitability of Colonial Englishes*, *Investigations in Sociohistorical Linguistics: Stories of Colonisation and Contact* (Cambridge) and *Sociolinguistic Typology: Social Determinants of Linguistic Complexity*.

# Dialect Matters
## Respecting Vernacular Language
### Columns from the *Eastern Daily Press*

PETER TRUDGILL
*University of Agder, Norway*

Pen and ink drawings by John Trudgill (1916–1986)

CAMBRIDGE
UNIVERSITY PRESS

# CAMBRIDGE
## UNIVERSITY PRESS

University Printing House, Cambridge CB2 8BS, United Kingdom

Cambridge University Press is part of the University of Cambridge.

It furthers the University's mission by disseminating knowledge in the pursuit of education, learning and research at the highest international levels of excellence.

www.cambridge.org
Information on this title: www.cambridge.org/9781107571457

First published 2016

Printed in the United States of America by Sheridan Books, Inc.

*A catalogue record for this publication is available from the British Library*

*Library of Congress Cataloguing in Publication data*
Trudgill, Peter, author. | Trudgill, John, 1916–1986, illustrator.
Dialect Matters : respecting vernacular language : Columns from the Eastern Daily Press / Peter Trudgill ; Pen and ink drawings by John Trudgill (1916–1986).
Cambridge : Cambridge University Press, [2016] | Reprinted from the Eastern Daily Press, of Norwich, England.
LCCN 2015041123| ISBN 9781107130470 (hardback) | ISBN 9781107571457 (paperback)
LCSH: English language – Dialects – England. | English language – Dialects – Social aspects. | English language – Dialects – Periodicals. | English language – Provincialisms – England. | Language change – England. | BISAC: LANGUAGE ARTS & DISCIPLINES / Linguistics / General.
LCC PE1711 .T67 2016 | DDC 427–dc23
LC record available at http://lccn.loc.gov/2015041123

ISBN 978-1-107-13047-0 Hardback
ISBN 978-1-107-57145-7 Paperback

In memory of my vernacular-speaking grandparents, Jane Fish, George Gooch, May Carver and George Trudgill

## The principle of error correction

"A scientist who becomes aware of a widespread idea or social practice with important consequences that is invalidated by her/his own data is obligated to bring this error to the attention of the widest possible audience."

## The principle of the debt incurred

"An investigator who has obtained linguistic data from members of a speech community has an obligation to use the knowledge based on that data for the benefit of the community when it has the need of it."

William Labov (1982) "Objectivity and commitment in linguistic science", *Language in Society* 11: 165–201

## The principle of linguistic gratuity

"Investigators who have obtained linguistic data from members of a speech community should actively pursue positive ways in which they can return linguistic favors to the community."

Walt Wolfram (1998) "Scrutinising linguistic gratuity: a view from the field", *Journal of Sociolinguistics* 2: 271–9

# Contents

# Foreword

Since 2012, I have been writing a weekly column on language and dialect for the *Eastern Daily Press*, the daily newspaper printed and published in the city of Norwich, which is in the county of Norfolk, in eastern England. The *EDP* is the biggest-selling regional morning newspaper in England, with a circulation of over 40,000, apparently implying a readership of over 100,000. It is the only newspaper in the country which outsells the tabloid newspaper *The Sun* in its circulation area, which consists of Norfolk, northern Suffolk and eastern Cambridgeshire.

This book is a collation of the first three years or so of my columns, which have been annotated and edited for this volume. The columns were obviously aimed first and foremost at a readership based in the circulation area, and so there are frequent references to the local dialects of East Anglia and to other regional features such as place-names. Some local knowledge on the part of the readership was assumed, so in this book *Background notes* have been added to many of the columns for the benefit of those readers who do not have this local knowledge. The *Background notes* to many of the columns also contain explanations aimed at readers from outside Britain, to help with any references to British places, people, institutions and history which may not be entirely clear to them.

All the columns are about language in some shape or form and contain linguistic information with, I hope, insights which will also be of interest to university students and teachers of linguistics, as well as to high-school English Language teachers and their classes. For the benefit of such readers, most of the columns in this book also have attached to them some brief *Linguistic notes* of a more technical nature, which general readers need not bother with unless they want to achieve a more academic understanding of the issues involved.

This book has two basic overall messages. The first is that language is a mysterious and fascinating and enjoyable phenomenon which not enough people know enough about: most of us can get great pleasure from finding out more about this most fundamental of human attributes.

The second message is one of anti-prescriptivism, anti-linguicism and respect for demotic linguistic practices. *Prescriptivism* is a form of negativity which is so widely accepted in the English-speaking world that it is taken by many people to be axiomatic. Prescriptivists believe that there is only one way in which English "ought" to be spoken and written, and that any deviation from this is "ignorant" or "wrong". If you ask them what is their justification for claiming, for instance, that it is "wrong" to say *I done it*, they may well answer that "everybody knows" that it is. In this book, I try to show that this is not so; and I try to oppose such negative attitudes, which are sadly held even by many highly educated and otherwise thoughtful people, by proposing that we cultivate a positivity towards the multifarious ways in which English is spoken around the world.

By the term *linguicism* I refer to a phenomenon which is, in its way, every bit as pernicious as racism and sexism, and which is these days more publicly and shamelessly demonstrated than those other evil phenomena now are: linguicism consists of negative sentiments towards, and discrimination against, individuals and groups of human beings because of their accent, dialect or native language. My columns are intended to support and argue in favour of the language of ordinary people, in terms of nonstandard dialects versus standard dialects; vernacular usage as opposed to puristic and politically correct language; everyday vocabulary as opposed to business-school jargon; and minority languages versus majority languages.

I am very grateful to the *Eastern Daily Press* for granting me a platform for arguing the case against prescriptivism and the evil of linguicism, as well as giving me the opportunity to try to show that language is an extraordinarily interesting and thrilling phenomenon, especially when we do our best to think about it analytically, and positively, without preconceptions and prejudice. I hope that readers of the book will also think that the columns are enjoyable and informative, and that they will find them as interesting and entertaining as many of the readers of the newspaper have been kind enough to let me know that they have found them. Nothing is more important to human beings than language; and I hope that in these columns I have succeeded, at least to an extent, in illustrating the degree to which languages and dialects – all languages and dialects – are not only worthy of respect and preservation but, as fascinating creations of human societies and of the human mind, are also highly rewarding and pleasing to discover more about.

# Acknowledgements

I am very grateful to all the Peters at the *Eastern Daily Press* – Pete Waters, Peter Hannam, Pete Kelley – and especially to my current editor Trevor Heaton for their help with the publication in their newspaper of the columns on which this book is based. Very many thanks also go to Keith Skipper, Ted Peachment, Rosemary Cooper and Ashley Grey at FOND (Friends of Norfolk Dialect) for their help and advice.

I am also indebted to the following people who have very kindly helped me with research towards the writing of the columns, as well as with ideas and advice: Dr Enam Al-Wer, Prof. Lars-Gunnar Andersson, Bernhard Bamberger, Prof. David Britain, Neil Brummage, Prof. Andy Butcher, Tom Carver, Prof. Magdalena Charzynska-Wojcik, Dr Jan Chromý, David Clayton, Prof. Piotr Gąsiorowski, Carol Geddes, Marta Gruszecka, Prof. Ian Hancock, Prof. Ernst Håkon Jahr, Prof. Mark Janse, Prof. Brian Joseph, Prof. Geoffrey Khan, Prof. Agnieszka Kielkiewicz-Janowiak, David King, Dr Jacob King, Dr Stephen Laker, Prof. Eva Lehečková, Dr Mary Macmaster, Prof. Hans Frede Nielsen, Prof. Jan-Ola Östmann, Dr Lynn Preston, Janet Rees, Dr Ian Roe, Dr Alexander Rumble, Prof. John Sandford, Prof. Jürg Schwyter, Prof. Barbara Seidlhofer, Janet Smith, D. J. Taylor, Dr Stephen Trudgill, Prof. Wim Vandenbussche, Dr David Willis, Dr David Woodman and Angela Wynne. I am sure I have forgotten others who I ought to thank – I apologise, and thank them too. And special thanks go also to Prof. Lars-Gunnar Andersson, Arne Kjell Foldvik and Prof. Elizabeth Gordon, who showed the way in their own newspaper columns in Sweden, Norway and New Zealand respectively.

Last but most: I am extremely grateful to my wife Jean Hannah, who advised on, read, helped with and edited every single one of these columns, and this book.

Elm Hill

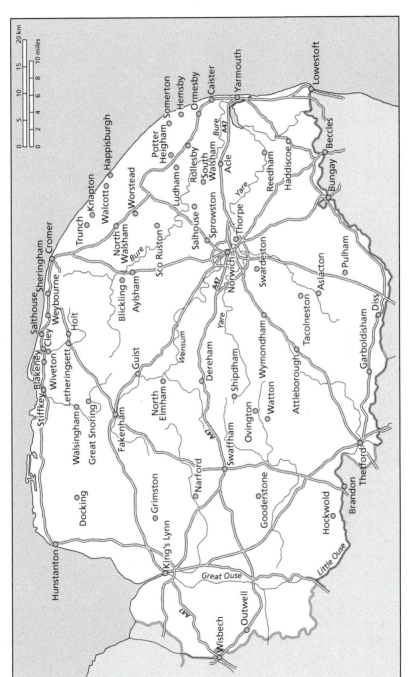

Norfolk

# Themes

I often refer in these columns to the following local Norfolk themes and topics.

**Norwich City Football Club** makes frequent appearances: the club and the team are supported in the *EDP* circulation area by very many more than the 27,000 or so spectators who turn out to watch them at every home game at the **Carrow Road** ground, and who represent just the tip of the iceberg when it comes to local interest and concern about how "City" are getting on. I mention **Norwich Market** rather often: this is said to be the largest permanent open-air market in England (it runs six days a week), and has been on the present site, in the heart of the city, since the eleventh century; I always think of the market as being the heart of working-class Norwich. See www.visitnorwich.co.uk/shopping/shops/listing/norwich-market.

**Radio Norfolk** also makes several appearances: this is our local BBC Radio Station, one of the most successful in England, with a weekly listenership of about 200,000.

FOND is the **Friends of Norfolk Dialect** organisation, which was founded in 1999, with Keith Skipper as one of the prime movers: the society is dedicated to conserving and recording Norfolk's priceless linguistic heritage, to engendering positive attitudes to the dialect and to keeping the dialect alive. See www.norfolk dialect.com/index.htm.

The **"Boy John" letters**, which are cited a number of times, were written to and published in the *EDP* between 1946 and 1958. Sidney Grapes, their author, was the proprietor of a bicycle shop, later a garage and motor business, in Potter Heigham, in the Broads area of eastern Norfolk. In the years before World War II, he acquired a reputation as an amateur Norfolk dialect comedian, performing at social functions in many parts of the county and on the radio. His highly entertaining letters appeared in the newspaper at irregular intervals – Grapes would simply write them when he felt like it – and they were always signed "The Boy John". They are a work of not a little genius, and are a brilliant and accurate representation of the Norfolk dialect of his time.

**Thorpe** is the eastern Norwich suburb where I was born and grew up. See http://en.wikipedia.org/wiki/Thorpe_St_Andrew.

**Jarrold & Sons Ltd** is the local family firm where my father and mother both worked. Jarrolds have a large department store in central Norwich, which was where my parents were both working when they met – I still always shop there out of gratitude (though not only for that reason!). And the firm used to have a highly successful printing works, plus a publishing department which my father became manager of in the late 1940s. See http://en.wikipedia.org/wiki/The_Jarrold_Group. The company were always very good to my father and to our family, and I am very grateful to them.

The admonition to **"do different"**, which turns up frequently in these pieces, is traditional in Norfolk, and has been made the official motto of the University of East Anglia in Norwich.

# 1 History: how things came to be this way

This section of the book is devoted to pieces which offer glimpses into the history of the English language: in Norwich, in Norfolk, in East Anglia and in Britain generally. The section starts, however, where English also started, on the European mainland; and the Prologue takes us even further back into our remote Eurasian Indo-European past.

## Prologue: Sir William Jones and his revolution

About 230 years ago, Sir William Jones made an amazing intellectual break-through. He was a gifted learner of languages, and by an early age he had mastered Greek, Latin, Hebrew and Arabic. He had even translated Persian into French. In 1783, arriving in Calcutta where he had been appointed as a judge, he started learning Sanskrit, the ancient classical language of northern India – one of the first Britons to do so.

He was astonished by what he found. Could it just be a coincidence that the Latin word *pater*, Greek *patér* and Sanskrit *pitár* all meant 'father'; and that Latin *frater*, Ancient Greek *phrater* and Sanskrit *bhratar* all meant 'brother'? After all, Sanskrit had been spoken 3,500 miles from Italy, where Latin had been spoken. The similarities, however, were undeniable, especially in the grammar: for example, Latin *est* ('it is') was *asti* in Sanskrit, *sumus* ('we are') was *smas*, and *sunt* ('they are') was *santi*.

In a famous lecture, Jones argued there was "a stronger affinity" between Sanskrit, Latin and Greek "than could possibly have been produced by accident". Others had also noticed this, but Jones' breakthrough was to state that the affinity was so strong that no linguist could examine the three languages "without believing them to have sprung from some common source, which, perhaps, no longer exists".

That was the big new idea: that there had been an earlier parent language *which had since disappeared*. Previously, scholars had misguidedly wondered which of the world's existing languages had been the "first" language – Hebrew was often mentioned. But Jones argued that the only way to explain these affinities, over such a large geographical area, was to assume that there had once been a language which had gradually turned into Latin, Greek and Sanskrit – and Celtic, Iranian and

Germanic – just as Latin itself had changed into the Romance languages Italian, Spanish, Rumanian and French; and just as Sanskrit had turned into the vernacular north Indian languages – Sanskrit had ceased to be spoken as a native language around 500 BC and morphed into languages like Hindi, Punjabi, Gujerati and Bengali.

From Irish in the west to Bengali in the east, from Icelandic in the north to Maldivian in the south, the languages of most of Europe and much of west and south Asia developed over time out of that same single source, which has now not existed for 5,000 years. Today we call it Indo-European.

Sir William died in 1794, aged only 41. But he revolutionised our way of thinking about language history.

## LINGUISTIC NOTES

- Irish or Irish Gaelic is the indigenous language of Ireland. It is a member of the Celtic branch of the Indo-European language family. The other Celtic languages are Scottish Gaelic, Manx, Welsh, Cornish and Breton. Irish is an endangered language, with perhaps 30,000 native speakers, although the numbers are disputed, not least because of the rather large numbers of speakers in Ireland who have learnt Irish as a second language.
- Bengali, which is the main language of Bangladesh as well as of the Indian state of West Bengal, is one of the descendants of Sanskrit. It has about 220 million native speakers, and is one of the biggest languages in the world. It is a member of the Indo-Aryan sub-branch of the Indo-Iranian branch of the Indo-European language family. The other main Indo-Aryan languages are Hindi-Urdu, Punjabi, Marathi, Gujerati, Sindhi, Nepali, Assamese and Sinhalese (the majority language in Sri Lanka/Ceylon). The Gypsy language Romany is also an Indo-Aryan language (see 1.10).
- Icelandic is, like English, a member of the Germanic branch of Indo-European. It has about the same number of native speakers as Maldivian.
- Maldivian, the language of the Maldive Islands in the Indian Ocean, is another Indo-Aryan language. It is also known as Dhivehi, and is rather closely related to Sinhalese. It has about 350,000 native speakers.
- The geographical spread of the Indo-European language family can be judged from the fact that Ireland and Bangladesh are about 5,000 miles or 8,000 kilometres apart, and the distance from the Icelandic capital of Reykjavik to Malé, the largest city in the Maldives, is about 6,000 miles or 9,500 kilometres.

## 1.1  Our ancestors across the sea

I am sitting at my laptop, in the county of Norfolk, about 17 miles or 30 kilometres from the North Sea, writing about English, in English. That is a very new thing to be able to do. I do not mean because laptops are a recent invention; and I do not mean because people of relatively humble origins like me have only recently known how to write, although both of those things are true. What I mean is that the English language itself is very recent. Human language is probably about 200,000 years old; but English has not been around for even 1 per cent of that time.

Five thousand years ago there was no such language as English, not even here in Norfolk which, I reckon, is where English was born. But there is an important respect in which the language I am writing in did already exist then: there actually was a language which *became* English. Five thousand years ago, the language-which-became-English was not spoken anywhere in Britain. You would have had to travel eastwards from Norfolk at least 500 miles (800 kms) across the North Sea to hear the forerunner of modern English being spoken. Around 2500 BC, the linguistic ancestors of modern English speakers were living in southern Scandinavia – in southern Sweden and on the Danish islands in the region where Copenhagen and Malmö are today.

During the millennia since, the language they spoke there has changed so much, as languages do, that if we could hear it today it would be unrecognisable and incomprehensible. But the English dialect I grew up speaking in Norfolk, on the other side of the North Sea, really is a direct descendant of that ancient language of southern Scandinavia, a descendant passed down directly from one generation to another over many centuries.

We have no idea what name the speakers of that language had for it – if it had a name at all – but today linguists call it Proto-Germanic. Two hundred generations later, my native language is called English by its speakers; but there is a direct line of transmission from the one language to the other. Proto-Germanic no longer exists, but it has not died out. It has simply become transformed, over the millennia, into English – and also Dutch, Afrikaans, Frisian, German, Yiddish, Swedish, Danish, Norwegian, Icelandic and Faroese, the sister languages of English in the Germanic language family.

It is very hard to imagine what the lives of our linguistic ancestors 200 generations back were like. But we owe them our language. If they hadn't spoken like that, we wouldn't be speaking – and writing – like this.

### BACKGROUND NOTES

*The city of Norwich, where I wrote this, lies about 17 miles / 30 kms from the east coast of the county of Norfolk in eastern England, which is in turn about 120 miles / 200 kms across the North Sea from the west coast of the Netherlands, and 340 miles / 540 kms from the west coast of Denmark.*

## LINGUISTIC NOTES

- How long human language as we know it today has existed is a question we do not really know the answer to. Evans suggests that language dates back to "long before" 150,000 years ago; see Nicholas Evans (2010) *Dying Words: Endangered Languages and What They Have to Tell Us*, Oxford: Blackwell, 14.
- The suggestion that English was "born" in Norfolk is a little bit cheeky, but the earliest and densest patterns of Anglo-Saxon settlement do seem to be focussed on Norfolk, and on Kent and Sussex; see Peter Trudgill (2014) "The spread of English", in M. Filppula, D. Sharma & J. Klemola (eds.), *The Oxford Handbook of World Englishes,* Oxford University Press.
- Proto-Germanic is generally dated from about 2500 BC. to 500 BC. It later divided into West Germanic; North Germanic, which was ancestral to the Scandinavian languages; and East Germanic, which developed into the languages of the Burgundians, the Vandals and the Goths, including the Visigoths who ended up in Spain. There is some indication that a form of Gothic survived in the Crimea until the eighteenth century; see http://en.wikipedia.org/wiki/Crimean_Gothic – but there are no East Germanic languages surviving today.

## 1.2 The oldest English word

The Norwich Castle Museum has been hosting a fascinating exhibition on the Roman Empire, including items from the Middle East and North Africa, as well as Europe. Amongst the European materials, there are displays from Walsingham, Hockwold and Hoxne – the Romans were here in East Anglia, too, for over 350 years.

How did we get on with these Romans who came over here, invading our country? Maybe "we" is not the right word. The people who lived in Norfolk when the Romans arrived were not English-speaking. They were the Iceni, Celts who spoke a language we now call Brittonic, which was the ancestor of Welsh, Cornish and Breton. Famously, to start with, the two groups got on very badly indeed; and the Iceni queen Boudica led a brave but ultimately doomed revolt against the Romans.

Not surprisingly, though, after centuries of increasingly peaceful contact with the Romans, the Brittonic language acquired many Latin words from them, as we can see in Modern Welsh words like *pont* 'bridge' and *llafur* 'labour'. But in much of Roman Europe, the linguistic consequences were much greater. The Celts in Portugal, Spain, France and Italy, under the influence of Roman culture, gradually abandoned their native tongues altogether and shifted to Latin.

Why did that not happen here? Well – it did! As the Roman legions were pulling out of Norfolk in AD 410, perhaps most of the Celts walking around the streets of Venta Icenorum (Caistor St Edmund) would have been speaking Latin: many of them would have actually been bilingual in Latin and Celtic, just as the Celts were in France.

Linguists believe that the dialect of Latin which was spoken here in southern England would eventually have ended up being very like Old French. Norfolk would have gone from being, if you like, Welsh speaking to being French speaking.

So what stopped this happening? Well, *we* did – depending once again on who you mean by "we". Our linguistic ancestors, the Anglo-Saxons, sailed across the North Sea to these shores, and subsequently came to dominate the Romano-Celts politically, culturally and linguistically. They brought with them the Germanic language which eventually became English. The very oldest word of written English ever discovered anywhere was found engraved on a bone in the Anglo-Saxon graveyard in Caistor. It reads RAIHAN 'roe deer'.

You can see that in the Castle Museum too.

## BACKGROUND NOTES

*Norwich Castle was built by the Normans on the orders of William the Conqueror, in the aftermath of the 1066 invasion. It now contains the Norwich Castle Museum, which houses permanent local art, natural history, archaeological and other exhibits, as well as temporary presentations such as the 2014 exhibition on the Roman Empire.*

*Walsingham and Hockwold are villages in, respectively, the northwest and southwest of the county of Norfolk, while Hoxne is in Suffolk.*

*Caistor St Edmund is a village just to the south of Norwich. The remains of the Roman town, which was constructed in the aftermath of Boudica's revolt in AD 60, are just outside the village. A local saying has it that "Caistor was a city when Norwich was none – Norwich was built with Caistor stone." The later Anglo-Saxon graveyard is on a hill nearby.*

## LINGUISTIC NOTES

– A form of Celtic was the first Indo-European language to arrive in Britain and, at the time of the Roman invasion of England in AD 43, it was spoken over all or at least most of our island in the specifically British form of Brittonic (also called Brythonic).

*cont.*

- The modern Welsh words *pont* 'bridge', and *llafur* 'labour' descend from Latin *pontem* (the accusative case of *pons*) and *labor* respectively, and can be compared to French *pont* 'bridge' and *labeur* 'toil, labour'.
- The *Icenorum* in Venta Icenorum is the Latin genitive plural of Iceni, so 'of the Iceni'. *Venta* is a Brittonic word which probably meant something like 'market' or 'meeting place'. It appears in Modern Welsh in the place-name Gwent – *Cas-gwent* is the Welsh name for Chepstow.
- The word *Caistor* was borrowed into Old English from Latin *castra*, singular *castrum*, which originally referred to a Roman military encampment. Caister-on-Sea in Norfolk has the same origin, as do many other English place-names such as Chester, Winchester, Leicester, Lancaster.
- The suggestion that colloquial Latin as spoken in southern England would have ended up very like Old French, if it had survived, is due to Peter Schrijver (2009) "Celtic influence on Old English: phonological and phonetic evidence", *English Language and Linguistics* 13.2: 193–211.
- The raihan inscription is written using an early form of the Germanic runic alphabet. It has been dated to the early AD 400s. It is thought that the deer bone which it was written on may have been used as part of some kind of game; see David & Hilary Crystal (2013) *Wordsmiths and Warriors: The English-Language Tourist's Guide to Britain,* Oxford University Press.

## 1.3 Ouse

You might be familiar with the well-known Scottish song which goes "Campbeltown Loch, I wish you were whisky". If we translate this into East Anglian terms, I suppose there might be some *EDP* readers who would not object at all if the Great Ouse, or even the Little Ouse, flowed with whisky as well. What they might not know, however, is that there is an interesting connection between the names of those rivers and the name of the drink.

Whisky is an alcoholic beverage which we owe to our Gaelic neighbours in Ireland and in northern and western Scotland. The English word *whisky* is an abbreviated version of an older form *whiskybae*, which was an anglicised form of the Gaelic term *uisge-beatha*.

Irish and Scottish Gaelic were once the same language – the Hebrides and the Scottish Highlands were originally settled by Gaels from Ireland. In both forms of Gaelic, *uisge-beatha* means 'water of life', which would originally have been a translation of Latin *acqua vitae*, like the French *eau de vie*.

The second part of *uisge-beatha* comes from Old Irish *bethu* 'life', which is related to the Greek root *bio-*, which we have borrowed into English in words like *biology* and *biography*. (Linguists talk about languages "borrowing" words from others, even though there is no intention of giving them back.)

The first part comes from Old Irish *uisce* 'water', which is from the ancient Celtic root *utso*, later *usso*. This is also where *Ouse* comes from – there are several rivers with this name in Britain.

In fact, many river names in England are, like the Ouse, pre-English in origin, deriving from the Celtic language of the peoples who inhabited Britain before the arrival of our Germanic ancestors.

*Thames* was Celtic for 'dark river'. *Yare* is Brittonic Celtic, perhaps meaning something like 'babbling river'. *Avon* is simply the Brittonic word for 'river' – in modern Welsh it's *Afon*. We can imagine Saxon incomers pointing to a river, asking its name, and the local Celts assuming they were just asking what their general word for a river was. So River Avon means 'river river'!

River Ouse means 'river water': one possible scenario in our part of the world is that newly arrived Angles heard native Celts referring to the water in the Ouse as *usso* and wrongly thought that was the name of the river. *Usso* later became *Uss*, and then *Uus* or *Ouse*.

So, even if the Ouse isn't whisky, *Ouse* and the *whis* part of whisky were originally the same word.

---

**BACKGROUND NOTES**

*The Little Ouse forms the western end of the southern boundary of Norfolk. It flows from east to west, and runs into the (Great) Ouse along the western boundary of the county. The Yare is the river that rises in central Norfolk, runs along the southern edge of Norwich, and reaches the sea at (Great) Yarmouth. There are several rivers called Avon in Britain.*

---

## 1.4 Detective work: our ethnic background

We were told at school that the Germanic invaders who crossed the North Sea to Britain in the fifth century were the Angles and Saxons. The Saxons, who came from northwest Germany, settled in Essex, Middlesex, Sussex and Wessex. The Angles, who were from southern Jutland, dominated everywhere else, including Norfolk and Suffolk – thus "East Anglia".

If anyone doubted the truth of what our teachers said, it can be demonstrated rather nicely through a little bit of linguistic detective work on our local place-names. Think about the Suffolk village called Saxham, near Bury St Edmunds. This name meant 'the home of the Saxons'. That might seem to contradict what we were told at school, but of course it doesn't. The village was called that because there was something unusual in Suffolk about being a Saxon. Everyone else was an Angle! Because there was nothing distinctive about being an Angle in Norfolk or Suffolk, we have no place-names with 'Angle' as an element. Where you do find such names is in Wessex. Englefield, in Berkshire, means the 'field of the Angles', which tells you very clearly that everybody else round there was a Saxon.

But East Anglia did have something of an ethnic mix – there were not just Angles and Saxons here. We also had Frisians, who made it over to England from their homeland along the Dutch/Belgian coast. We can see this from the Suffolk village names Friston and Freston, 'the village of the Frisians'. There were also other Germanic tribes hanging around. Swabia today is the part of Germany around Stuttgart, but the Swabian tribe spread far and wide in those days: the name of our Norfolk town of Swaffham meant 'the home of the Swabians'. Flempton in Suffolk, also near Bury, indicates the presence of Flemings, who had come from areas just inland from the Frisians.

As another part of this fascinating ethno-linguistic mix, East Anglia also had plenty of survivors from the original Celtic population. On the Norfolk coast, just across the sea from the Frisian homeland, is the village of Walcott, which in Old English meant 'the cottage of the Welsh'.

So Celts, Angles, Saxons, Frisians, Flemings, Swabians – there was a rich mix of peoples in early East Anglia. With such a diverse gene pool in our ancestry – not forgetting the Danes who came along later – it is no surprise that the native people of modern Norfolk and Suffolk are such a fine bunch.

## BACKGROUND NOTES

*The names Essex, Middlesex, Sussex and Wessex are derived from the geographical labels for the East Saxon, Middle Saxon, South Saxon and West Saxon kingdoms. The first three are now names of traditional English counties (and their cricket teams). Wessex was never a county but is the name of a region which is generally held to consist of Hampshire, Wiltshire, Berkshire, Dorset and Somerset, plus southern Gloucestershire and Oxfordshire, corresponding roughly to the limits of the Anglo-Saxon kingdom of Wessex: Alfred the Great was King of Wessex from 871 to 899.*

**LINGUISTIC NOTES**

- The Angles, Saxons and Frisians were all speakers of West Germanic dialects that are generally grouped together under the heading of North Sea Germanic or Ingvaeonian, and from which English, Scots, Frisian and Low German are descended. The other West Germanic groupings were Weser-Rhine Germanic or Istvaeonic, which gave rise the language of the Franks, and later on to Dutch and related German dialects; and Elbe Germanic or Irmionian, which produced modern High German as well as the ancient language of the Lombards.

## 1.5 Anglo-Saxon kingdoms and "the Sheres"

In a piece I wrote for the *Eastern Daily Press* a while ago, I used the expression "the Sheres", but the editors cut it out and it did not appear in print. I do not know why they did that, but I wonder if it was because they did not know what it meant. *Sheres* or *Sheers* is our way of referring to that part of the outside world which lies immediately beyond East Anglia.

If you have never heard the expression before, you can still work out where it comes from. The names of some English counties always have *shire* (pronounced "sheer") at the end: Yorkshire, Berkshire. Others sometimes do and sometimes don't: Somerset(shire), Devon(shire). And others never do: Sussex, Surrey. The names of the East Anglian counties of Norfolk, Suffolk and Essex are never followed by the suffix *shire*.

East Anglia is surrounded on three sides by the North Sea and the River Thames, and on the other side by counties whose names end in *shire*. If you leave East Anglia by land, you inevitably do so via Lincolnshire, Cambridgeshire or Hertfordshire; and beyond those counties again you come to Huntingdonshire, Northamptonshire and Bedfordshire. So if you are brave enough to decide that you really do want to leave East Anglia, however briefly, you have no choice but do so through the Sheres.

Perhaps when we speak this way we are reminding ourselves that until AD 870, East Anglia was a separate kingdom in its own right, alongside Anglo-Saxon Northumbria, Mercia and Wessex. If that is what we are doing, though, it is not quite right. Our kingdom was bordered by the River Cam and the River Stour and never included Essex, which was a separate, rather minor kingdom. The people of Essex were Saxons – East Saxons. We – the North Folk and the South Folk – were Angles.

But then, over the centuries, East Anglia annexed Essex through its dialect: Essex became part of linguistic East Anglia, as much influenced by the speech of the East Anglian capital Norwich as by the speech of the national capital London. Norfolk and Suffolk people traditionally said *he go, she swim, that do* and did not drop their *h*'s; and traditionally that was true of Essex too.

So if you want to be sure of hearing local dialect speakers say *he goes, she swims, it does*, you will have to pluck up your courage and cross over the border into Mercia, or as we say today, the Sheres.

---

## BACKGROUND NOTES

*Modern East Anglia is a region which everybody in England knows about but which has no official status. It is the same kind of area as the English Midlands or the American Midwest. Everyone agrees that the counties of Norfolk and Suffolk are prototypically East Anglian, although some would argue about the inclusion of the Fenland areas of the western part of the region; and I have treated modern Essex in this piece as East Anglian as well. Many other people, on the other hand, would extend the boundaries to include Cambridgeshire or at least eastern Cambridgeshire, which used to be part of the ancient Anglo-Saxon East Anglian kingdom; and some would extend the boundaries even further than that.*

*For much of its length, the River Stour forms the boundary between Suffolk to the north and Essex to the south. It flows eastwards out into the North Sea, with its estuary lying between the Suffolk port of Felixstowe and the Essex port of Harwich. The River Cam flows through the modern city of Cambridge.*

---

## LINGUISTIC NOTES

- *Shire* was the original English word for county, with *county* being of French origin and meaning 'area controlled by a count': the modern French word is *comté*. (A *sheriff* was originally a 'shire-reeve', where *reeve* meant a king's officer.) As a lexeme in its own right, *shire* is pronounced so as to rhyme with *fire*, but in county names *shire* rhymes with *fear*, hence "the Sheres".
- Grammatical forms such as *he go, she swim, that do* are referred to as demonstrating third-person singular (present-tense) zero. This feature is referred to a number of times in this book.

## 1.6 The Great Heathen Army

My great-grandfather Henry Trudgill came from a south Norfolk village which, about 1,150 years ago, was the scene of a dramatic and probably rather traumatic event.

We know about this from the name of the village itself, Aslacton. In Norfolk, most of our place-names are Anglo-Saxon. They are composed of elements made up of Old English words such as *ham* 'homestead' and *ton* 'enclosure'. You can see this in names like Walsham and Runton, where the first elements come from names of Anglian leaders like Walh and Runi.

Norfolk also has some names of Scandinavian origin. These use elements made up of words from the Old Norse language of the later Viking colonisers, such as *by* 'settlement'. They include names like Scratby and Mautby, where the first elements are from the names of Danish leaders like Skrauti and Malti. Research suggests that these Scandinavian place-names are often found in locations which were less readily habitable than those which had already been taken by the Angles, who had got there first.

But there are a few names which have a more complicated history and which indicate that the Danes did not always settle on virgin territory. These are names which end in an Old English element like *ton*, but begin with a leader's name which was not English but Norse. Aslacton is one of these: Aslak was, and still is, a Scandinavian man's name.

These hybrid names came about because of the Great Heathen Army, as the Anglo-Saxons fearfully called it. That was how our Anglian ancestors referred to the very large Viking army which landed on the East Anglian coast in 865, intent on conquering the Anglo-Saxon kingdoms. The army spent their first winter at Thetford, in southwestern Norfolk, and then marched north to take control of York. But in 869 they returned, and defeated and killed the East Anglian king, Edmund. The invaders then remained in control of East Anglia for fifty years, until it was retaken by the English in 918.

After they had seized East Anglia, the men of the Great Heathen Army shared out the land which they now had under their control between them. After four centuries of Anglian ownership, the south Norfolk village which was later to be my great-grandfather's home fell to the Vikings. And its dispossessed English Christian population came under the rule of alien warriors led by a pagan called Aslak.

The inhabitants of the village we now call Aslacton were probably not very happy.

---

**BACKGROUND NOTES**

*Aslacton is about 15 miles / 25 kms south-southwest of Norwich.*

**LINGUISTIC NOTES**

- The North Germanic language of around AD 800 is often referred to as Old Norse. Most of the Great Heathen Army were from Denmark and spoke the form of Old Norse called Old Danish. The modern North Germanic or Scandinavian languages are Icelandic, Faroese, Norwegian, Swedish and Danish.
- Place-names like Aslacton are often called "Grimston hybrids". There are a number of places called Grimston in England, including one in Norfolk: Grimr was, like Aslak, a man's name in Old Norse.

## 1.7 Danes and Angles in the swamps

The far east of Norfolk must have been the scene of very considerable ethnic and linguistic contact, and maybe even conflict, a thousand or so years ago. It is well known that in the ninth century there was very heavy Viking Scandinavian settlement on the island of Flegg by the North Sea coast of Norfolk. The names Filby, Mautby, Ormsby, Scratby, Stokesby, Ashby, Oby, Thrigby, Herringby, Billockby, Clippesby, Hemsby and Rollesby all have the Old Norse ending *by* 'village/settlement', corresponding to modern Danish *by* 'town'. Flegg itself was an Old Danish word referring to a swampy, boggy area overgrown with marsh-plants such as flag iris.

But the Old Danish speakers in Flegg Hundred were surrounded by people who spoke Old English. (*Hundred* was the old Germanic label for a subdivision of a county, which was in official use until 1894.) To the north of Flegg Hundred was Happing, an Anglo-Saxon name meaning the followers of a man called Hæp (as also in Happisburgh), dating back to an Anglo-Saxon settlement which had been there for 400 years before the Vikings arrived. And Flegg's other neighbour across the River Bure, Walsham Hundred, also had an English-language name: it meant the *ham* (modern *home*) or homestead of an Anglian leader called Walh.

But the Scandinavians did not even have Flegg all to themselves. There must have been an ethnic dividing line across the area, because immediately to the north of Hemsby, Rollesby and Ashby there are places with names like Bastwick, Martham and Somerton. Place-names ending in *ham, ton* (modern *town*) and *wick* go back to the original Anglo-Saxon settlement of our county; so in the north there were English speakers, with Norse speakers on their southern flank.

But we cannot be certain about the actual location of the language boundary. Repps, in the Danish–English borderlands between Bastwick and Ashby by the

River Thurne, is thought by some experts to be an English name deriving from the Anglo-Saxon word *ripel*, meaning 'a strip of land'. But others maintain that it is from Old Danish *rep*, meaning 'community'.

The River Thurne is also linguistically ambiguous. The river is named after the village of Thurne. That name, according to experts, comes either from Old English *thyrne*, meaning 'thorn bush' – or from Old Norse *thyrnir* meaning, well, 'thorn bush'. The two languages were not that very different in many respects. It is very likely that someone from Bastwick and someone from Ashby, coming across each other as they quanted around the marsh, would have been able to talk to each other without too much difficulty.

Let's hope it was a friendly conversation.

**BACKGROUND NOTES**

*Flegg is now no longer an island but an area of higher ground surrounded by marshland.*

*"Quanting" is the same as punting, propelling a boat by pushing on the bottom of a waterway with a long pole or "quant"; see 11.7.*

**LINGUISTIC NOTES**

– The extent to which Old English and Old Norse were mutually intelligible in the ninth, tenth and eleventh centuries is a controversial, interesting and important topic. For a good discussion, see Matthew Townend (2002) *Language and History in Viking Age England: Linguistic Relations between Speakers of Old Norse and Old English*, Turnhout: Brepols.

## 1.8 The "saint" and the poet

A long time ago, I was a pupil at St Williams Primary School, on St Williams Way in Thorpe. Next door to the school was the place where I first became interested in languages, St Williams Way Library, with its wonderfully helpful librarian Janet Smith; and opposite the library was the field where my friends and I loved playing football and cricket.

It is rather sad for me, therefore, that St William himself is something of an embarrassment. As far as we know, there was nothing particularly saintly about William. He was just an unfortunate 12-year-old boy who was murdered in 1144; his body was found on Mousehold Heath by a Henry de Sprowston.

A chapel dedicated to William was built on Mousehold, and the ruined foundations are still visible. In the old days they were hard to find, but my grandfather knew how to get there and took me to see them. Grandad explained that William had been turned into a revered martyr through anti-Jewish racism. There was a belief that Jews carried out ritual murders of Christian children – "the blood libel" – and Norwich citizens falsely accused the local Jews of killing William. This was the same terrible bigotry which led to the slaughter of Jews in Norwich in 1190, and to the total expulsion of the Jews from England by King Edward I in 1290.

William was an English boy who spoke English. The Jews, who had arrived in England with William the Conqueror in 1066, spoke French, like the brutal Norman overlords and King Edward himself; so they were set apart from the English by their language as well as their religion, which no doubt added to the hostility directed towards them.

The Jews also knew Hebrew, which they used as their language of religion and literature. It should be a matter of pride for us that a famous mediaeval Hebrew poet lived in the city, probably in the area by the Haymarket; he is known as Meir ben Elijah of Norwich. But he was never revered by the citizens, and he was expelled with the rest of the Jews in 1290.

Now, though, we have made some atonement for this: his works have recently been translated and published in Norwich as *Into the Light: The mediaeval Hebrew poetry of Meir of Norwich*. I can't help thinking that it would have been much less embarrassing if my school had been named after Meir rather than the unfortunate "saint" William.

---

**BACKGROUND NOTES**

*Primary schools in England, at the time when I was a pupil, catered for children aged 5–11. Mousehold Heath is an elevated – by Norfolk standards – heath and woodland enclave which is now entirely contained within the boundary of Norwich. It was formerly very much bigger; see* http://en.wikipedia.org/wiki/Mousehold_Heath. *The Meir of Norwich reference is: Keiron Pim (ed.) (2013)* Into the Light: The Mediaeval Hebrew Poetry of Meir of Norwich, *Norwich: East Publishing.*

---

**LINGUISTIC NOTES**

– By the twelfth century, the dialect of French spoken in England had become a distinctive variety, often known as Anglo-Norman. This was a Norman French variety with an admixture of other northern French dialects, such as Picard, which had over the generations become significantly differentiated from continental Norman; see Richard Ingham (2012) *The Transmission of Anglo-Norman: Language History and Language Acquisition*, Amsterdam: Benjamins.

## 1.9 Those Normans and their handwriting

There are things to be grateful to the Normans for – Norwich Cathedral, for a start. But they did cause us many problems when they first arrived in 1066, and they are still causing us problems.

Here is one example. The normal way of representing the short u sound in English is with the letter *u*, as in *cup, up, butter*. But, mysteriously, there are some words where we do not use a *u* and spell the sound with an *o* instead: *above, come, dove, honey, London, love, monk, some, son, wonder* . . .

Why on earth do we do that? For children learning to read, and for foreigners learning our language, this is a problem. How are you supposed to know that *on* is "on" but *son* is "sun"?

To explain this strange state of affairs, we can look at the spelling used by our Anglo-Saxon forebears, before the Norman Conquest. Their orthography was much more sensible than our modern spelling. In Old English, *above* was spelt <abufan>, *come* was <cuman>, *dove* <dufe>, *honey* <hunig>, *London* <Lunden>, *love* <lufu>, *monk* <munuc>, *some* <sum>, *son* <sunu> and *wonder* <wundor>.

So why did the Normans start messing things up by abandoning this perfectly sensible Anglo-Saxon system and starting to use a letter which normally stood for the short *o* sound as in *on* to stand for the short *u* sound as in *son*?

The clue comes from noting that, in each of the words I have listed, the letter *o* comes before an *m*, *v* or *n*. The Norman scribes used a system of joined-up handwriting where, if you had too many *u*'s and *v*'s and *m*'s and *n*'s together, you could not tell where one letter stopped and another one started. If the kind people at the *EDP* will print the nonsense word *umunuvum* for me, you will be able to see the breaks between the letters; but if you imagine how it would look in certain styles of handwriting, you can work out what the problem would have been. By writing *o* instead of *u*, the scribes made it possible to see where the divisions between the vowel and the preceding and following consonants were located, and that made texts easier to read even if it made the spelling more difficult.

Because this *o* spelling is ambiguous and misleading, problems are occurring today with some place-names, because non-local people come along and are, well, misled. Ovington near Watton was, in Anglo-Saxon times, the settlement (*tūn*) of the people (*ing*) of a man called Ufa; the village name used to be spelt Uvington and was pronounced with the short *u*. But these days, I am told, there are people who call it "Ovvington" with the *lot* vowel. Blame the Normans.

**BACKGROUND NOTES**

*Watton is a market town about 20 miles / 32 kms west of Norwich.*

**LINGUISTIC NOTES**

- The convention in linguistics is that forms cited in < > indicate spellings rather than sounds.
- It is by no means just Norfolk place-names which are affected in this way. The form *Bromwich* as it occurs in the name of West Bromwich in the English West Midlands is now generally pronounced with the short *o* vowel, but was originally pronounced /brʌmɪdʒ/ or, in the local accent, /brʊmɪdʒ/, the etymological origin being *brōm-wic*, a *wic* ('settlement') where the shrub *broom* grew.
- Surnames are also affected: *Compton* originally had the short *u* vowel, but many speakers now pronounce it with the short *o*. And it is not just names, either: *covert*, originally pronounced like *cover* with a *t* on the end, is now often pronounced to rhyme with *overt*. For more on spelling pronunciations, see 14.2.
- Words with the original Anglo-Saxon spelling <wu> were also affected in the same way, e.g. *worry, worm, wort, wonder*.

## 1.10 There's likewise a wind on the heath

"There's night and day, brother, both sweet things; sun, moon, and stars, all sweet things; there's likewise a wind on the heath. Life is very sweet, brother; who would wish to die?"

These are the famous words attributed by George Borrow to the Gypsy character Jasper Petulengro in his autobiographical novel *Lavengro: The Scholar, the Gypsy, the Priest,* published in 1851. As is well known in this part of the world, the conversation between the novel's protagonist, no doubt a version of Borrow himself, and Petulengro, in real life called Ambrose Smith, took place on Mousehold Heath.

Borrow was born in Dereham and, like Nelson, went to Norwich Grammar School. At one time he lived on Willow Lane in Norwich. He was good at learning languages, though how well he acquired them we do not really know. One of the languages he learnt, perhaps on Mousehold itself, was Romany, the language of the Gypsies. Romany is in origin a language from northwestern India, quite closely related to Hindi/Urdu and Punjabi, but it has been transformed as a result of contact with other languages as the Gypsies migrated over the centuries through Afghanistan, Iran, the Middle East and the Balkans into Western Europe.

Quite a lot of words have been borrowed into English from the Romany language. *Lollypop* and *lolly* meaning 'money' are Gypsy words; so are *pal* and *cosh* 'bludgeon'; and *moosh*, as a disrespectful form of address used to a man, comes from the Romany word for 'man'.

Strictly speaking, though, many of these words have come into English not from Romany itself, but from Anglo-Romany. This is an in-group form of language which employs English pronunciation and English grammar but uses Romany words. It is still spoken by many Romany people in this country and in North America, and is sometimes used as an "anti-language", which is a language designed to prevent other people from understanding what you are saying.

Our Norfolk speech owes something to the language of the Gypsies, who probably arrived here in the late Middle Ages. The dialect word *cooshie* 'a sweet' is probably a Romany word. And so is the word *rum* 'strange'. This is a peculiarly British word – Americans often do not know what it means – and it has nothing to do with rum, the drink. It comes from the Romany word *rom*, which meant 'man', and in English originally meant 'exceptionally good'. Then it gradually came to mean 'exceptional', and now it means 'odd'.

Where would we be in Norfolk if we were not able, from time to time, to exclaim: *'Ass a rumm'n!*

## BACKGROUND NOTES

*George Borrow (1803–81) was a novelist and writer of travel books. In addition to* Lavengro, *he is best known for* The Romany Rye *(another autobiographical work about his relationship with Gypsies),* The Bible in Spain *and* Wild Wales.

*Dereham is a town about 15 miles / 25 kms to the west of Norwich. In some official contexts it is called East Dereham to distinguish it from the village of Dereham in the Fenland area of western Norfolk.*

*On Nelson, see 1.13.*

*'Ass a rumm'n!" [= That's a rum one] is a well-known jocular East Anglian phrase meaning 'That's strange/unusual . . . '.*

## LINGUISTIC NOTES

 – Romany or Romani is a language that appears to be most closely related to Central Indo-Aryan languages such as Hindi, and to Northwestern Indo-Aryan languages like Punjabi. It is thought to have left the Indian sub-continent around AD 1000, and has been greatly influenced by the languages it came into contact with as the Gypsies migrated westwards, notably Greek.

*cont.*

- Anglo-Romany, which is also called Pogadi, is one of a group of mixed Gypsy languages known to linguists as Para-Romani. Others include Scandoromani, as spoken in Sweden, and Caló in Spain. For more on Anglo-Romany, see Peter Bakker (2000) "The genesis of Angloromani", in T. Acton (ed.) *Scholarship and the Gypsy Struggle: Commitment in Romani Studies,* Hatfield: University of Hertfordshire Press, 14–31; Ian Hancock (1984) "Romani and Angloromani", in P. Trudgill (ed.) *Language in the British Isles,* Cambridge University Press, 367–83; Yaron Matras, H. Gardner, C. Jones & V. Schulman (2007) "Angloromani: a different kind of language?", *Anthropological Linguistics* 49: 142–84.
- For more on anti-languages, see 4.9.

## 1.11 Germanic tribes in Grandad's kitchen

The Proto-Germanic noun *thwahila* has done a lot of travelling over the last 2,500 years.

Proto-Germanic was our ancestral language: it was spoken in and around southern Sweden about 500 BC. The language had a verb *thwahan,* meaning to wash, and *thwahila* was derived from that. It referred to anything used for washing things, like a washcloth.

As the Germanic people gradually moved south into Germany and Holland over the next few centuries, they took their word with them. And when, much later, some Germanic tribes moved even further south during the sixth century AD, they took the word with them again. As the Lombards moved into northern Italy, the Visigoths into Spain and the Franks into France, the local Latin-derived Romance languages borrowed the word from them. It survives today as Italian *tovaglia,* meaning 'cloth', and Spanish *toalla* 'towel'; in Old French it was *touaille.*

During the 1100s, after the Norman Conquest, *touaille* was borrowed across the English Channel into Mediaeval English, to give us our modern word *towel.* (English had lost the original Germanic word during the Anglo-Saxon period, but now got it back again because of the Norman invasion!)

While all that borrowing was going in southern Europe, the original word also stayed where it was, in the north. It had morphed into *dwahila* in Old High German, as spoken in southern Germany between AD 500 and 1000; and later we see it in mediaeval Dutch in the form of *dweile.*

Eventually it crossed the sea once again; this time it was the North Sea that was crossed, in the direction of East Anglia. The *English Dialect Dictionary* shows that the word never made it any further west than eastern Cambridgeshire. Perhaps it came with the Strangers, the Dutch-speaking refugees who formed an important part of the Norwich population in the early 1600s.

*Thwahila* arrived here, of course, in the form of *dwile*, the well-known Norfolk-Suffolk word for a floorcloth or dishcloth. In his 1830 book *The Vocabulary of East Anglia*, the Rev. Forby wrote that in the Norfolk dialect of the late 1700s, a *dwile* was "a refuse lock of wool" or "a mop made of them" or "any coarse rubbing rug".

So after two and half millennia of travelling, that ancient Germanic word from southern Sweden ended up, twice over, in my grandparents' kitchen in New Catton. My grandfather called the new spin-dryer "a terl in a tin" – he pronounced *towel* as "terl" – and of course there was a dwile in that kitchen as well.

---

**BACKGROUND NOTES**

On the Germanic migrations, see http://en.wikipedia.org/wiki/Migration_Period.

New Catton is a northern area of Norwich just outside the mediaeval city walls. It grew up in the late nineteenth and early twentieth century, filling in the area between the original old Norwich and the village of Catton, which is now officially called Old Catton.

On the Strangers, see below 1.12.

---

**LINGUISTIC NOTES**

– The spelling <terl> is intended to represent the pronunciation /tɜːl/. I assume that this form reflects the results of "smoothing" (J. C. Wells's term; see 13.5) of an earlier pronunciation /tʉːəl/, where the stressed vowel resembles the vowel in the original French *touaille*. This perhaps indicates a borrowing or re-borrowing into Norwich English which occurred later than in mainstream varieties of English, where Old French /uː/ had become Modern English /au/ as a result of the Great Vowel Shift. A later borrowing into Norwich English – maybe even from the French-speaking Walloon Strangers – which post-dated the Vowel Shift would account for this distinctive form, with the /uː/ remaining undiphthongised.

## 1.12 Refugees and asylum seekers

In the last ten years or so, the population of Norwich has increased rapidly and enormously. Amazingly, there are now about 60 per cent more people than there used to be.

This sudden dramatic increase has not been the result of exceptionally high fertility on the part of young Norwich couples; and it is not due to a sudden influx of people from rural areas around the city either. It is all down to immigration.

Forty per cent of the population of the city are now refugees and asylum seekers who have arrived from overseas. These immigrants do not look very different from Norfolk people; and they are Protestant Christians – but they do not speak English. If you walk down St Benedicts or St Giles, you are almost as likely to hear people speaking Flemish or French as you are Norfolk English.

The immigrants have arrived in their hundreds from places like Antwerp, Ghent, Bruges and Lille, escaping from their Spanish Catholic persecutors, executioners and torturers. They are all foreigners – or "Strangers" as they are called in sixteenth-century English – for this is the late 1500s we're talking about.

It is interesting to try and imagine what it must have been like here in the city after the arrival of the Strangers. Overcrowded, certainly; and multilingual. How did people communicate? Did the Strangers already know some English? Were the Walloon French speakers able to speak Dutch to the Flemings? Could the Flemish people speak French? Did the indigenous Norwich people pick up any Dutch?

Norwich remained a trilingual city for at least 200 years: French and Dutch were used in the city well into the 1700s. Many of us must have ancestors who came from the Low Countries, so surely this must have had some effect on our local dialect? *Dwile* 'dishcloth, floorcloth', an English word used only in East Anglia, is certainly the same as the Dutch word *dweil*; and *lucam*, a weaver's long attic window, is from French *lucarne*. What else?

Visitors to our city often wonder why, when London has Leicester Square, Grosvenor Square and Langham Place, Norwich has Palace Plain, St Andrew's Plain, Bank Plain, St George's Plain . . . I was recently invited to go to Belgium, to the Royal Flemish Academy in Ghent, to talk about the influence of Flemish on East Anglian English. Around the corner from my hotel was an open area called Sint Veerleplein, 'Saint Veerle's Plain'.

You can be sure I mentioned that.

## BACKGROUND NOTES

*The historical background to the arrival of the refugees was the Revolt of the Spanish Netherlands, in which the inhabitants of the Low Countries rebelled against Catholic Spanish rule and the repression of their Protestantism. In 1567, King Philip of Spain sent the Duke of Alva with an army of 20,000 Spaniards to the Low Countries to quell this anti-Spanish, anti-Catholic revolt. Many prominent people were executed, estates were confiscated and opposition was ruthlessly suppressed. Penal edicts against "heresy" led to persecution and torture of Protestants: see Frank Meeres (2012)* Strangers: A History of Norwich's Incomers, *Norwich: HEART (Norwich Heritage Economic and Regeneration Trust).*

*St Benedicts Street and St Giles Street, like other ancient Norwich streets named after churches dedicated to particular saints, are normally referred to locally without the word* Street – St Andrews *rather than* St Andrews Street *(see also 14.13).*

*For more on* dwile, *see below 11.6.*

## LINGUISTIC NOTES

- The words *strange* and *stranger* were borrowed into English from French during the 1200s and originally meant 'from elsewhere, unknown'. The meaning 'peculiar, unusual, unexpected' developed only about a hundred years later. The modern French word *étranger* still means 'foreign, foreigner, abroad' as well as 'strange'.
- The refugees discussed here were mostly from what is today Belgium, and were mostly speakers of dialects of Flemish. Today Flemish is often, though not totally uncontroversially, regarded as a variety of Dutch. There were also many Walloons, who were speakers of Romance dialects often regarded as varieties of French; and even some speakers of Franconian dialects of German from Lorraine, which is now part of France.
- I have argued that the lengthy trilingual period which Norwich went through is in part responsible for the absence of third-person present-tense singular -s in East Anglian English dialect verb forms, as in *he go, she run*; see Peter Trudgill (1996) "Language contact and inherent variability: the absence of hypercorrection in East Anglian present-tense verb forms", in J. Klemola, M. Kytö & M. Rissanen (eds.), *Speech Past and Present: Studies in English Dialectology in Memory of Ossi Ihalainen*, Frankfurt: Peter Lang, 412–25; and Peter Trudgill (1998) "Third-person singular zero: African American vernacular English, East Anglian dialects and Spanish persecution in the Low Countries", *Folia Linguistica Historica* 18.1–2: 139–48.

Strangers Hall

## 1.13 Revolt and rebellion

The national census shows that Norwich is the least religious place in the United Kingdom, 43 per cent of us professing to have no religion at all compared to the national average of 25 per cent. According to a leader that appeared in the newspaper after these figures came out, the *EDP* finds this "rather curious". But it isn't really. Norfolk people are admonished to "do different". We don't much like to conform to what other people think is normal. When our team were bottom of the third flight of English football, stubborn Norfolk supporters still turned up a Carrow Road in their many thousands. In the old days, Norwich was known as the place where large numbers of women went to the pub, although that was not respectable elsewhere. And as the Rev. Robert Forby wrote in his 1830 book, "we so stubbornly maintain that the first and third person are of the same form, 'I love, he love'" in our dialect.

Norfolk has always been rather oppositional. Kett's famous rebellion is honoured in the names of pubs and streets – and one rather steep hill in Norwich. During the Civil War, Norfolk opposed the Royalist establishment and supported the insurrectionary forces of the Parliament. And like Nelson, Norfolkman that he was, disobeying orders at Copenhagen, we do not much like being told what to do. Our Horatio did not actually say "Doon't you come along hair with none-a that ol' squit", but that was probably what he was thinking. "You can allus tell a Norfolkman, but y' can't tell 'm much" is an old joke, but a true one.

Usually, though, it has been the city people of Norwich itself who have "done different" the most. The farm labourers of East Anglia were the subject of a book called *The Deferential Worker*. My country grandfather believed in "salut'n" – touching his forelock to the boss; but my city grandmother lay down on the tram lines during the General Strike of 1926 and stopped the public-schoolboy strike-breakers from driving through.

Norwich rebelliousness goes back to the 1272 attack on the French-speaking clerics at the Cathedral by the English-speaking citizens: buildings were burnt down, monks killed, and the priory sacked. It is said that citizens fired burning arrows into the priory precinct from the tower of St George Tombland church on Princes Street. And maybe the sixteenth-century influx of nonconformist Flemish-speaking Strangers from the Low Countries helped to maintain this oppositional mindset. Perhaps centuries of being the underdog, number two city to London's number one helped too. If London did the one thing, we did the other. Even today when Norfolk and the whole United Kingdom are governed by the Conservatives, Norwich does not have a single Conservative councillor.

In the 1600s, rebelliousness meant being pious, anti-Royalist, religious believers, and that is what the citizens of Norwich were.

Now it doesn't, and they're not.

## BACKGROUND NOTES

*The percentage figures referred to here are from the UK census results of 2011.*

*Carrow Road is the location, and therefore also the name, of the Norwich City football ground.*

*Kett's Rebellion was a revolt against land enclosures which took place in 1549. It was led by Robert Kett, a farmer from the Wymondham area of Norfolk to the southwest of Norwich; see http://en.wikipedia.org/wiki/Kett%27s_Rebellion.*

*Lord Horatio Nelson, Admiral of the Royal Navy, was the commander of the victorious British fleet at the Battle of Trafalgar in 1809. There is a probably apocryphal story that, at the Battle of Copenhagen against Napoleon's Danish–Norwegian allies, he failed to see a signal ordering him to retreat because he deliberately held his telescope to his blind eye. Nelson was born and brought up in Burnham Thorpe, Norfolk.*

*The book on farm labourers is Howard Newby (1977)* The Deferential Worker: A Study of Farm Workers in East Anglia, *Harmondsworth: Penguin.*

## LINGUISTIC NOTES

– The Forby reference is to Robert Forby (1830) *The Vocabulary of East Anglia,* London.
– The spelling <hair> for *here* is intended to indicate the pronunciation /hɛ:/ – the NEAR and SQUARE vowels are merged in the Norfolk dialect area. (For more on NEAR, SQUARE and other key words for John Wells's lexical sets, see J. C. Wells (1982) *Accents of English*, Cambridge University Press.)
– *Squit* is a dialect word meaning 'nonsense' (see 11.6). *Allus* is 'always'.

# 2 Prescriptivism and other useless pastimes

This section deals with prescriptivism – the idea that some forms of language are "correct" and others are "wrong". This view is propagated by people who feel that they have some kind of entitlement to prescribe how other people should speak and write – which is most often how they speak and write themselves. They feel – quite unjustifiably – that they have some kind of authority which enables them to instruct the rest of us that certain of the grammatical forms which are used by ordinary people in their everyday lives are "incorrect".

Prescriptivism in English has usually been levelled at three different types of grammatical phenomenon. First, prescriptivists dislike nonstandard dialects: they believe that nonstandard grammatical forms like *I done it* are "wrong" even though they are used by a majority of English speakers around the world. Secondly, they object to normal Standard English forms which are at odds with the grammar of Latin, such as *It's me* and *I've got a new car I'm very pleased with* – prescriptivists think we should say *It is I* and *I've got a new car with which I am very pleased*. And, thirdly, they protest about new forms and usages: in the 1970s, prescriptivists railed against the new usage of *hopefully* as a sentence adverbial as in *hopefully it won't rain today*; now nearly everybody says this. Prescriptivism is based on a false premise, and it is a waste of time: it does not work, and all it succeeds in doing is making speakers and writers insecure and inarticulate.

Anyone wanting to read more about informed, rational and analytical arguments against prescriptivism might like to look at the *Language Log*, which comes out of the University of Pennsylvania http://languagelog.ldc.upenn.edu/nll/, and in particular at the category called "Prescriptivist Poppycock".

## 2.1 Against uniformity

If you mention to English-speaking people that there are two versions of the past tense of the verb *to light*, some of them are likely to want to know which one is right. Is it wrong to say *I lighted the fire*, or is it a mistake to say *I lit the fire*?

I have a different question. Why does one of them have to be wrong and one of them right? How about: they are both right? Why can't they both be perfectly legitimate alternatives? Americans say *sidewalk* and we say *pavement*, but we do not claim that we are right and they are wrong, do we? It would be foolish if we did. Variation in language is normal. We should accept this for the fascinating fact that it is, and not keep trying to make judgements about "correctness".

But we cannot blame people if they are worried about whether to say *burnt* or *burned*. They have been made nervous about it by their schoolteachers; and you cannot blame the teachers either. They were made nervous about whether they should say *in the circumstances* or *under the circumstances* by the people who taught them. For the last 300 years, we have been browbeaten by a gang of interfering pedants who think they know how to speak our language better than we do, even if we have been speaking it all our lives!

Their problem is that they are offended by variation. Alternatives make them uneasy. It must be some kind of neurosis they are suffering from: variability upsets their sense of order, perhaps.

They try and deal with this uneasiness by employing one of two strategies. One is to announce that all the variants except one are "wrong". Well, we didn't authorise them to tell us what was right and wrong, did we?

Their other strategy is to claim that, if there are two variants, then they must mean different things. American pedants are even worse at this than ours are. Believe it or not, they have invented a *further–farther* rule. They declare that *further down the road* is wrong because – well, I won't bore you with the details, it's not worth it.

Let's worry about something important – there are children starving out there. If anyone wants to know which is right out of *this is different from that, this is different to that* or *this is different than that*, we have a good Norfolk answer for them: all on 'em.

## LINGUISTIC NOTES

– *Lighted* and *lit* have both been used for very many centuries in English as the past tense of the transitive verb *to light*. In England, *lit* has become more common, and *lighted* correspondingly less common, over the past hundred years. (In the diaries that my mother wrote during the 1930s and 1940s, she consistently wrote that she "lighted the fire"; I would have written "I lit the fire".) *Burnt* and *burned* have also both been used for centuries as the past tense of *burn*. The regular form *burned* is more common in North American English, *burnt* in the English of the British Isles; see Peter Trudgill & Jean Hannah (2008) *International English: A Guide to Varieties of Standard English*, 5th edn, London: Hodder Arnold.

*cont.*

- Some prescriptivists suffer from the "etymological fallacy": they believe that a word ought to mean what it meant originally, especially if it has been borrowed into English from some other language (see also 7.3). *Circumstance* was originally borrowed into mediaeval English, via French, from Latin, where *circum* meant 'around' and *stare*, which our -*stance* part comes from, meant 'to stand'. Since, many centuries ago, Latin *circum* meant 'around', the pedants say that we should use **in** *the circumstances* so as to retain the sense of something being surrounded by something else. It is true that we have retained the 'around' meaning in our not very common two-part word *circumnavigate* 'to sail around'; but modern English *circumstance* is not perceived by English speakers as consisting of two parts: it is a single unit which simply means, well, 'circumstance' – which is why we naturally feel it is just as normal to use *under* as it is *in*. The American linguist Arnold Zwicky reports that a Google search gave 3,310,000 instances of *in the circumstances* and 3,980,000 of *under the circumstances*.
- An excellent and highly readable text on the subject of prescriptivism in English is: James Milroy & Lesley Milroy (2012) *Authority in Language: Investigating Standard English*, 4th edn, London: Routledge.

## 2.2 Wrong

Most of us would agree with the sentiments expressed in the title of the famous novel by the late UEA professor Malcolm Bradbury: *Eating People Is Wrong*. It is not a controversial point of view.

But this does remind us that there are different types of "wrong". First, there is the Lisbon-is-the-capital-of-Spain and 3 x 3 = 8 kind of wrong. As the *Oxford English Dictionary* says, these are wrong in the sense of "not in consonance with facts or truth; incorrect, false, mistaken". It is inherently true that Lisbon is the capital of Portugal, and that 3 x 3 = 9. If these things were not true, the world as we know it would be a very different place.

Then there is the hitting-someone-on-the-head-and-taking-their-money kind of wrong. Eating people is presumably of this second type, though even worse. This is wrong in the *OED* sense of "deviating from equity, justice, or goodness; not morally right or equitable; unjust, perverse".

Sadly, quite a lot of people also seem to think about our language in terms of right and wrong. If you say *we done it*, that is "wrong" because it "should be" *did*. But what kind of wrong is this? It is not inherently true that the past tense of *do* is *did*. It would make no difference to anything important if all English speakers said *we done it* rather than *we did it* – and in fact, most of them do already! And saying *we done it* is hardly deviating from equity, justice or goodness.

So perhaps it is the putting-your-elbows-on-the-table kind of wrong? This is what the *OED* describes as "contrary to, or at variance with, what one approves or regards as right". So basically it is wrong because, according to some people, it is not right. This does not really get us very far: who are those people, and what authority do they have to say that putting your elbows on the table, or using a grammatical form which is a natural part of the dialects spoken by millions of people, is wrong?

The fact is that, though *we done it* is not part of the Standard English dialect, it is the natural and correct form in the grammatical systems of the dialects spoken by a majority of native English speakers around the world, including our Norfolk dialect. That's not the same as wrong.

---

### BACKGROUND NOTES

*UEA is the University of East Anglia, which is on the western edge of Norwich.*
*Sir Malcolm Bradbury (1932–2000) taught at the University of East Anglia, where he became Professor of American Studies and where he started the famous MA in Creative Writing course, from 1965 to 1995.* Eating People Is Wrong *was published in 1959.*

---

## 2.3 On starting with a conjunction and ending with a preposition

When children go to school, they are taught arithmetic because they do not know arithmetic. They have French lessons because they do not know French. And teachers teach them geography because they do not know geography.

English is different. In this part of the world, children are not taught English because they do not know it. When they arrive at school, they already know English. If they didn't know English, they could not be taught arithmetic or geography – or anything. Teachers teach children to read intelligently; they teach them to write effectively; and they teach them English vocabulary. They also, I hope, teach them about the grammar of English and other languages: everyone needs to know something about grammatical categories like nouns, verbs and conjunctions.

But what else is there left for them to teach? Not much. When I went to school, they could have taught us about English dialects, or the history of our language. But they didn't. Instead they invented things to teach. They took some made-up "rules" and taught them to us. They could do that because the rules were fantasy rules. Since they were not real, we did not know them, and so the teachers could spend time telling us about them! What a foolish waste of time and energy.

One of these imaginary rules was: "You must not start a sentence with a conjunction." My response is: Why not? Who says? But an *EDP* correspondent has kindly written to query the fact that I start sentences with *and* and *but* myself, and says she believes it is important that one should not do this.

I am always genuinely grateful to people who care about language, but in this case I would like to refer her to the respected *Chicago Manual of Style* which says that this "rule" has "no historical or grammatical foundation". Conjunctions do conjoin, but they can conjoin sentences just as well as they can conjoin phrases into sentences. English conjunctions have always been used to start sentences, though we have to note that the idea of the sentence itself is a relatively new one. After all, no one speaks in sentences. The notion that a written sentence should begin with a capital letter, contain at least one verb and end with a full stop dates only from the 1600s.

Another imaginary rule we were taught at school was: "You mustn't end a sentence with a preposition." We did not know that rule either – because there is no such rule! In English a preposition has always been a good thing to end a sentence with.

---

**BACKGROUND NOTES**

This piece is, rather obviously, written from the point of view of someone living in a part of England where traditionally all children entering school have been native speakers of English. Obviously, English teachers who have non-native speakers in their classes do need to teach the basic rules of the language to such children if they can.

English speakers have always begun written sentences with conjunctions, and it is a total myth that this practice should be avoided. You can confirm this by picking up more or less any book, including those written by our most distinguished authors. Just one example: "And even Mary could assure her family that she had no disinclination for it." – from Jane Austen's Pride and Prejudice.

---

**LINGUISTIC NOTES**

– The notion that it is "wrong" to end a sentence with a preposition comes from the historical inferiority complex that some English speakers felt with respect to the Latin language where, as for the most part also in modern French, it was not possible for prepositions to end sentences.

## 2.4 Grammar questions for an expert

Dear Mr Gove,

I have seen in our local newspaper, the *Eastern Daily Press*, that you are keen on testing children in our schools on their knowledge of the rules of English grammar. I think this is a good idea. Grammar is an important subject. I am rather worried, though, as there are a number of grammatical rules which I am not too sure about myself. I would be very grateful if you – I suppose you are very much an expert on the subject? – could explain them to me. If children are going to be tested about rules, it would be good if adults were in a position to help them and answer any questions they might have.

Here are some of the things I am worried about. It is correct grammar to say *a big new red house* but not *a red new big house* or *a new red big house*. I think I am right, aren't it? But why is that exactly? What is the rule?

It is also true, I think, that according to the rules of English grammar the negative of *you may* is *you may not*, but the negative of *you write* is not *you write not*. Why is this? What is the rule? It seems rather odd. Has it got anything to do with the fact that the interrogative of *you write* is *do you write?*, but the interrogative of *you may* is not *do you may?* I would be glad to have the rule explained, please.

It is correct, too, to say *I know him very well* but not to say *I am knowing him very well*. Can you please tell me why this is? And another mysterious thing is: you can say *I turned the light out* and *I turned out the light*; but, while you can say *I asked my friend out*, you can't say *I asked out my friend*. There must be a rule there. But what is it? How does that work?

I also notice that it is good grammar to say *I like, you like, we like, they like* but not *she like*. Why not? You are supposed to say *she likes*. But what is the point of that *s* there? In Norfolk we don't bother with it, but perhaps we should? Is it important? If so, why is that?

All of your expert opinions will be very gratefully received.

Yours sincerely,

Puzzled of Norwich

---

### BACKGROUND NOTES

*Michael Gove is a Scottish Conservative politician who was the Secretary of State for Education in the British Government – though strictly speaking with responsibility only for England – from 2010 to 2014. He was often criticised by the National Association of Head Teachers, who accused him of producing a climate of bullying, fear and intimidation. Their conference passed a vote of no confidence in his policies, as did the three other teachers' unions.*

## LINGUISTIC NOTES

- The rules for the ordering of adjectives in English are very complex. They are discussed at some length in Randolph Quirk, Sidney Greenbaum, Geoffrey Leech & Jan Svartvik (1985) *A Comprehensive Grammar of the English Language*, London: Longman, sections 17.113ff. A less technical account can be found at http://learnenglish .britishcouncil.org/en/english-grammar/adjectives/order-adjectives.
- The answer to the second question posed in this piece has to do with *do*-support, which refers to the grammatical requirement in English for negation and interrogation involving full verbs like *write, go, make* to be performed through the usage of the auxiliary verb *do*. Modal verbs such as *may, can, will* do not have this requirement; see the Quirk *et al.* grammar, sections 2.49, 3.37; and 6.1 in this book.
- For the third question, see below, 3.10.

## 2.5 Aren't there any rules?

"So aren't there any rules?" someone has asked me. They were referring to my writing in these columns that there is no reason why you should not end a sentence with a preposition – *She's someone I'm very fond of* is a perfectly good, grammatical English sentence. And to my maintaining that there is no reason why you should not begin a sentence with a conjunction like *and* or *but* – as in the case of this sentence, which is also perfectly grammatical. And that there is no reason why you should not say *The man who I saw* – it does not have to be *whom*.

But, people say, "we were always taught" that there are these rules. Yes, we were always taught these things; but what we were taught was wrong. There is a very good reason why 2 x 2 = 5 is incorrect. But there is no reason why putting a preposition at the end of a sentence in English is wrong. This is just a "rule" which someone who had no authority to do so simply invented.

But, yes, there really are rules – lots of them, and they are rather strict. We were just not "always taught" these at school because, by the time we were four years old, we knew them already.

Here is a very strict rule of English grammar: always put an adjective before a noun, not after it. It is right to say *the huge car* and wrong to say *the car huge*. People learning English as a foreign language are "always taught" that, but no one taught us this rule: we worked it out for ourselves, without realising we were doing so, as small children. And we figured out all the other rules about English adjectives too – like how it is correct to say *the huge new black car* and not *the black new huge car*.

Here is another rule: stative verbs should not be used with the progressive aspect. You didn't realise you knew that? Well, all it means is that it is right to say *I need this* and wrong to say *I am needing this*, which would be breaking a real rule of English grammar. People learning English as a foreign language have trouble with that one.

Rules can vary as between one dialect and another too. In the Norfolk dialect, it is wrong to say *He was a-hitten it* and right to say *He was a-hitten on it*. And no one taught us that either.

**LINGUISTIC NOTES**

– Further grammatical rules of English are illustrated in 2.9.

## 2.6 *Fewer* and *less*

In a light-hearted column in the *EDP*, new grandfather Paul Durrant came to some entertaining decisions about what role he could play in the new baby's life. A couple of his decisions, though, seemed a bit questionable to me. First, Paul wants to make sure his grandson will be able to recite the names of the West Bromwich Albion side that won the FA Cup in 1954. Really? Surely what he actually means is the names of the Norwich City side that made it to the semi-final replay in 1959?

And he wants the little boy to know the grammatical difference between *less* and *fewer*. I think he is on to a loser there too. Paul has probably been listening to self-appointed grammar experts who reckon that *less* should apply only to singular nouns, while *fewer* applies to the plural: *less cheese, less water, less time, less money*; but *fewer biscuits, fewer drinks, fewer minutes, fewer coins*.

*Less of it*, they say, but *fewer of them*. But millions of people do actually say *less biscuits, less drinks*. English-speaking people have always done that, ever since the time of King Alfred. The *"less–fewer* rule" was invented at the end of the eighteenth century by someone who had nothing better to do; so I do not think we can be at all surprised if normal English-speaking people say *less drinks*. It has been normal in English for a millennium and a half.

And, anyway, what these would-be grammarians tell us is that the use of *fewer* versus *less* is a purely automatic consequence of whether these words modify plural or singular nouns: plural – *fewer*; singular – *less*. That's it.

But if an alternation is totally automatic, then it is useless. It does not do any work. It does not tell you anything. It has no significance. There is no point in differentiating between the alternatives at all, so it is no surprise if people don't.

After all, what is the opposite of *less cheese*? *More cheese*.

What is the opposite of *fewer people*? *More people*.

---

**BACKGROUND NOTES**

*Norwich City is the name of the local football (soccer) club in Norwich. The team have played for 53 of the last 54 years in one of the top two divisions of the English football league. During the season 1958–9, however, when Norwich were a club with much lower status and had been a third-division side for many years, the team achieved national recognition and fame by beating many famous first-division clubs, such as Manchester United, in the English Football Association FA Cup knock-out competition, and made it to the semi-finals. No local person born before 1950 has ever forgotten the excitement and the enjoyment of it all.*

*West Bromwich Albion is a football club from the West Midlands of England.*

---

If *more* works perfectly well for both singular and plural, then *less* can do the same. If we do not need a separate word for *more* in the plural, then we don't need *fewer* either.

However, if you do prefer to say *fewer of them* – and why not, if you want to – be sure to pronounce it in the correct Norwich way. So that will be: "Fur on 'em".

**LINGUISTIC NOTES**

- The *fewer–less* "rule" is most often presented in technical works on English grammar not as a matter of plural versus singular, but as having to do with count nouns versus mass nouns. Count nouns are those which are countable, so they can be pluralised, as in *one coin, two coins*; mass nouns such as *money* cannot be pluralised – one cannot say *\*one money, two moneys*.
- For the pronunciation of *fewer* as "fur" /fɜː/ as a result of "smoothing", see 13.5.

## 2.7 Apostrophe's

Some people are very keen on apostrophes. Some people don't like apostrophes. Jeremy Clarkson doesn't like apostrophes. Some people don't like Jeremy Clarkson.

Is any of this important?

I reckon apostrophes come into the class of things which are "quite important but not as important as some people think". They play a role in distinguishing between *well* and *we'll*, *hell* and *he'll*, *shell* and *she'll*, *wed* and *we'd*, *shed* and *she'd*, *were* and *we're*, and sometimes *ill* and *I'll*. But nothing very serious will happen if you write *Im* instead of *I'm*, *hes* instead of *he's*, *theyre* instead of *they're*, *dont* instead of *don't*. Perhaps someone could confuse *cant* with *can't* if you omit the apostrophe, but I doubt it.

It is obvious that apostrophes cannot be enormously important, because we don't use them when we are speaking. Some clever journalists have written about how it is absolutely vital to get the possessive apostrophe right: people will be confused, they say, if you do not distinguish between plural *cats*, singular possessive *cat's* and plural possessive *cats'*. But that cannot be right: when we're speaking we pronounce all three exactly the same, and I don't ever remember wondering, in all my many decades as a native English speaker, whether someone was really referring to more than one cat or not.

But if you are going to use apostrophes, it is a good idea to get them right (though even the self-appointed experts don't agree about everything – are we supposed to mind our *ps* and *qs* or our *p's* and *q's*?).

For instance, writing *cat's* for *cats* is a Bad Idea; and in fact writing *cat's* when you mean *cats* is much worse than writing *cats* when you mean *cat's*. It makes it look as if you are trying hard to get things right but even so you are not clever enough to succeed. So if you advertise *cucumber's* and *cabbage's*, potential customers might just think that you are not a very successful greengrocer, either. A good rule of thumb for using apostrophes before an *s* would seem to be: if in doubt, leave them out; and if you put them in, get them right.

Often when Im sending emails, I dont use apostrophes. Im such a slow typist that anything that saves time for me is a bonus. I also expect that if I leave some out when Im writing for the *EDP*, theyll put them back in for me. Lets see.

---

## BACKGROUND NOTES

*Jeremy Clarkson is a British journalist and TV presenter, especially well known for his motoring programme* Top Gear. *He is notorious for being highly opinionated, and reactions to him on the part of the British public tend to be very polarised.*

*British greengrocers are famously but pointlessly ridiculed for misplaced apostrophes on signs advertising* cucumber's *and* cabbage's *outside their shops.*

*The* EDP *did in fact insert the apostrophes that I had omitted in the last paragraph in the version printed in the newspaper!*

## LINGUISTIC NOTES

- The current conventional wisdom about how possessive apostrophes should be used – that the non-possessive plural is *cats*, singular possessive *cat's*, and plural possessive *cats'* – was established only rather recently in the history of the writing of our language; it became fully established only in the middle of the nineteenth century. We managed pretty well without it before then.

## 2.8 Spelling-punctuation-and-grammar

The *Daily Telegraph* says that Mr Gove plans to "re-introduce" spelling-punctuation-and-grammar into our classrooms. My fellow *EDP* columnist Sharon Griffiths has also written about spelling-punctuation-and-grammar.

This rather common lumping together of these three very different aspects of writing English makes it seem as if they all hang together and are all equally important. But they are not. Punctuation is by far the most important of the three.

Writing is very deficient as a language medium compared to speech. When we are speaking, we can pause, slow down, speed up, speak more or less quietly, hesitate; and in particular we can use intonation, changing the pitch of our voice to convey all sorts of different and subtle meanings. We cannot do those things in writing, and punctuation is our way of trying to make up for this inadequacy. Think of the difference between *You're leaving today, You're leaving today!* and *You're leaving today?*

This usage of punctuation to compensate for the deficiencies of the written medium does not include apostrophes. With apostrophes, it is the other way round. The difference between *the girl's house* and *the girls' house* is a distinction which cannot be made in speech. And if we manage without the distinction when we are speaking – which we do – it is hard to argue that it is a matter of life and death in writing, though clearly it is helpful if everybody gets it right.

But commas, full stops, colons, semi-colons, dashes, quotation marks, question marks and exclamation marks are very different from apostrophes. Punctuation will never be able to bring writing up to the level of subtlety and expressiveness of the spoken word, but there are many types of writing where we should try.

Speech is more important than writing in many ways. Human beings developed speech many, many millennia before they developed writing. Most languages even today are not written down. We learn to speak effortlessly in infancy, while learning to write is much more challenging and comes much later. And according to one calculation, English speakers on average utter about 16,000 words a day – few people write that many words, not even the hard-working journalists at the *EDP*.

**BACKGROUND NOTES**

*Sydney Grapes's "Boy John" letters to the* EDP *(see* Themes) *purported to be reports of events in the Boy John's village. In addition to the Boy John – a farm worker – they featured as their main characters his Aunt Agatha, Granfar and old Mrs W, their neighbour. Most of the letters ended with a PS containing one of Aunt Agatha's aphorisms, which became famous throughout the county, such as "Aunt Agatha she say: all husbands are alike, only they have different faces so you can tell 'em apart." For the letters, see Sydney Grapes (1958)* The Boy John, *reissued 1974, Norwich: Wensum Books.*

But writing obviously enables us to preserve language and transmit it from one place to another – and from one time to another. We can still read the wonderful "Boy John" letters that Sidney Grapes wrote to the *EDP* in the 1940s and 1950s. As he himself advised: "Aunt Agatha, she say, trust no memory however bright, put it down in black and white." I reckon th' ol' Boy John put all them commas in the right place, doon't you?

**LINGUISTIC NOTES**

– For a linguistic discussion of the "Boy John" letters, see Peter Trudgill (1999) "Dedialectalisation and Norfolk dialect orthography", in I. Tavitsainen, G. Melchers & P. Pahta (eds.), *Writing in Nonstandard English*, Amsterdam: Benjamins, 323–30.

## 2.9 *Me, myself, I*

Some while ago, two interesting linguistic things happened in the *EDP* on the very same day. First, a letter-writer wrote asking what had happened to the word *me*: he reckoned people are saying *myself* instead. And, secondly, one of the *EDP* columnists wrote in their column that "it is not good form for we linguistically lazy Brits to criticise . . . ".

I agreed with the letter-writer: you can hear footballers avoiding the word *me* every Saturday around 5pm: "myself and Holty worked very well together". And I also wholeheartedly agreed about our linguistic laziness in not bothering to learn foreign languages. But I could not help observing that Norfolk speakers know that it is not good grammar to say "it's not good form for we . . . ". Obviously it should be *for us*.

Fascinatingly, these two things are linked. The letter-writer gave a clue as to how. People "with less grammar" than the Queen, he wrote, say *me and my husband*. But, actually, while it may not be polite to put yourself first, *me and my husband* is perfectly good grammar. Natural English uses *I* and *we* only as the single subject of a verb: *I like it*; *We like it*. Otherwise, we use *me* and *us*: *John likes me*: *He likes John and me*; *He likes us*; *John and me went*; *Us Norwich fans are a rum lot*. And in answer to the question: *Who's there?* we say *Me!* French is the same. You cannot reply *Je* ('I') in answer to the question *Qui est là?* ('Who is there?'); it has to be *Moi* ('Me').

Sadly, the English language has been plagued by generations of self-appointed "experts" with an inferiority complex about Latin who think English ought to have nominative (subject) and accusative (object) cases. It is "wrong", they pontificate, to say *John and me went* because *me* is accusative (it isn't!).

This clash between the grammar of natural English and the pseudo-Latin grammar of the "experts" has got people confused, and so sometimes they *hypercorrect* – they try and speak "correctly" and overdo it, using *we* when *us* would be correct, as in *for we Brits*, as the columnist did. And sometimes people are so uncertain about what to say that they develop clever escape strategies. If you do not know whether to say *I* or *me*, well, you can just say *myself* instead, and avoid the problem.

If only the self-appointed "experts" had let people feel comfortable about using the natural grammar of their own native English dialects, there would never have been a problem in the first place!

---

**BACKGROUND NOTES**

*Holty is a reference to the very popular Norwich City footballer Grant Holt, who played for the club from 2009 to 2013.*

---

**LINGUISTIC NOTES**

– Hypercorrection is a form of hyperadaptation, a process whereby native speakers of a particular accent or dialect attempt to reproduce or accommodate to another accent or dialect, whose structure they then misanalyse. Hypercorrection refers specifically to the process whereby speakers inexpertly attempt to reproduce a variety which they believe to be more "correct" than their own. A well-known example from the English of England is that of northerners who have no contrast between the vowels of FOOT and STRUT, with the FOOT vowel in both sets: in attempting to reproduce south-of-England forms, they may introduce the STRUT vowel into FOOT words as well as STRUT words. (The use of key words such as FOOT and STRUT to identify vowels and the lexical sets associated with them is due to J. C. Wells (1982) *Accents of English*, Cambridge University Press.)

*cont.*

> – The English pronouns *me, him, her, us, them* are not accusative. They are technically referred to as "oblique pronouns". They are used as direct objects: *John saw me*; indirect objects: *John gave me a book*; prepositional complements: *John did it for me*; subject complements: *It's me!*; under ellipsis: *Who's there? Me!*; and in coordinated noun phrases: *John and me went*. The only situation where the oblique pronouns cannot be used is where the pronoun is the single, non-coordinated subject of a verb: *I did it*, cf. *John and me did it*. For a full discussion, see Randolph Quirk, Sidney Greenbaum, Geoffrey Leech & Jan Svartvik (1985) *A Comprehensive Grammar of the English Language*, London: Longman, sections 6.2–6.5; see also 6.8, below.

## 2.10 The next couple is ...

People have been asking me for my professional opinion about *Strictly Come Dancing*. As you might suppose, I do not actually know my Salsa from my Samba or, come to that, my Artem from my Anton. So they are not consulting me about the actual dancing. People are perplexed about some of the language used in the show. In homes and pubs all across our county, *Strictly* watchers are discussing one particular phrase used by the show's presenters: *the next couple is ...*

It sounds really odd, which is why people are arguing about it. It is odd because it is not what any normal British person would ever say. We would say *the next couple are ...*

So why do these presenters use *is* instead? It is because they have been told to; and they have been told to because someone, somewhere, thinks it's "wrong" not to.

But it isn't wrong. With collective nouns like *couple, team, committee* you can in principle choose to treat them either as singular, which they are grammatically, or plural, which they are semantically (in terms of their meaning). And *couple* does, after all, mean 'two'! In all the dialects of English we speak in this country, it is natural and normal and correct for us to prefer to go with the semantics.

My wife, on the other hand, finds *the next couple is ...* entirely normal. That is because she is American. Americans tend quite naturally to go with the grammatical agreement. In this country we can alternate between *the government is* and *the government are*, while Americans favour *is*. But when it comes to sport, we really part company with them. Americans do actually say things like *Norwich City is playing well – it's going to be the league champion*.

I do not like to bandy the words "right" and "wrong" about too much. If, however, a Norwegian student of mine said *Norwich City is brilliant*, I would of course entirely agree with the sentiment; but I would tell them that, if they thought they were speaking British English, they were wrong. For us, there is a very big (and very useful) difference between *England are rubbish* and *England is rubbish*. The former is a frequently heard remark at Wembley Stadium. The latter is a much more serious accusation, and one that strikes at the very heart of our nation.

Maybe someone should write a letter to *The Times* asking the BBC to tell Tess not to use American grammar. That will work.

---

## BACKGROUND NOTES

Strictly Come Dancing *is a very popular BBC TV programme which has run since 2004 and which features celebrities with professional dance partners competing against each other.* Artem Chigvintsev *and* Anton Du Beke *were two of the professionals at the time I was writing this, and* Tess Daly *is one of the presenters who have appeared on the show.*

Wembley Stadium *is the northwest London venue where the England football team often play international matches.*

Writing a letter to The Times *will of course not make the slightest difference to anything.*

---

## LINGUISTIC NOTES

–  Collective nouns like *army, audience, company, crew, enemy, family, group, gang, council, team, committee* can either take singular verb forms and be pronominalised with *it* and *which* – this can be referred to as grammatical concord; or they can take plural verb forms and be pronominalised with *they/them* and *who* – this can be referred to as notional concord:

The team, which was selected yesterday, has played well so far. It looks very promising.
    The team, who were selected yesterday, have played very well so far. They look very promising.

This also applies, as we have seen, to the names of sports teams: *France are winning; Germany were the better team; Australia never lose.* In British English it is more or less compulsory to use the plural with sports clubs and teams – it sounds very odd if you do not. This also applies to the names of companies: *Microsoft have made a huge profit.*

–  Using plural verb forms and *they/who* probably indicates that the collective noun is being thought of as referring to a collection of individuals – this is more common in British English than in North American and Australian/New Zealand English – while the use of singular verbs and *it/which* indicates that the collective noun is being thought of as referring to a single entity.

*cont.*

– There is also a prescriptive element at work here: some New Zealand newspapers take reports of English football matches written by British journalists and systematically change all plurals to singular – they seem to have the idea that grammatical agreement is "better" than notional agreement. On notional vs grammatical agreement, see Randolph Quirk, Sidney Greenbaum, Geoffrey Leech & Jan Svartvik (1985) *A Comprehensive Grammar of the English Language*, London: Longman, section 10.35.

## 2.11 Singular *they*

I do not have to sit on committees anymore, but I sometimes do still have nightmares about a former English university colleague who insisted that all official references to students should use both the masculine and feminine pronouns: *any student who does not complete his or her work ...; if a student fails, then he or she must ...*

This was an improvement on the earlier situation where our students were referred to as *he, him, his* even though most of them were female; but I argued that his wordings were incredibly cumbersome and that we should use *they, them, their* instead: *if a student fails, then they must ...* He hated this idea, pontificating that it would be wrong because *they* is plural, so it cannot refer to a single person.

Now the pronoun *they* is plural, of course, but it can also be singular. English speakers have been able to use it for hundreds of years as a highly convenient way of referring to a single person when that person could be either male or female. We have examples of this from written English going back to at least the 1300s. From 1526, we find: "If a psalm escape any person, or a lesson, or else they omit one verse or twain ...". Here the pronoun referring to *any person* is *they*, because obviously a person can be male or female, and writing *they* is a lot more sensible than writing *he or she*.

Singular *they* is entirely normal, very common and utterly correct. Jane Austen and Shakespeare used it. The *Oxford English Dictionary* states that *they* can be used in "reference to a singular noun or pronoun of undetermined gender: he or she; especially in relation to a noun phrase involving one of the indefinite determiners or pronouns 'any, each, every, no, some, anybody, anyone'". You can tell it truly is singular by the way in which speakers sometimes say things like *anyone who hurts themself* rather than ... *themselves*.

In fact, singular *they* is so normal in grammatical constructions involving indefinites like *any* that we use it even when we do know the sex of the unknown person being referred to. Before the election of the current pope, BBC reporters were using expressions such as "whoever the next pope is, they will have to . . . ".

So it was my colleague who was mistaken. If you have such a colleague, do tell them they are wrong.

## 2.12 Grammar and conkers

Anne Atkins is not very popular in this part of the world. She is the woman who infamously said on BBC Radio 4: "No more chestnut trees lining the streets of Norwich in case the conkers fall on your head – as if that would make a difference in Norfolk." She said it was "a joke" and refused to apologise to us, the people of Norfolk.

Now she has been talking nonsense again, on the "Thought for the Day" feature, about language. She said that "good grammar helps you think clearly". Anne has no background of research, as far as I know, in psycholinguistics. Fancy addressing that piece of wisdom to the nation when you actually have no idea what you are talking about!

Unfortunately when people like Anne say "good grammar", they mean the grammar of Standard English, as if there was something "bad" about Norfolk grammar and the grammar of other dialects. Anne's father was headmaster of a boarding school, and she was educated privately and at Oxford. I think we can assume that Standard English is her native dialect; so when she says "good grammar" she means "my grammar".

I would be glad if one day Anne could explain how saying *I did it* helps you think more clearly than saying *I done it*. Certainly she herself is not thinking very clearly. She admitted on "Thought for the Day" that her family, having received an invitation ending "please let us know if you can come", did not reply because they could not go. She claimed that the wording should have had *whether*, not *if*.

Unless this is another bad joke, this was surely a rather impolite and supercilious thing to do. It was also based on a faulty analysis of English grammar. *Let us know if you can come (or not)* is a perfectly normal English grammatical construction and is totally equivalent to " . . . whether you can come (or not)". The two conjunctions *if* and *whether* do of course behave differently in many grammatical contexts. No native English speaker would normally say *he didn't know if to go*; we would say *whether*. And we would not say *please pop in whether you have time* – we'd always say *if*. But in indirect questions with *or* (implied or not), both are equally normal.

Being a native speaker of Standard English has not helped Anne to achieve very much clarity of thought. Maybe there are lots of chestnut trees on her street.

## BACKGROUND NOTES

Conkers are horse chestnuts. They are known by this name especially in the context of the traditional children's game in which two players each have a conker threaded on a piece of string and the players take turns to hit the other's conker with their own until one breaks.

Norwich City Council did in fact discuss the possible dangers posed to passing pedestrians by falling chestnuts.

"Thought for the Day" is a regular 3-minute feature on the BBC Radio 4 programme *Today* which consists of a "reflection from a faith perspective on topical issues and news events. Speakers from across the world's major faiths offer a spiritual insight rooted in the theology of their own tradition." In 1996 Anne Atkins used a "Thought for the Day" slot to attack Anglican bishops for supporting a twentieth-anniversary celebration of the Lesbian and Gay Christian Movement in Southwark Cathedral. This led to the Church of England's first ever official complaint about the programme. In the programme referred to here, the implication was rather clearly intended to be that people in Norfolk are stupid.

## LINGUISTIC NOTES

– For a much fuller discussion of the use of *whether* and *if* in English, see Randolph Quirk, Sidney Greenbaum, Geoffrey Leech & Jan Svartvik (1985) *A Comprehensive Grammar of the English Language*, London: Longman, section 15.6.

## 2.13 Norwegian classrooms

Norway is one of the most democratic, egalitarian countries in the world. It is also one of the happiest and most successful – many commentators believe that this is not a coincidence.

Norway is currently the top country in the world on the United Nation's Human Development Index (Britain is 14th). It is second on the worldwide Happiness Index (Britain is 22nd). It is also the second richest, after Luxembourg, in terms of GDP by population (Britain is 23rd). It comes third on the Quality of Life index (Britain is 27th). And it has the fifth lowest murder rate in the world (Britain is 30th, USA is 117th).

Norway is also an enormously tolerant place. Its tolerant egalitarian philosophy manifests itself in attitudes to the way people speak. In England, speakers can be criticised for "speaking badly" or for their "bad English". There is nothing like that

in Norway: if you started talking about "bad Norwegian", no one would understand what you meant – they would be baffled. As far as Norwegians are concerned,
there are no dialects and accents of their language which are "bad".

There is a long history of English children being told that the way they speak is
incorrect: "Don't say *I ain't got none* – it's wrong." In Norway, that would not
happen. No Norwegian educator would want to say things like that, but even if
they did, they would not be allowed to. It is against the law there to try to "correct"
the way children speak.

In 1917 the Oslo Parliament approved a passage in the School Law which
read, in translation: "Pupils are to use their own spoken variety, and teachers
shall as far as possible adapt their natural spoken variety to the dialect of their
pupils." Teachers were not allowed to try and make children speak like them:
if anything, it was to be the other way round.

Today Norwegians still accept that pupils should use their local dialect in school.
The current school law translates as: "For spoken language in the classroom, pupils
and teaching staff decide for themselves which variety they will use. Staff and
school managers, in their own choice of vocabulary and expression, shall also take
into consideration as much as possible the local dialect of the pupils."

Achieving a more respectful and less hostile attitude to local accents and dialects
in England might not make us as rich or successful as Norway. But it would surely
make this country a fairer and happier place.

# 3 Language change: observing and accepting it

Changes in language – in pronunciation, grammar and word-meaning – are inevitable and unstoppable. They are also a little mysterious. All languages change through time, but it is not easy to say why. It seems simply to be a built-in characteristic of human languages that they change. This is fascinating, but it can also be disturbing. This section of the book is devoted to arguing that we should prefer to be fascinated by linguistic change rather than be disturbed by it.

## 3.1 *Fing* and *bruvver*

Right now is a very exciting time to be doing research on the English language. All languages change: if you heard Shakespeare, you would find him hard to understand; and if we had recordings of Anglo-Saxon, you would not understand it at all. The sounds of English have changed enormously over time.

Why is this? We do not really know. It is just an inherent characteristic of human languages that they change. We do not fully understand *how* changes take place, either, so when we do have a chance to observe a change as it is happening, that is exciting. It is too late to observe how the change from Chaucer's "k-nicht" – his way of saying *knight* – to our "nite" happened; but here in England we can now very happily study, while it happens, a fascinating new change involving the two *th* sounds, as in *thigh* and *thy*. Older Norfolk people will have noticed that many younger people no longer have these sounds. They replace them with *f* and *v*, as in *fing* and *bruvver*.

When sounds fall together like this, it is technically called a merger. This particular merger is known as TH-*fronting*. It started in London around 1850 and had spread to Bristol by 1870. It was reported in Reading around 1950, Norwich in 1960, Hull 1970 and Glasgow 1980. There is a clear pattern of geographical spread: it has not arrived in Liverpool yet, but it probably will.

Some people are not as excited about TH-fronting as I am. They complain about it. They are part of the venerable Complaint Tradition which is repeated in every generation: older people hear youngsters speaking differently and object.

There is nothing wrong with TH-fronting, however. Nothing terrible comes of it. True, it means that some words now sound the same that did not before: *thin = fin*.

But if you can think of a sentence where that might cause misunderstanding, please let me know!

If you are part of the Complaint Tradition, you might consider that your own speech is also full of the results of earlier mergers inherited from your ancestors – unless, that is, you don't pronounce *meet* and *meat* the same?

TH-fronting is not lazy or careless or bad. It isn't good either. It just IS. I have been criticised for my "go with the flow" attitude to language change; but there is no other course to take. By all means complain if it makes you feel better, but bear in mind that there is as yet no record of any sound change ever being halted by a letter to *The Times* – or even to the *EDP*.

## LINGUISTIC NOTES

– Chaucer's pronunciation of *knight* would have been [knɪçt].
– The change /θ/ > /f/ and /ð/ > /v/ was first called TH-fronting by John Wells; see J. C. Wells (1982) *Accents of English*, Cambridge University Press. There is some evidence that it was at least sporadically present in London English much earlier than the date given here: we find occasional spellings such as *Lambeffe* for *Lambeth* in writings from as early as the sixteenth century.
– On the Complaint Tradition, see James Milroy and Lesley Milroy (2012) *Authority in Language: Investigating Standard English*, 4th edn, London: Routledge.

## 3.2 Going with the flow

A correspondent has written an interesting letter to the *EDP* about my column on pronunciations such as *fing* and *bovver*. I wrote that when it comes to natural language changes of this type, we have no choice but to – as another correspondent put it – "go with the flow". Her response to what I wrote was to say "er, no actually", i.e. we do have a choice. Well, I think she is wrong about that because we can be absolutely certain that she has already has gone with the flow, whether she likes it or not.

I have never met this correspondent, but I know for a fact that her own speech demonstrates very clearly the truth of what I say. Does she pronounce *meet* and *meat, see* and *sea, teem* and *team* the same? Of course she does, which means that she has gone with the flow. Pairs of words like this were originally pronounced differently, which is why they are not spelt the same today. But then the two vowels merged, as *th* and *f* are doing now; and nearly all English speakers have gone with the flow.

Does she pronounce the *k* in *know*? Of course she doesn't. All English speakers used to pronounce this *k*, which is why there is a *k* in the spelling, but now no one does.

Do people in this part of the world have the original hard *g* at the end of words such as *long* and *tongue*, like people from Liverpool and Manchester? No we don't. People from the northwest have not gone with that particular flow yet, but we have.

Do you pronounce *Wales* and *whales* the same? *Fur* and *fir*? *Moor* and *more*? Many Scottish people have not gone with these flows, but most of the rest of us have, including even those East Anglians who dislike *fing* and *bovver*.

Does our letter-writer pronounce the *r* in *car* and *cart*, as Americans do? I would be very surprised. If she does not pronounce *farther* and *father* differently, then she has gone along with everybody else in the southeast of England in accepting this change. No doubt when the *r* sound in these words was being lost by younger people, older people complained that they weren't "enunciating" clearly, but that made no difference.

Old English used to have an *h* sound at the beginning of words like *ring* and *roof*. If you feel your ancestors were remiss in going with the flow and not enunciating these *h*'s, you are of course free to start saying *hring* and *hroof* if you want to. But I think you'll be on your own.

## LINGUISTIC NOTES

– The FLEECE merger (J. C. Wells, 1982, *Accents of English*, Cambridge University Press) – the merging of Middle English /e:/ and /ɛ:/, as in *see* and *sea*, on /i:/ – was completed in the southeast of England by 1700. The /k/ in *know, knit* etc. started being lost during the 1500s. NG-coalescence, when word-final [g] stopped being pronounced after [ŋ], happened in the decades around 1600. The merger of /w/ and /hw/, or /ʍ/, is still on-going: the two remain distinct, as in *wine* and *whine*, in Scotland, Ireland and parts of the southeastern USA. The merger of the three Middle English short vowels before /r/ as in *fur, fir, fern*, such that all now have /ɝ/ or /ɜ:/, has not been carried through in many Scottish accents, which still have /fʌr, fɪr, fɛrn/.

– Note that all these changes demonstrate what in German is famously called the *Ausnahmslosigkeit der Lautgesetze*, or "the exceptionlessness of sound laws". This principle was first proposed by the nineteenth-century German linguists known as the Neogrammarians (in German the *Junggrammatiker*), and was the biggest breakthrough in historical linguistics, enabling linguists to reconstruct unattested earlier stages of languages with some confidence. The Neogrammarians came to realise that when, for example, /k/ and /g/ were lost before /n/, this was not a haphazard process: they were lost in every single word where word-initial /kn-/ and /gn-/ occurred. See Lyle Campbell (2013) *Historical Linguistics*, 3rd edn, Edinburgh University Press.

## 3.3 *K*-dropping

Am I alone in suffering from how deplorably badly young people are speaking these days? It is quite shocking to listen to them gabbling away to each other on the streets. Far too many of them have become so careless and slovenly in their pronunciation that it is hard to even understand what they are saying sometimes, though perhaps, from the way some of them look, that might be just as well. The fact is that they seem to communicate in a series of grunts half the time.

Some of these young people have become so sloppy in their language that they cannot even be bothered to pronounce all their letters properly. Have you heard how they are saying the word *knife*, for instance? You must have noticed how more and more teenagers are actually pronouncing it nowadays without the letter *k*! I am sure that all right-thinking people will agree with me in finding that this sounds really horribly ugly. Dropping your *k*'s is a deplorable and careless modern habit. Maybe they think it sounds really cool – all very seventeenth century I'm sure! – but when I hear youngsters pronouncing *knee* as "nee", I can't help shouting at them "Don't you know that there's a *k* in knee! K-nee, k-nee, k-nee!"

Many of these youths are not content with just dropping their *k*'s. They can't even be bothered to say their *g*'s in word like *gnaw* and *gnat* either! Is it really so much effort?

Happily, the better class of citizens do not descend to these depths: we must be glad that the people at the court of King James have not yet lowered themselves to pronouncing *kneel* without the *k*! No, it is the lower classes who are guilty, but we must make sure to band together to stop this *k*-dropping plague from infecting the speech of the offspring of our more important citizens before it is too late. Even Mr Shakespeare thinks it is in order to make a pun out of *nave* and *knave*!

Can you imagine what would happen if everybody ended up pronouncing *knight* as if it were the same as *night*! And if everybody confused *knew* and *new*? Where would we be then? Bewilderment and chaos will be the result. It will be the end of civilisation as we no it, and the nation will be brought to its nees.

| BACKGROUND NOTES |
| --- |
| *Here I am imagining what letters of complaint to the* EDP *might have looked like if the newspaper had been available in the early seventeenth century.* |

## 3.4 Enough rejoicing

Dear *EDP* Letters Page,

Am I the only reader who is getting rather fed up with all these older people who keep on writing to your newspaper to say how much they appreciate the speech of youngsters today? I entirely agree that youth speech is greatly superior to the English which we remember our parents and grandparents speaking, and the English which we use ourselves. I, too, therefore feel extremely optimistic about our language – it is clearly getting better all the time, and we may actually be approaching a Golden Age in the development of the English language.

But do these people have to keep going on about it? And do you have to keep publishing their letters? Can we not, please, call a moratorium on all this praise for modern speech?

I totally agree with the correspondent from Ashwellthorpe who so much appreciates the glottal stop in words like *butter* (bu'er), *better* (be'er) and *city* (ci'y) that she felt moved to write to the *EDP* to express her enthusiasm. I like it too, and am increasingly finding the older pronunciation ugly and unpleasant. But I don't see why it was necessary for her to write to the paper and say so.

It is also true, as the gentleman from Taverham wrote, that we all feel positive about the usage of *f* rather than *th* in words like *fing*, *fistle* and *fimble*. Getting rid of unnecessary consonants like *th* is an excellent thing, as he quite rightly says, because it increases efficiency. Why talk about *thatching* your roof when you can just as well say *fatching*? But there is no need to keep belabouring the point, is there? Can't we just accept that things are getting better and leave it at that? Why write a letter to the paper just to impart the information that you really like people saying *fing* and *bruvver*? Would you write a letter to the *EDP* to say "I really like porridge"? I don't think so.

I admit that I, too, personally rejoice in locutions such as "She was just like walking along the pavement when this cyclist like ran into her" – it is so much better, I feel, than using *sort of* or *kind of* as we used to. And I so enjoy hearing *was like* instead of *said*: "I was like 'wow' and he was like 'yeah'!" Wonderful!

But I wouldn't dream of writing a letter to the paper about it.

Yours sincerely,

Puzzled of Norwich

---

**BACKGROUND NOTES**

*Just in case anybody is in doubt – this column was intended ironically. No one has ever written to a newspaper saying that they think our language – or any language – is getting better and approving of the changes which young people have introduced into the language.*

---

## 3.5 Reasons to be cheerful, part I

All languages change through time. Older people can find that annoying. People do not like change. It is very irritating to get used to something and then suddenly find you have to get used to something else. It still annoys me that I can't drive up Prince of Wales Road and round Castle Meadow.

When it comes to linguistic change, however, there is nothing we can do about it. You can tell how unhappy that makes some people by looking at the letters columns of the *EDP*. It is not always easy to feel positive about changes in your own language, like the pronunciations "fing" for *thing* and "bovver" for *bother*.

For this reason, I have been compiling a list of things about language change that we can all try and feel happy about. Here is my first attempt – *Linguistic change: Reasons to be cheerful, part I*.

1. English and German are different languages. We are happy about that, aren't we? Would you want it otherwise? Two millennia ago they were the same language – West Germanic – and if it had not been for different changes occurring in different places, we would not have had our own language.
2. Old English had three grammatical genders and five grammatical cases. There were six ways of saying 'ship(s)' depending on the grammar: *scip, scipes, scipe, scipu, scipa, scipum*. Linguistic changes that have taken place in the last thousand years have removed these complexities – which must surely mean that English as a Foreign Language courses are shorter and therefore cheaper than they would have been.
3. If it was not for linguistic change, people in the south of England would still pronounce *paths* to rhyme with *maths*, and *budding* to rhyme with *pudding*, like northerners do. Isn't it rather fun that there is now a difference? Such distinctions can be useful, too, when Norwich City are playing Hull City and you want to know which supporters are which.
4. If it was not for language change, there would be no such thing as the Norfolk dialect. Our dialect is distinctive because of changes that have taken place here that have not taken place elsewhere – and vice versa. When we say "Come you on!", we are using an older form that has been lost elsewhere. When we make *road* and *coat* rhyme with *good* and *put*, we are using an innovation which is all our own.
5. And – one more good thing – we no longer have to go around pronouncing the *k* in Knapton.

---

## BACKGROUND NOTES

*The title of this piece is a tribute to the 1979 recording by Ian Dury and the Blockheads* Reasons to Be Cheerful, Part 3.

*The introduction of the Norwich one-way traffic system which meant that drivers could drive in only one direction along Prince of Wales Road occurred in the 1960s.*

*The Hull City football team colours are not totally dissimilar to those of Norwich City: yellow (amber) and black, as opposed to yellow and green.*

> **LINGUISTIC NOTES**
>
> – The different Old English forms *scip, scipes, scipe, scipu, scipa, scipum* are respectively: nominative and accusative singular; genitive singular; dative singular; nominative and accusative plural; genitive plural; dative plural.

## 3.6  Don't blame the Yanks

I was on the 25 bus in Norwich the other day, travelling from the University to the city. The students getting on at UEA asked to go to the "train station". An old bloke at the stop on Bluebell Road asked for "Thorpe Station", as I would have done. And then some middle-aged people on Unthank Road wanted tickets for the "railway station". So there we had, encapsulated in a just a few minutes and just a mile or so, visible and audible evidence of a change in speech. (The bus itself had Rail Station on the front, but no one ever says that.)

The gradual disappearance of *Thorpe Station* from Norwich people's usage is due to external factors. Since there is only one railway station in the city now, it is no longer necessary to specify which one you want, though it is interesting that there has been a time-lag of a good thirty years for this to even start taking effect. It is less easy, though, to explain why people have stopped saying *railway station* and started saying *train station*. I do not recall hearing anybody in this country, apart from small children who didn't know any better, calling it that until about twenty years ago.

But *train station* is what Americans have always said, at least as far back as I remember (and that is getting to be quite a long time now). It is true that Paul Simon is an American, and that his famous song "Homeward Bound" begins "I'm sitting in the railway station" ... But he did supposedly write it at Widnes station, and of course the two syllables of *railway* fit the melody. But in all the modern books which describe differences between US and British English, the opposition between *train station* and *railway station* is mentioned, and that is my experience too.

So we can blame the Americans then? Hardly. If we stop using our term and start using theirs, that is our doing. It is nothing to do with them. And the change cannot be explained in terms of young people casually throwing Americanisms into their speech in order to sound trendy. Sometime in the last two decades, older British people in positions of authority have made the decision to take down old signs saying *railway station*, including expensive electronic signs, and replace them with new ones reading *train station* – at Gatwick Airport, for instance, and many other places.

Don't blame the Yanks. That was us what done it.

## 3.7 *Lay* and *lie*

Our ancestral Anglo-Saxon language used to perform lots of grammatical operations by alternations between the vowels of related words. In modern English we do this much less, but we still have quite a few traces: *foot–feet, take–took, song–sing–sang–sung, know–knew, write–wrote–written, stink–stank–stench*.

Another example is this: if you *fell* a tree, it *falls* down; if you then *raise* it up again, it *rises*. Obviously *fall* and *fell*, and *rise* and *raise*, are related words. Verbs like *fell* and *raise* are called causatives: *to fell* means 'to cause to fall', *to raise* means 'to cause to rise'. Lots of the world's languages have fully developed systems of grammatical causatives; but, although Old English used to have many pairs like this, modern English has only a very few of these old-style Anglo-Saxon causatives left.

We do still have *sit* and *set*: if you *set* a child down in a chair, you cause it to *sit*. And we do also still have *lie* and *lay*: *to lay* means 'to cause to lie'. But we have lost the mediaeval English word *sench*, which meant 'to cause to sink' – these days, if you want to a boat to sink, you do not *sench* it, you *sink* it. And nowadays it would occur to only a very few people that *drench* is derived from *drink*, or that *wend* means 'to cause to wind'.

Even the causatives that we do have are gradually going the way of *sench* and being lost: in our Norfolk dialect it is very normal to say "please set down" when you want someone to take a seat. Nobody misunderstands you.

And the distinction between *lay* and *lie* is also being lost in most forms of English. This process is being helped along by the fact that *lay* is not just the present tense of the verb *to lay* but also the past tense of *to lie*. Very many of us these days tell the dog to lay down, and then perhaps go and have a nice lay-down ourselves. Some people do not like this – they think it is "careless". But I think it is rather likely that in a couple of hundred years time the verb *to lie*, in the sense of being in a horizontal resting position, will probably have disappeared totally in favour of *lay*. No one will misunderstand: after all, if you *stand* things on the table, they *stand* on the table. Just as, if you *lay* the carpet, it will *lay* on the floor.

## LINGUISTIC NOTES

- The alternation between the vowels of *sing–sang–sung* is a relic left over from a very ancient phenomenon which goes back 6,000 years to our ancestral language Indo-European, which extensively and regularly used a form of "vowel gradation", known by the German term of *Ablaut*, for grammatical purposes. The alternations between *foot* and *feet*, and *fall* and *fell*, on the other hand, are a few thousand years more recent – they date from perhaps the fourth century AD – and are part of the *i*-umlaut phenomenon found in the Germanic languages. What this means is that back vowels changed to front vowels, and open front vowels became closer, under the influence of an /i/ or /j/ in the following syllable, with the following syllable subsequently disappearing; so singular /muːs/, plural /muːsi/, became /muːs, myːsi/ and then /muːs, myːs/, later /muːs, miːs/ which gives us modern English *mouse, mice*. See Lyle Campbell (2013) *Historical Linguistics*, 3rd edn, Edinburgh University Press.
- Turkish is a good example of a language with a fully developed grammatical system of morphological causatives. For example, *gülmek* means 'to laugh', while *güldürmek* means 'to make someone laugh'; *durmak* means to stop, as in "the car stopped", while *durdurmak* means to cause to stop, as in "the driver stopped the car".
- For more on *wend*, see 12.3.

## 3.8 Controversy

There is a controversy about the word *controversy*. Should it be CONtroversy or conTROVersy? There is also controversy about the word *contribute*: at least one *EDP* reader finds the pronunciation CONtribute irritating and feels it should be conTRIBute. Some objectors even claim that CONtribute is an "Americanism" (it isn't) – which of course means that they don't like it.

It might help to reduce this irritation a little if we can look at this issue historically, because what is going on here is actually part of a very long-term historical trend. As far back as about 1000 BC, our ancestral language Proto-Germanic regularised stress on the first syllable of all words, something which distinguished it from all the other Indo-European languages like Proto-Celtic and Proto-Italic, which never did this.

By the time of Old English, say AD 500, this rule still applied – the norm for all words was stress on the first syllable unless that was a prefix, as in *be*-NEATH or *be*-FORE; and this is still the system today in our basic English vocabulary.

But in 1066, the Normans invaded and starting messing things up. English began to borrow words from French – which descended via Latin from Proto-Italic and did not have the first-syllable stress rule.

The word *contribute* was borrowed into English in the late 1300s. This, and the many other words like it, complicated the originally straightforward English word-stress system, not least because stress could also shift as between related forms like *contribute* and *contribution*.

Ever since these French borrowings arrived, there has been a tension in the English language between the original Germanic system and the upstart French system. There has also been a tendency for the English language to try and resolve this tension by fitting inconvenient French-origin words into the natural Germanic system: there has been a drive to shift to pronunciations like CONtribute, with stress on the first syllable. *Balcony* was pronounced balCONy until the 1920s, but is now BALcony. Other borrowed words which used to have stress on the second syllable but now do not include comPENsate, conCENtrate, conTEMplate and reCONcile.

But, to be honest, things aren't quite so simple as this. The tension between the two systems actually leads to all sorts of contradictions and complications. It used to be more usual to say CONtroversy, as it still is in the USA. But nowadays a majority of people in this country say conTROversy. I wonder if this Briticism irritates Americans.

## LINGUISTIC NOTES

- The regularisation of first-syllable stress was one of a number of changes which set off the Germanic languages from other Indo-European language families. Another such change was the First Germanic Sound Shift or Grimm's Law; see 12.7. Both of these developments have been hypothesised by some scholars to be substratum effects. That is, they might be the results of the language of Indo-European incomers having been acquired by original inhabitants who, as they shifted from their native language to an Indo-European dialect, transferred elements of their own pronunciation into their new language.

# 4 What is happening to words?

This section is mainly concerned with the various ways in which words can travel, and how they may change their form and meaning over time – in some cases during the course of an individual's life-time, in other cases over periods as long as several thousand years.

## 4.1 Latte?

If you go into the coffee bar in Jarrolds book department in Norwich and ask for a *latte*, you will get a cup of coffee. If you go to a coffee bar in Milan and ask for a *latte* you will probably get a glass of milk; you will certainly not get a cup of coffee. The Italian word *latte* means milk. *Latte* as used by English speakers is an abbreviation of Italian *caffè latte*, which means 'coffee (with) milk'. We can only abbreviate it to *latte* because we do not know, most of us, what *latte* means.

This is a common type of occurrence when words are borrowed from one language to another. French speakers have borrowed our word *foot*, for instance, but it does not mean 'foot' to them: they have their own word for that, *pied*. For French-speaking people, *le foot* means 'football'. The French language borrowed our word *football* – we invented the game, after all – and then abbreviated it. We could not have done that because, obviously, to us *foot* already meant something else.

Funny things happen when words are borrowed from one language to another. The French word *living* means 'living room'; and *lifting* means 'face lift'. In German, a *Smoking* is a dinner jacket. In Swedish, a *fitness* is a gym.

The strangest thing of all is when languages borrow words which do not actually exist. The German word for a mobile phone is *Handy*. It's a non-English English word. So is *Pullunder*, which is the German word for a sleeveless pullover.

We do similar things. The French term for a cul-de-sac is not *cul de sac* but *voie sans issue* or *impasse*. (We have borrowed the word *impasse* from them, but we only use it metaphorically to refer a situation where no progress is possible, not to a street where you have to turn round and go back.) In French, *petite* is the feminine form of the adjective which simply means 'small'; but in English it is used very specifically to refer to a woman who is small and slim in an attractive way.

The Italian word *panini* means 'sandwiches' (plural), but we use it to mean a particular type of sandwich – if we had known about Italian grammar we would have said *panino* instead. *Spaghetti* is also plural in Italian: it means 'little strings'. We ought to say, really, "these spaghetti are very tasty". *Vermicelli* means 'little worms'. The Greek word for moussaka is *moussakáss*, with the stress on the last syllable. The Greek word for taramasalata is *taramosaláta*.

I could go on, except I'm now off to Jarrolds for a *macchiato* (that's Italian for 'spotted').

> **BACKGROUND NOTES**
>
> *On Jarrolds shop, see the Themes section at the beginning of this book.*

## LINGUISTIC NOTES

- *Latte* as an abbreviation of *caffè latte* is first recorded in American English from the 1980s. The Italian word descends from Latin *lac, lactis* 'milk', which we can also see in English borrowings from Latin such as *lactate*.
- French *cul-de-sac* literally means 'bottom of a sack or bag'; and *voie sans issue* means 'way without outlet'.
- The Greek word *moussakáss* (μουσακάς) is originally from Turkish *musakka*, which is itself originally from an Arabic word *musaqqā*. Greek *taramáss* (ταραμάς) 'preserved fish roe' is also originally from Turkish.
- Italian *macchiato* goes back to Latin *maculatus*, which was the past participle of the verb *maculare* 'to spot, stain'. The English loan-word from Latin, *immaculate*, originally 'without stain', has the same origin.

## 4.2 Danish pastries

The term *Danish pastry* first hit the English-speaking world when confections of that type were served in Washington, DC, at the wedding of President Woodrow Wilson in 1915. The pastries then took New York by storm and became so common in the USA that nowadays Americans who want one generally just ask for "a Danish". The phrase *Danish pastry* did not arrive in this country until the 1930s, when it turned up in London, presumably along with the pastries themselves, from America; but I do not recall ever having heard the term here in Norwich until very many decades indeed after that.

But why *Danish*? Any search for an explanation has to follow a trail from New York back to Copenhagen, where these confections were first baked in the 1850s, and where the bakers who brought them to the US came from.

But what do they call them in Denmark? Obviously it is no good asking for a *Danish pastry* in Denmark: all pastries in Denmark are Danish! Well, if you want a

Danish pastry in Copenhagen, you have to ask for a *wienerbrød* – meaning 'Viennese bread'.

But why Vienna? Well, it seems they were first baked in Copenhagen by bakers who had arrived there from the Austrian capital, when Danish bakers were on strike. So then the interesting question arises: what are *wienerbrød* called in Vienna, where everything is Viennese? According to native informants consulted by this column, they do not have a single word for them: there are so many different types of these pastries there that the usual thing is to ask for a particular sort by name. But the German-language version of Wikipedia tells us that the original Viennese pastry which found its way to Copenhagen from Austria was of the type called a *golatsche*.

So where did the word *golatsche* come from? It turns out that it is not actually German in origin; the Viennese borrowed this word from the Czech language of Bohemia, at that time part of the Austro-Hungarian Empire, but now across the border in the Czech Republic. The Czech word is actually *koláč*, and there is a suggestion that this comes from the Czech word for wheel, *kolo*, because a Bohemian *koláč* is typically round.

If so, this circularity is appropriate. According to native Czech informants consulted by this column, if you are in Prague and want a Danish pastry, the most usual thing is, again, to specify the particular type you want. But there is also a rather new Czech term you could use if you wanted to. This is *dánské pečivo*. You can guess what that means. *Dánské* is the Czech word for 'Danish'. And *pečivo* means 'pastry'.

## 4.3 "It's not American"

While the football World Cup was being played in Brazil in 2014, there was an interesting little item on National Public Radio in the USA which I happened to hear. A presenter was complaining, albeit not very seriously, about the use of the word *nil* in American sports broadcasting, and its apparently rather rapid spread into general public usage in the United States. It is "not American", he protested.

This was of course *nil* as in "Brazil are losing seven–nil" (or as Americans would say, "Brazil is losing seven–nil").

Americans never used to say *nil*. Before 2014, they would have phrased it as "seven to nothing" or "seven–zero" or "seven–zip".

However, the employment of large numbers of British expert soccer commentators and co-commentators on the American TV networks to describe and analyse the World Cup matches ("games" as they are called in the USA) led to lots of Americans using a number of sporting "Briticisms", as the presenter named them, at least in the football (soccer) context.

This complaint about Briticisms is really rather amusing, given the number of complaints there have been over the decades in this country about Americanisms and how dreadful they are. It is rather entertaining to see the boot on the other foot and to hear Americans protesting about the evil linguistic influence from our side of the pond.

But *nil* meaning 'nothing' was not originally an English word anyway. Its usage in English only dates back to the 1830s, and it comes from the Latin word *nil*, which was a contraction of *nihil* 'nothing', which we can still see in its full form in our word *nihilism*.

The word *zero*, as formerly preferred by Americans, is not originally an English word either. It has a rather long history. It came into English from French *zéro*, which was borrowed from Italian *zero*, which came down from Mediaeval Latin *zephirum*, which in turn originated from Arabic *sifr*, which itself was a translation of Sanskrit *sunyam* 'empty place, desert'. *Sifr* is also, via French, the source of our word *cipher*. That, too, originally meant 'zero' but was then extended to all numerals, and then to secret codes (because these often involved substituting numbers for letters).

The word *nothing*, though, really is an ancient English term, and so is *naught/ nought*. In our part of the world, we have an innovative version of *nought* which involves a reinterpretation of original "a nought" as "an ought". Let's hope that this season Norwich City are not going to lose seven to nothing, seven–zero, seven–zip, seven–nil and especially not seven–ought.

## LINGUISTIC NOTES

- The use of *ought* rather than *nought*, as the result of the reanalysis of *a nought* as *an ought*, is paralleled by other cases which are found in all forms of English, such as *an adder*, which was originally *a nadder* (see also 10.3); the related German word for this snake is *Natter*. *Umpire* was also originally *noumpere* in Middle English. This came from Old French *nonper*, later *nomper*, from *non* plus *per* 'peer', so 'peerless, without equal', hence the modern meaning of 'person in charge, arbitrator'.
- For more discussion of *naught/nought*, see 6.7.

## 4.4 Weakening and bleaching

Languages change all the time. Why? Well, they just do. The sounds change. The grammar changes. And the meanings change.

The study of meaning is called *semantics*. One type of meaning change involves a process called *semantic weakening*, in which the meaning of a word gets less strong in some way. Extreme weakening is called *semantic bleaching*: that is when a word is more or less emptied of all its meaning. This happens over time with most place-names. In Anglo-Saxon times, Norfolk people would have known that Acle meant 'oak wood', but now it does not mean anything at all except . . . Acle.

Bleaching also occurs if words become more and more grammatical. If you say "I have seen it", it is really rather hard to say what the meaning of the word *have* is there. It certainly does not have anything to do with "having" anything.

Lesser forms of semantic weakening are common enough too, especially with words which have some kind of emotional loading. *Terrible* used to mean 'inspiring terror'. Nowadays, when people tell me that my handwriting is terrible, I have to agree, but I know it does not actually terrify anybody. *Awful* used to mean 'producing awe', but in modern English it just means 'not very good'; or, if you like, 'not terribly good', or even 'not awfully good'.

Older people reading the *EDP* may have noticed that the same sort of thing has been happening to the word *hero*. All the soldiers in Afghanistan now are heroes, not just the ones who have stormed machine-gun nests single-handed, as would have been the case when we were younger. Farmers who have pulled cars out of snow-drifts with their tractors are heroes too. When Russell Martin goes up to head a ball in the penalty area, surrounded by opposition players, even he is being "heroic".

I am not saying there is anything wrong with that. There isn't. It is perfectly normal. But it is a very interesting example of the sort of change that happens in language; and there is absolutely nothing to worry about. Languages take care of themselves. It is true that we can no longer use the word *terrible* in the old, very strong way; but we can perfectly well say *terrifying* instead. Somebody seeing Norwich Cathedral for the first time these days can no longer indicate how extremely impressive it is by saying that it's "awe-ful". But they can easily use the word *awe-inspiring* instead.

Or as, Norfolk people might say, "quite good".

## BACKGROUND NOTES

*Acle is a small town between Norwich and the east coast of Norfolk.*
  *Russell Martin is a Scotland international footballer who joined Norwich City in 2010 and was appointed club captain in 2013.*
  *The main building work on Norwich Cathedral was carried out between 1096 and 1145.*

## LINGUISTIC NOTES

– On semantic bleaching, see Eve Sweetser (1990) *From Etymology to Pragmatics: Metaphorical and Cultural Aspects of Semantic Structure*, Cambridge University Press.
– According to the *Oxford English Dictionary* (*OED*), the usage of *terrible* meaning 'bad' dates from the late 1700s, and of *awful* to the early 1800s.

Norwich Cathedral

## 4.5 Wood for the trees

One of the most fascinating things about languages is that they change. This is an inherent characteristic of human language: all languages change through time. Speakers change their languages; but they do not know they are doing it, and they certainly do not do it on purpose. It just happens; why they do it is not fully understood.

One way in which languages change is in the meanings of words. This happens gradually, and changes are usually subtle to start with. You can see rather clearly how this happens by comparing English with the languages it is most closely related to, in the sense that they have all descended from a single common Germanic ancestor over the last 2,000 years.

The Norwegian word *kinn* has the same origin as our word *chin*, but it means 'cheek'. Swedish *ben* is the same as our *bone*, but it refers to the leg. Danish *sky* doesn't mean 'sky' but 'cloud'. German *Zeit* comes from the same root as English *tide*, but it means 'time'. Dutch *bos* is related to English *bush*, but it means 'wood' or 'forest'.

In fact, Germanic words for wood are very interesting generally. The German word for tree is *Baum*; the Dutch word is *boom* – these have the same source as English *beam*: a beam is, after all, made from a tree. English *tree* corresponds to Norwegian *tre*, but in Norwegian *tre* also refers to wood as a material, as if we were to say "this desk is made out of tree". The corresponding German word for wood as a material is *Holz*, which is the same word as the name of our Norfolk town *Holt*, where it meant 'a small wood'.

Our word *wood* corresponds to Norwegian *ved*, but that means 'fire-wood'. If you want to refer to a wood or forest in Norwegian, you have to say *skog*. We do not have this word in English – except that in our region we actually do. The *Sco* in Sco Ruston, earlier Scouriston, comes from the Old Norse word *skogr*, meaning 'wood' or 'forest' in the language of the Viking settlers. And Haddiscoe was originally 'Hadd's wood', with the *scoe* part again coming from that Old Norse word.

We have no idea who Hadd was, but his name lives on in Norfolk, as do all these different Germanic words for wood, albeit with their meanings subtly changed in different ways in the different languages.

**BACKGROUND NOTES**

Sco Ruston and Haddiscoe are villages in, respectively, the northeast and southeast of Norfolk.

**LINGUISTIC NOTES**

– The Dutch word *boom* has been borrowed into English as our word *boom*, the sailing term referring to spars that are used to run along the bottom of sails.

## 4.6 Curb kerb

A reader wrote to the *EDP* during the winter pointing out that a car which had skidded off an icy road had mounted a kerb, not a curb as reported in the newspaper. The letter-writer was right. A *kerb* is a stone edging to a raised path. A *curb* is a restraint on something.

Except that in the USA they do spell *kerb* "curb". We regard *curb* and *kerb* as two different words; Americans think of them as being the same. Historically speaking, they are right.

In English, a curb was originally a strap bent round the jaw of a horse in order to restrain it – to curb it. The word came from Old French *courbe*, which descended from Latin *curvus* 'bend' – also the source of our word *curve*. By 1500, *curb* had also come to refer to a bent enclosed framework, and later it was applied to the edge of a garden bed, bent or not. Then, by 1800, the meaning had been extended to include the edge of a street-side path. This was a meaning so different from a strap round a horse's jaw that it is easy to see why it was no longer perceived as the same word; and it is not surprising that an alternative spelling developed for the newer meaning.

The same thing happened with *flower* and *flour* – they were originally the same word, too. *Flower* was borrowed from Old French *flor* 'flower, blossom' and through time also came to mean 'the best of its kind' – especially, by about 1250 or so, the best part of the wheat, i.e. wheat after the bran had been removed, the 'flower of the wheat'. Eventually this meaning became divorced from the 'bloom' meaning, and the words started being spelt differently to avoid confusion.

Another example of the same phenomenon is provided by *metal* and *mettle* – again, they used to be the same word. English acquired the word from Old French *metal* 'metal, material, stuff'. In Shakespeare's time, the two spellings were used interchangeably, for both the literal sense of metallic stuff and the metaphorical sense of 'stuff that a person is made of', i.e. their character. During the 1700s, the two spellings began to be used systematically to apply to the literal and metaphorical meanings respectively, and we now no longer think of them as being the same word.

And if we think of them as being different words, then they are different words.

## LINGUISTIC NOTES

- Another American–British difference of the *curb–kerb* sort is *check* vs *cheque*: both words have the same origin, and in the USA they are spelt the same.
- Cases such as those of *flower* and *flour*, and *mettle* and *metal*, pose an interesting descriptive problem for linguistic scientists. Where the same word has two or more related meanings, we are happy to say that this is a case of *polysemy*. An example of this is *wood*, which can refer to wood as a material, or to a tree-covered area (on words for wood in the languages related to English, see 4.5). *Flour/flower* clearly started life as a single polysemous lexical item of this type, but now we have to say that they have become two separate words which are *homonyms*, i.e. words which sound the same but mean different things.

## 4.7 But

Where words come from is something which many people find very interesting. There is something rather fascinating about the fact that the etymology of the word *person* lies in the Latin word *persona*, which meant the role taken by an actor in a play.

*Persona* originally meant 'mask': Roman actors wore masks made of wood or clay which depicted the face of the character they were playing. The word probably originally came from Latin *personare*, where *per* meant 'through' (as in *percolate*) and *sonare* meant 'to sound' (as in *resonate*): the actor had to speak through the mask. Two and a half millennia later, this two-part compound Latin word has turned into a single English word with a very different meaning.

The portion of our English vocabulary that descends from Latin includes lots of rather grand etymologies like this. But what about some of our humble little Germanic-origin words? Every word, however small, has to have come from somewhere. What about *but*, for instance?

Intriguingly, this also used to be a two-part compound: the *b* and the *ut* parts actually have their origins in two different words! In Anglo-Saxon, *but* was *butan*. It originally meant 'outside' and then later on 'unless'; and it came from an earlier form, *be-utan*.

In our West Germanic parent language, *utan* 'from outside' was derived from *ut* 'out', so the second element of modern *but* has the same origin as modern *out*.

And the *be-* part is just as interesting. There was an ancient Indo-European word *bhi*. This came down into Greek as the second element of *am-phi* 'round', as in *amphitheatre,* and it also appeared as the second part of Latin *am-bi*, as in *ambidextrous*.

The corresponding form in ancient Germanic was the adverb of place *bi*, also meaning 'around, about'. Some etymologists say that this then developed through time down two different paths. In one direction, they say, it became the Scandinavian word *by*, meaning a settlement – the area around a place where people lived. We can still see this today in many English place-names ending in *by* which are found in areas which were settled by the Danes.

In the other direction, in Anglo-Saxon it became *bi* meaning 'by, near, in', which survives as our modern word *by*. But Anglo-Saxon *bi* also had a weak, unstressed form *be-* which occurred in compounds like *be-yond*, *be-neath*, *be-fore* and *be-tween* – and *be-utan*.

So the *b* in *but* and the *by* in *Hemsby* may originally have been the same word!

## 4.8 How many words do you know?

Have you ever wondered how many English words you know? Have a guess, and I'll tell you in minute. Of course it depends a bit on what you mean by "a word". If we are going to make a proper count, we do have to decide that *walk, walks, walked* are not three different words, but just different forms of the same word. We have to make the same decision about *car* and *cars*. And we have to think about problems such as: is *bookshop* one word or two?

There is also a problem with what "know" means. It cannot necessarily mean that you actually use a word yourself. We all have much bigger passive vocabularies than active vocabularies; but who is to know if it really is "passive" anyway? My American wife and I have been together now for more than thirty-five years, and she still occasionally comes out with an American word I have never heard before; and vice versa. It makes you think that there are probably lots of words we all know which we only use once every thirty-five years, or even less often.

Linguistic scientists, though, do have a pretty good idea of average vocabulary size. The normal way to test it is not very sophisticated or complicated, though it is rather time-consuming. We take, say, every fiftieth page in a dictionary, see how many words on those pages different individuals know, and then multiply the result by fifty. If you do that with a large enough number of people, you get a very good picture of the situation, although it is interesting that the bigger the dictionary is, the more words it seems to show that people know!

Anyway, I bet your guess about your own vocabulary size was too low. Most adults know at least 35,000 words or so, and very educated people probably know as many as 50,000 – some estimates even suggest double that number.

We have to remember too that, here in Norfolk, most people will know more words than that, because we know quite a lot of local dialect words which are actually not in the dictionary. Even non-dialect-speaking incomers may benefit. If you have tried Keith Skipper's Saturday *EDP* quiz recently, you will know by now that *to hain* means 'to raise' and that *to dudder* means 'to shiver'. So that makes 50,002, then.

> ## BACKGROUND NOTES
>
> *Keith Skipper is a well-known local author, journalist, humourist and broadcaster in Norfolk who is very proud of his Norfolk roots. The* EDP *runs a local knowledge quiz that he sets every Saturday. He is also the founder of FOND – the Friends of Norfolk Dialect society.*

## LINGUISTIC NOTES

– "Different forms of the same word": the relevant linguistic term for "the same word" here is *lexeme*: http://en.wikipedia.org/wiki/Lexeme. *Walk, walks* and *walked* may or may not be the same word, depending on how you think about it, but they are the same lexeme.

## 4.9  Give us a butcher's

The subject of rhyming slang was raised in a letter to the *EDP*. Rhyming slang is an interesting phenomenon. We tend to associate it with Cockney, but it is also well known in Glasgow, Australia and other places. You know the sort of thing: in Cockney slang, *plates* means 'feet', and *dog* means 'phone'.

Most people know how it works: you disguise a word by taking a phrase which rhymes with it, and then omitting the rhyming word. The word *stairs* is disguised by taking the phrase "apples and pears" and then leaving out *and pears*, so that *apples* means 'stairs'. *Plates* is from "plates of meat", *dog* is from "dog and bone".

Some of these words have moved into general usage and their origins have been forgotten. If everyone knew what the origin of *bottle* ('courage') or *cobblers* ('nonsense') was, some people might decide not to use them anymore.

When I was at school, I knew perfectly well what "give us a butcher's" meant, but I had no idea that its origins were in *look* disguised in the phrase *butcher's hook* with the rhyme left out. I did not realise that "use your loaf" was a shortened version of *loaf of bread*, i.e. *head*. I certainly did not know that "on your tod" (= 'alone') came from *Tod Sloan*; and I was totally ignorant of the fact that Mr Sloan was an American jockey who became famous after riding five consecutive winners here at Newmarket in 1898.

Rhyming slang is creative – anyone can invent their own – and fun; but it does have a purpose. One of its functions is to operate as an "anti-language", a way of speaking which is designed to be intelligible only to insiders, like the Gypsy language Anglo-Romany, which I have also written about.

But rhyming slang is not always a particularly serious barrier to communication; you can often work out what a word means, even if you have never heard it before. Sometimes the rhyming word is not even left out: "Would you Adam and Eve it?" It is probably more important as a way of signalling that you are a member of some particular in-group.

But rhyming slang did permit the writer of the letter to smuggle a couple of rather indelicate terms into the *EDP* which I do not think the editor would have allowed him to use if he had not disguised them. I am sure the letter-writer knew what he was doing. If he says he didn't, we will know he is telling porkies.

---

### BACKGROUND NOTES

*Cockney is the traditional working-class dialect of London.*
   *Adam and Eve = 'believe'. Bottle is short for 'bottle and glass'; and cobblers for 'cobblers' awls'. Porkies is derived from pork pie. Readers will no doubt be able to supply the rhymes for themselves.*

**LINGUISTIC NOTES**

- *Anti-language* is a term due to Michael Halliday (1976) "Anti-languages", *American Anthropologist* 78.3: 570–84. It refers to "a variety of a language, usually spoken on particular occasions by members of certain relatively powerless or marginal groups in a society, which is intended to be incomprehensible to other speakers of the language or otherwise to exclude them. Examples of groups employing forms of anti-language include criminals, drug-users, schoolchildren, homosexuals and Gypsies. Exclusivity is maintained through the use of slang vocabulary, sometimes known as argot, not known to other groups, including vocabulary derived from other languages. European examples include the anti-languages Polari and Anglo-Romani. Some such varieties rely on phonological or other distortion processes to make them incomprehensible" (Peter Trudgill, 2003, *A Glossary of Sociolinguistics*, Edinburgh University Press).
- For more on Anglo-Romany, see 1.10.

## 4.10 Feet and inches

Our word *foot* comes from Anglo-Saxon *fot* and is related to Norwegian and Swedish *fot*, Danish *fod*, Dutch and Afrikaans *voet*, West Frisian *foet*, North Frisian *fötj*, German *Fuss* and Low German *Foot*. It is an ancient Germanic word for a fundamental part of our anatomy.

It is also an ancient natural measurement, based on the length of the foot of a typical adult male. A twelfth of a foot is called an *inch*, which is often taken to be equivalent to the width of a man's thumb.

Another natural unit of measurement is the *fathom*, which was originally the length of the outstretched arms, from fingertip to fingertip. A fathom is equivalent to six feet, and these days it is mostly used in measuring the depth of water. It, too, is an old Germanic word, and is related to the modern Swedish verb *famna*, which means 'to embrace'. Obviously, if you are going to embrace somebody, you start with your arms stretched out.

In western Europe, natural measurements of this type disappeared in those countries (which was most of them) that had been conquered by Napoleon, who imposed the new and more logical – but less natural – French metric system on them. In Britain we were not conquered by Napoleon, and so we could choose to stay with the same natural measurement system which had served us so well for a thousand years and more.

But even in many of those nations which were not able to hold out against Bonaparte, the foot and inch and fathom still survive as units of measurement today, 200 years after Waterloo. Scandinavian carpenters may still talk in thumbs or inches, for instance. And in Norway, the length of a boat is always still quoted in feet. In Sweden, the depth of the sea is often measured in fathoms. Internationally, too, it is still widespread practice to give the height at which aeroplanes are flying in feet.

It is the intuitive naturalness of measurements like inch, foot and fathom which make them hard to get rid of. We like them because we can relate to them.

The other day I was in a stationery shop in Norwich, buying some plastic folders. The young woman serving me showed me the folders they had, and I wanted to know if they were the right size. I asked how many inches wide they were. She said: "I don't know anything about feet and inches" and gave me the dimensions in millimetres.

Then I asked her how tall she was. "Five foot seven", she replied.

## LINGUISTIC NOTES

– The French word *pouce* 'thumb' also means 'inch'. So does Italian *pollice*. In Hungarian, *hüvelyk* means both 'inch' and 'thumb', but 'thumb' can also be *hüvelykujj* 'inch-finger'.

## 4.11 Surnames

English-language surnames always mean something, or at least they used to. There were four major sources for our surnames. Some of them were occupational names, like Turner. Others were *patronymics*, where sons were named after their fathers, like Jackson and Howson ('son of Hugh'). There were nicknames, like Ruddy and Fox and Bunn (from French *bon* 'good'). And there were place-names, like Barnett and Whittaker (there are a number of 'white-field' or 'wheat-field' place-names in Britain); and Pilkington, a place in Lancashire. These names were generally the place of origin of people who had moved elsewhere: there would have been no point in calling people who still lived in Pilkington by that name because then everybody there would have had the same name.

Surnames did not really get established in England until the late Middle Ages. That is when names started getting passed on from one generation to another. Boys started being called Turner or Jackson because their father was called Turner or Jackson, not because they turned lathes themselves or because their father was called Jack.

I keep being asked about my own name; and I think it is quite interesting from a dialect point of view. It is actually an occupational name like Turner. The original form was Threadgold, the nickname which was given to men who embroidered the vestments for the clergy – they literally threaded gold.

Over the centuries, the second syllable of the name was reduced in pronunciation, giving Threadg'll. And then there was a special Norfolk/Suffolk dialect factor. Just as our dialect has *troshen* for *threshing* and *troshel* for *threshold*, so Threadg'll was Trodg'll in this part of the world. All Trudgills are descended from an eighteenth-century Harleston man called William Trodgill; and we are also obviously the result of a spelling mistake. Most people were illiterate in those days, so how your name was spelt depended on the vicar listening to what you said your name was, and then doing his best to write it down, hence the *u* rather than an *o*.

Anyway, that is why my name has a hard *g* in it. In the old days, I never had to tell anybody in Norwich that. People who had grown up in the area were used to us – there were enough of us around – but now incomers do not know and have to guess. And that is also why my name does not have an *h* in it, even if the *EDP* occasionally thinks it does.

---

**BACKGROUND NOTES**

---

*This column appears here in the form in which I sent it in to the* EDP, *the week after they had published a column of mine with my name spelt wrongly as Trudghill. When they printed the column, they omitted the last sentence.*

*The names used as illustrations in this article are all, with the exception of my own, those of footballers who were members of the Norwich City squad during the season 2012–13.*

---

**LINGUISTIC NOTES**

---

– On English language surnames, see P. H. Reaney (1969) *The Origin of English Surnames*, London: Routledge & Kegan Paul.

## 4.12 Maps and napkins

A Mr Napier kindly wrote to the *EDP* asking about the origin of his surname, which he believed had an interesting and ancient history. Well, he was certainly right about that!

In mediaeval England, if you had the name Napier, that was because you were a naperer. This term was derived from *nape* – a word we had borrowed from Old

French – which meant 'table-cloth'. *Nape* and the related word *napery* have now been lost in English, but we do still have the diminutive form *napkin*, which was *nape* plus the originally Flemish suffix *kin*.

The corresponding French diminutive form was *naperon* – a 'little cloth'. This was a borrowed into English as *napron*; and eventually *a napron* became *an apron*.

So a *naperer* was a person whose job it was to take care of the table linen: the corresponding Old French word was *napier*.

The question then is: where did the Old French word *nape* come from? Well, everyone agrees that it goes back to Latin *mappa*, meaning cloth or napkin. I say "everyone agrees" because it is slightly odd for a Latin *m* sound to turn into a French *n*, but that is clearly what happened. *Mappa* also meant 'map' in Latin, because maps were originally drawn on cloth, so it was the source of our word *map*, too.

But where did Latin *mappa* come from? The Roman rhetorician Quintilian wrote that it was a word which the Romans had borrowed from Punic. We have to accept what he says because we do not have any other evidence for it. Punic was the colonial dialect of Phoenician which was spoken in ancient Carthage, in North Africa. And Phoenician was a Semitic language which was originally spoken in the area where modern Lebanon now is.

We do not know a great deal about Punic, but Professor Geoffrey Khan, Regius Professor of Hebrew at Cambridge, has told me that Hebrew and Phoenician were very closely related languages, and that there actually was an old Hebrew word *mappa* which meant 'cloth, napkin'. So Quintilian was probably right.

We can suppose, then, that the word *mappa* left its original home in the Middle East some time in the 800s BC, when some Phoenicians departed to found Carthage. It then embarked on a very long journey – in different guises such as *map*, *nape*, *apron*, *napkin*, *naperer* – via North Africa to Europe where, three thousand years later, in twenty-first-century Norfolk, it still survives in the form of Mr Napier's surname.

## LINGUISTIC NOTES

– One account of the change /m/ > /n/ has it that *mappa* changed to *nappe* or *nape* because of *dissimilation*. This was a process which involved a change of bilabial /m/ to dental /n/ in order to avoid a sequence of two bilabial consonants, /m/ and /p/, in consecutive syllables. On the other hand, there was an Old French word *nate* which is, or at least was, found in the form of *nat* meaning 'mat' in some northern English dialects. This came from Latin *matta* (which has given us English *mat*), and here the change from /m/ to /n/ is described as assimilation!

*cont.*

- The Semitic languages are a sub-grouping of the major Afro-Asiatic language family. The main Semitic languages which remain extant today are Amharic (in Ethiopia), Arabic, Aramaic (which was the native language of Jesus, and which has small numbers of speakers in Syria and Turkey), Hebrew, Maltese, Tigrinya (in Ethiopia and Eritrea), Tigre (in Eritrea) and, along the southern coast of the Arabian peninsula, South Arabian languages such as Mehri, which is spoken in parts of Yemen and Oman. Phoenician and Hebrew were closely related Canaanite languages which were members of the historical Northwest Semitic sub-family. See also 5.7.
- For more on *napron/apron*, see 10.3.

## 4.13 No boys named Sue

It is rather well known that the famous English novelist Evelyn Waugh was once briefly married to a woman who was also called Evelyn. The couple were known to their friends as "he-Evelyn" and "she-Evelyn".

This was an unusual situation, since in our culture it is normal for given names to be gender specific – it is obviously helpful to be able to tell what sex someone is from their name. I am made very aware of this if someone writes to me from, say, Japan, where names are totally unrelated to the ones we know. Is a Japanese person called Kazuhiko a man or a woman? Similarly, is a Finn with the name of Terttu male or female? What about a Thai person called Nattapong?

But there are a number of English-language names which can be equally confusing. We have just noted Evelyn. Hilary is another. The famous British novelist Hilary Mantel is female, but the famous British politician Hilary Benn is male. The American actor and comedian Robin Williams was a man, but in the USA Robin is much more often a woman's name – even though it was originally a diminutive form of Robert – while it is almost entirely used for boys and men over here.

How did we end up with ambiguous names like Robin and Evelyn and Hilary? Why wouldn't we try to avoid the confusion that this might produce? Well, there is a very interesting pattern to this development. Nearly all of our ambiguous names started off being given to boys and were only later transferred to girls. Hilary was a boy's name for centuries and only began to be given to girls fairly recently – the transfer has been fairly rapid and is now almost complete, so that today it is Mr Benn's name that surprises us, not Ms Mantell's.

There are several other originally male names which have become ambiguous or even gone over to being entirely female: Ashley, Beverly, Joyce, Leslie, Lindsey . . .

Why is this? Why do parents give boys' names to girls, but not girls' names to boys?

Notice that we do this especially with the shortened, familiar forms of names. There are plenty of girls these days who, whatever their official names, are known to their friends as Sam, or Eddy, or Stevie, or Charley.

But, except in the well-known Johnny Cash song, there are absolutely no boys named Sue.

---

**BACKGROUND NOTES**

*"A Boy Named Sue" is a song which was written by Shel Silverstein and recorded by Johnny Cash. The record was released in 1969. The song deals with the hatred a young man feels for his father because he gave him a girl's name.*

---

**LINGUISTIC NOTES**

– For a highly interesting account of English-language personal naming practices in the modern period, see Richard Coates (1999) "Onomastics", in Suzanne Romaine (ed.), *The Cambridge History of the English Language*, vol. 4, *1776–1997*, Cambridge University Press, 330–72.

## 4.14 Aitch

There are twenty-six letters in the alphabet we use for writing English. Some of these letters are redundant. We could easily abolish *c*, and use *k* and *s* instead: *kathedral sity* would work all right. *X* is a bit pointless too – we could write *boks* instead of *box*. We could also, though, do with some extra letters, since we have no way of indicating the difference between the initial consonants of *thy* and *thigh*. And we have to write our single *sh* and *ch* sounds with two letters.

Mostly, the names we give our letters correspond to the speech sound the letter stands for: the name of the letter *b* begins with a "b" sound, and the name of the letter *f* has an "f" sound in it. But there are exceptions. *W* doesn't have a "w" sound in its name; and you cannot hear a "y" sound in the name of the letter *y* either. And in this part of the world, there is no "r" in the name of the letter *r* – we call it "ah" – even if Bristolians, Scots, Americans and Irish people do pronounce the *r*.

Another exception is the letter *h*, which is called "aitch" – there's no aitch in "aitch". Except that, now, there are quite a lot of people who do pronounce it "haitch", as you have probably noticed. Nearly all of them are under thirty-five. On the train from Norwich to London, you can tell how old the buffet-car staff are from whether they inform the passengers over the intercom that you can get a coffee in coach "aitch" or coach "haitch".

The only exception that I know to this age differentiation is that "haitch" has always been the normal form in the Irish Republic, and amongst people who went to Catholic schools in Northern Ireland. In the bad old days, it was said that you could be stopped in the streets of Belfast by men carrying guns and ordered to recite the alphabet. Australian Catholics tend to say "haitch" as well.

But why have so many younger people here in England started saying "haitch"? It seems like a mistake, doesn't it? Of course it does make the name of this letter fit into the general pattern that we use with our other letters. And perhaps some schoolteachers use that name because they think it will help small children with learning to read and write.

## LINGUISTIC NOTES

– The form *aitch* goes back to Middle English *ache*, which was from Old French *ache*. Like Spanish *ache*, and Italian *acca*, this is assumed to have come from a Latin form such as *ahha*, where the *h* sound appeared in the middle of the word.
– Hypercorrection (see 2.9) would be another obvious explanation for the change *aitch* > *haitch*. Speakers who had been led to believe that there was something wrong with saying *'ammer* and *'ouse* rather than *hammer* and *house*, as is very common in most regional accents in England and Wales, would have inserted an /h/ at the beginning of words beginning with a vowel in order to speak more "correctly" and overdone it, as also with pronouncing *apple* as /hæpəl/.
– For more on *aitch*, see 8.6.

## 4.15 Two

I think we can agree that there is something odd about the spelling of the word *two*. It is the same thing which is odd about *sword* and *answer* – and *Norwich*. These words have a letter *w* in the spelling, but the w is not present in the pronunciation.

This is because we used to pronounce the *w* in words like this, but it has been lost over the centuries through language change. In Old English the masculine form of the numeral *two* was *twegen*, while the feminine and neuter form was *twa* – which is the form that our modern word *two* descends from.

The "w" sound is still retained in most of the languages which are closely related to English such as Scots, where two is *twa*. In German the word is *zwei*. In Dutch and Afrikaans it is *twee*, in Frisian *twa*, in Swedish *två*, in Icelandic *tvö*, and in Faroese *tvey*. But the Danish word for two, which is *to*, has lost the "w" just like English.

The original *tw-* does actually survive in English, though, in many related words. *Twelve* was originally 'two-left' – that is, 'two are left if you subtract ten'. *Twenty* is 'two tens'. *Twice*, obviously, means 'two times'; and *twins* refers to two children born together.

*Twain*, an archaic word which still survives in phrases such as "never the twain shall meet" and splitting something "in twain", comes from the Old English masculine form *twegen*. *Twine* goes back to an Old English form meaning 'double thread', where the threads have been *twisted* – another related word – together. *Twill* was also originally a cloth woven from such double thread. And a *twig* originally meant a fork – a branch which divided into two.

*Between* and *betwixt* are derived from Old English forms of the number *two* preceded by *be*, which was a reduced form of *bi*, modern *by*. In Norfolk we also have the forms *atween* and *atwixt*, which go back to an Old English form with the prefix *on* rather than *bi*.

We have also kept the "w" in another set of words, where it appears as "u". Ancient Proto-Indo-European *dwo* meaning 'two' was the source not only of Old English *twa* but also of Latin *duo*. This Latin form appears in some words which we have borrowed from the classical language or from Italian, such as *duality* and *duet*.

So English has a dual origin for words related to *two*.

## LINGUISTIC NOTES

– For more on *be-/bi/by*, see 4.7 on *but*.

# 5 Languages and dialects in contact and conflict

In this section I look at contact: contact between people speaking different languages, and contact between people speaking different dialects. I examine the use of certain languages as lingua francas – that is, as languages of wider communication in multilingual situations. I also discuss issues to do with minority languages and dialects, including language conflict; and I explore different facets of bilingualism – the use of two languages – and bidialectism – the use of two dialects.

## 5.1 Julius and Cleopatra

A lot of people know that, as Julius Caesar was being stabbed to death, he turned to his friend Brutus, who was one of the assassins, and said *Et tu, Brute?*, the Latin for 'And you, Brutus?', or 'What, you too?'

A lot of people know this, because those were the words put into Caesar's mouth by William Shakespeare. But it is probably wrong. We do not know if Caesar said anything at all: we do not have any eye-witness reports. But we do know that if he did say something, he probably did not say it in Latin.

It is much more likely that his dying words were uttered in Ancient Greek. The Roman historian Suetonius – not an eye-witness either, as he was writing about the event over a century after it happened – claimed that what Caesar said was *Και συ τέκνον?* (Kai su, teknon?), the Greek for 'You too, my son?'

But surely the language of Ancient Rome was Latin? (It was.) So why on earth would Romans be speaking Greek? Well, most of them didn't: they spoke Latin. But the patricians – the toffs like Caesar – were bilingual in Latin and Greek, and they tended to speak Greek to each other.

When Caesar died in 44 BC, Alexander of Macedon had been dead for nearly 300 years; but it was Alexander the Great whose conquests had taken the Greek language across the Middle East and Iran into the places which are now Turkmenistan, Tajikistan, Uzbekistan, Afghanistan, Pakistan, northwestern India, and parts of Kyrgyzstan and Kazakhstan.

Greek became vitally important as the *lingua franca* – the language of wider communication – in a very large area of the eastern Mediterranean. Later on, even under the Roman Empire, Greek was the official language in the provinces of Libya,

Egypt, Arabia, Judea, Syria and Persia, as well as Greece and Asia Minor. This widespread knowledge of Greek, and its usage in the New Testament, greatly aided the spread of Christianity. And back in Ancient Rome itself, Greek became the prestigious language of learning and cultivation to such an extent that the upper classes actually spoke it amongst themselves.

Julius Caesar had a famous love affair with the 21-year-old Queen of Egypt, Cleopatra. (She was actually in Rome when Caesar was assassinated.) She might never have been able to seduce him in Alexandria, as she is said to have done, if Greek had not been her mother tongue – and Caesar's second language.

## LINGUISTIC NOTES

- *Brute* is the vocative case – the form used for calling to or addressing someone – of the name *Brutus*.
- The sociolinguistic situation in Rome would not have been unlike the elite bilingualism situation in nineteenth-century Russia, where the aristocrats used French amongst themselves; see Derek Offord *et al.* (eds.) (2015) *French and Russian in Imperial Russia*, vol. 1: *Language Use among the Eighteenth and Early Nineteenth Century Russian Elite*, Edinburgh University Press.
- A *lingua franca* is a language which is used in communication between speakers who have no native language in common. If English is used between native speakers of Swedish and Dutch, then it is functioning as a lingua franca. English is the most significant lingua franca in the world today, but other languages which are used as lingua francas in a large-scale institutionalized way in different parts of the world today include Swahili in East Africa and French in parts of West Africa.
- On Greek as a lingua franca, see Geoffrey Horrocks (2010) *Greek: A History of the Language and Its Speakers*, 2nd edn, Oxford: Blackwell.

## 5.2 Lesbian English

This August I spent a week teaching on a linguistics summer school on the Greek island of Lesbos. (I dare say that sounds idyllic, but I'd like you to know that it was very uncomfortably hot, at 40°C.) Doctoral and post-doctoral students came from all over the world: Venezuela, USA, England, France, Spain, Belgium, Holland, Austria, Albania, Turkey, Japan . . .

And everybody spoke English.

Of course, the Venezuelan and the Spaniard might greet each other in Spanish, and the Belgians and the Dutch might chat in Dutch; but the classes, presentations, discussions, announcements, meals – absolutely everything official or communal was conducted in English.

There was never any discussion about whether this was going to happen or not. It is what almost always happens these days at truly international meetings. English is the world language.

It is important to realise, though, that this is not because English is in any way superior to other languages; all languages are wonderful, and English is no more or less wonderful than any other. English became the world language for economic, military and political – not linguistic – reasons. The situation came about as a result of the British Empire's many decades of economic and political domination of the world and, later, the same kind of dominance as exercised by the USA, which had itself become English-speaking as a result of colonisation by the British Empire.

This state of affairs has now become so entrenched that it is not going to change. Some people have a developed a facile view that English will be replaced by Chinese as the world language. It won't. There is no reason why it should. Far too many millions of people in every part of the world have invested so much time and money and effort in acquiring and speaking and writing and printing and teaching English that this situation is here to stay.

It is very useful to have a language that everyone can use as a lingua franca. When Finns go on holiday to Greece, they do not expect Greeks to speak Finnish to them. They expect – and get – English. If a Spanish professor gives a lecture at a Japanese university, they will not do it in Spanish or Japanese, but English. If a Pole falls in love with a Dane, English is very likely to have been involved.

But there are disadvantages, especially for us British. Of all the people involved on that summer school, I was the most useless at speaking foreign languages. Because I didn't have to.

## 5.3 Mandarin or not?

A lot of people are learning Mandarin Chinese these days. That seems like a good idea, as it is the language in the world with the most native speakers. English, on the other hand, is the language which has the most non-native speakers – 500 million – with an additional 350 million of us who are native speakers.

Mandarin is one of a number of languages called Chinese; there are at least six. In Hong Kong, the local language is not Mandarin but Cantonese, which is spoken by about 70 million people in China as a whole. People speaking Mandarin and Cantonese cannot understand one another at all. In Taiwan the main language is Hokkien, which is also found in mainland China and amongst the Chinese diaspora in the Philippines, Indonesia, Singapore and Malaysia; it has nearly as many speakers as Cantonese.

Linguistic scientists are always very happy when they hear about people learning a foreign language. Everybody should learn at least one. And it is also a very good idea to find out what non-European languages are like: they can often be surprisingly and fascinatingly different from European languages. It really is best, though, if you can learn a foreign language properly so that you can read it and use it for talking to people. That is very hard work, however: learning a language is a massive task. Perhaps pupils passing GCSE French or German or Spanish with a high grade should be awarded two GCSEs, not just one?

It would really be excellent if all British people could study, learn and be able to speak, or at least understand and read, other European languages like French, German, Spanish, Italian, Swedish ... With these languages, you have a good chance of ultimately being able to read them successfully.

With Mandarin the chances are rather low. The writing system makes that enormously difficult. The language itself is not particularly hard, though you will be starting from scratch, unlike with western European languages where you will know lots of the words already. But the Chinese writing system is so complex that even Chinese-speaking children are not able to read a newspaper satisfactorily until quite late.

Of course, if you want to go and do business in China, it would be helpful to speak Mandarin. But unless you are very good indeed, it would be much safer to use a professional interpreter as well.

So why don't you learn, say, German or Spanish? You will find it a lot easier. You can readily travel to Germany or Austria or Switzerland, or to Spain or South America, read the newspapers there, find out what people are thinking, discover their literatures, and get some insight into the way they look at things.

Unless you are a really brilliant language learner and are willing to devote years of your life to learning the language, you are unlikely to get that far with Mandarin.

**BACKGROUND NOTES**

GCSE – the General Certificate of Secondary Education – is an academic qualification which is awarded to students in particular subjects in the United Kingdom (apart from Scotland), most usually at the age of 16.

**LINGUISTIC NOTES**

– The grammar of spoken Chinese causes very few difficulties for non-native learners. The phonology is more complex, since the different Chinese varieties are all tone languages in which an identical syllable in terms of vowels and consonants can form different words depending on voice pitch and movement. Mandarin has four word tones: level, rising, falling and falling–rising. Cantonese has six word tones, and many dialects of Hokkien have five.

*cont.*

- The Chinese writing system is logographic, i.e. a single character or symbol is used to represent a morpheme or single-syllable word. In order to read Mandarin at the same level as educated Chinese people, you would need to learn and recognise something like 4,000 characters.

## 5.4 English is not enough

An index of worldwide linguistic proficiency shows that the very highest levels of proficiency in English as a foreign language are found in Denmark, Holland, Sweden, Finland, Norway, Poland and Austria, in that order. The nations outside Europe with the highest levels of English proficiency are Malaysia, Singapore, the Dominican Republic and South Korea. The lowest levels in Europe (although we do not have information for many of the Balkan countries) are, starting from the bottom, Ukraine, Russia, France, Italy, Slovakia, Portugal and Spain.

The low position of France is rather remarkable. Although they are just across the Channel from us, the French are lower on the index than Hungary, Romania, Latvia and even Argentina. Maybe this is because there is a tradition in France of resisting English as the language of American imperialism, which of course it is; but perhaps they should consider that it is also the language of international communication, and one is at a disadvantage without it.

Talking of disadvantages, where would the British come on any worldwide index of foreign language proficiency? Pretty low, is my guess. Too many people here have the wrong attitude to the teaching and learning of foreign languages. Fewer pupils now study languages at school; language qualifications are no longer a requirement for university entrance; and, in a spate of academic vandalism, universities are closing down language departments.

Some people think that that is OK: why should young British people bother to learn other languages when everywhere else in the world there is such a strong emphasis on developing a very good command of English?

A high proportion of people in Denmark, Holland, Sweden and elsewhere speak English so well that, if necessary, they can use it fluently in their working lives, and with clarity and accuracy. Very many educated Swiss people speak Swiss German, Standard German, English and French, and then apologise for their bad Italian.

And we are not just talking about academics and top professionals: think of all those eloquent Dutch and Scandinavian footballers you can hear doing post-match interviews on TV.

So the real question that we should be asking is: why would an international business employ a young monolingual British English speaker when they could engage a bilingual (or trilingual or quadrilingual) Dutch, Austrian, Swiss or South

Korean person? By thinking that "English is enough", we are putting our country and ourselves at a disadvantage.

The truth is that English is not enough.

## 5.5  A tragedy and the Winter Olympics

On 7 October 1992, something really rather tragic occurred. An elderly gentleman called Mr Tecfik Esenc died in his sleep. This was of course very sad for his friends and family, but it was also a tragedy for all of us, because Mr Esenc was the last ever mother-tongue speaker of an ancient European language called Ubykh.

This was yet another nail in the coffin of worldwide linguistic diversity, adding to the growing list of dead and dying languages around the world. Experts predict that, of the 7,000 or so languages in the world today, 90 percent will disappear during the next two centuries or so. Each language that dies will take with it, for ever, a unique product of the human mind, and the unique product of a particular human society. A unique repository of a special human culture will have gone for all time.

Ubykh was no exception. All human languages are objects of wonder; but Ubykh was particularly amazing. If you look at the *Guinness Book of Records* you will see that, of all the languages in the world, it is listed as the one which had the most consonant sounds. English has quite a lot of consonants – like most Norfolk speakers, I have 24 – but Ubykh had 81! And it had many fascinating grammatical structures, too.

Ubykh was not related to any of the Indo-European languages like German, or Russian, or Greek, or English. Rather, it was part of a family of languages which had been spoken for millennia in the northwestern part of the Caucasus Mountains, by the Black Sea.

The language died out because in the nineteenth century its homeland was attacked and invaded by the Russians under Czar Alexander II. In 1864 the Ubykh people finally decided to leave in order to avoid subjugation at the hands of the Russian army, and to escape the massacres which were reported to have occurred elsewhere in the Caucasus as the Russians attempted to take these lands for themselves. The Ubykhs made for the neighbouring Ottoman Empire and settled in Turkey. There, over a few generations, as a minority in a foreign land, they gradually shifted over to speaking the majority language, Turkish.

One of the main centres of Ubykh language and culture which these unfortunate people were forced to flee from, taking their language and culture with them, was a place they called Soatshe. You may have heard of it. The Russians call it Sochi.

**BACKGROUND NOTES**

*This column was published in February 2014, during the Winter Olympic Games which were being held in Sochi, Russia. There was quite a lot of English-language journalistic discussion around the Games to do with gay rights, but there was nothing that I saw about the rights of the indigenous peoples of the area.*

**LINGUISTIC NOTES**

- Ubykh was a member of the Northwest Caucasian language family. The other members are Abkhaz, Abaza, Kabardian (or East Circassian) and Adyghe (or West Circassian). For more information, see George Hewitt (2005) "North-West Caucasian", *Lingua* 115: 91–145.
- Language death is important not just because linguists find studying languages fascinating. On what we are losing as a result of language death, see Nicholas Evans (2010) *Dying Words: Endangered Languages and What They Have to Tell Us*, Oxford: Blackwell.

## 5.6 Ukraine

The only time I ever went to Ukraine, most of the people I met there were speaking Hungarian. This was in the far southwest of Ukraine, which was part of Hungary until 1919, and then part of Czechoslovakia until 1945, when the Soviet Union took over. The town of Ungvar (in Ukrainian, Uzhhorod), on the border with Slovakia, is still Hungarian speaking.

Hungarian is by no means the only non-Slavic minority language in Ukraine. There are large numbers of Rumanian speakers, as well as speakers of German, Yiddish and Romany. In Crimea, while it would not be true to say that the Tatars, who speak a Turkic language related to Kazakh, are the original inhabitants, they have certainly been there much longer than the Russians and Ukrainians, who did not arrive until the 1700s. The Greeks were just one of many peoples who were in Crimea before the Tatars, and there are still Greek speakers in Ukraine.

As far as Slavic languages are concerned, there are about a million Polish speakers in western Ukraine. Polish is a West Slavic language while Ukrainian and Russian are East Slavic. About 25 per cent of Ukrainians – the figures are not totally reliable – are native speakers of Russian, but interestingly, only 17 per cent claim to be ethnic Russians. And, as we have been hearing in the news, most Russians are concentrated in the south and east of the country.

Early in 2014, the Ukrainian government foolishly repealed a law that allowed Russian, Hungarian, Rumanian and Tatar to be used in courts and for other official purposes, but fortunately they quickly repealed the repeal.

Ukrainian and Russian are closely related languages – probably about as close as Italian and Spanish – and some communication is possible between their speakers, since the two languages have more than 60 per cent of their vocabularies in common. But when we see pictures on TV of Ukrainians and Russians speaking to each other, they are probably speaking Russian, since many Ukrainians have learnt it as a second language. Ukrainian was banned under the Tsars and was repressed by Stalin.

The close relationship between Russian and Ukrainian has led to there being a long history of linguistically prejudiced Russians disrespectfully denying that Ukrainian is actually a language at all, claiming that it is really just a rather inferior peasant dialect of Russian. The last Russian Tsar, Nicholas II, also known as Nicholas the Bloody, once said exactly that.

He was, of course, executed in 1918.

**BACKGROUND NOTES**

*The occasion for this piece was the outbreak of armed conflict in the east of Ukraine between Russian-speaking rebels and the Ukrainian government and their supporters – as well as the annexation of Crimea by Russian government forces in 2014.*

**LINGUISTIC NOTES**

– Ukrainian and Russian form part of the East Slavic (or East Slavonic) dialect continuum which also includes the dialects of Belarusian (also known as Byelorussian, Belorussian, White Russian). This has the consequence that in some areas, certain dialects of Russian and Ukrainian are very much more similar to one another than the standard varieties are.

## 5.7 Semitic

Some commentators have pointed out that it is a tactic used by the Israeli political establishment to argue that foreign criticism of Israeli government policies is motivated by anti-Semitism. In fact it is obviously perfectly possible to disapprove of Israeli government actions without being at all anti-Semitic: *anti-Semitic* means demonstrating prejudice against or hostility to Jews as an entire ethnic or religious group.

For a linguist, though, the interesting thing here is that, while the word *anti-Semitic* is widely used to mean anti-Jewish, *Semitic* does not mean Jewish. Although, in deeply racist Victorian England, the term *Semite* came to be used as a kind of distorted euphemism for *Jew* – a word which was considered "not very nice" in polite society (much as in living memory we used to say *Negro* instead of *Black*) – *Semitic* actually refers to many more peoples than just the Jews.

In linguistics, Semitic refers to the family of languages which descend from Proto-Semitic, which was spoken somewhere in the Middle East in about the fourth millennium BC. Hebrew, which most of the Old Testament was written in, was one of many ancient Semitic languages. Another was Aramaic, which eventually became the most powerful language in the Middle East. By the first century BC, the widespread adoption of Aramaic had led to the death of Hebrew and other local languages like Canaanite; Jesus and his disciples would have been mother-tongue speakers of Aramaic.

Hebrew did survive as the liturgical language of the Jews; and after many centuries it was artificially resurrected as the national language of modern Israel. A number of linguists, however, argue that modern Hebrew – they prefer to call it Israeli – is as much a European as a Semitic language, since many of its structures come from Slavic languages like Polish and from the Germanic language Yiddish.

Aramaic is still spoken by small endangered groups of Syriac Christians, Moslems and Jews in parts of Iran, Iraq and Syria. But the major Semitic languages in the world today are Amharic, which is the official language of Ethiopia; the Tigre and Tigrinya languages of Eritrea; and Arabic, which is actually better regarded as a group of related languages.

You may not realise that one of the official languages of the European Union is also Semitic: that's Maltese. But if you do feel like criticising Malta for some reason, no one is going to call you anti-Semitic.

## LINGUISTIC NOTES

- On the linguistic classification of modern Israeli Hebrew, see Ghil'ad Zuckermann (2003) *Language Contact and Lexical Enrichment in Israeli Hebrew*, Basingstoke: Palgrave Macmillan.
- For more on Semitic languages, see 4.12.

## 5.8  What we can learn from the Welsh

The original language of our country, or rather the earliest language that we know about, was Welsh. Three thousand years ago, and possibly much earlier, everybody in Norfolk, and in fact everybody in Britain, spoke Welsh – or, more accurately, its ancestor, Brittonic Celtic.

By the year AD 1000, however, this ancient language had been pushed back to the far west of our country – Cornwall, Devon, Wales, the Lake District, and Galloway in southwestern Scotland. And now, although Welsh is not doing too badly, there are only some areas of Wales where a majority of people use the language on a daily basis.

One difficulty Welsh people encounter in trying to preserve their language, and pass it on to future generations, is the problem of the large numbers of monolingual English people who are moving in. Because North Wales is a beautiful area, people want to go and live there – and some of them then expect everybody to speak English to them. Some even object, disgracefully, to the local language being used in schools, in a way they would never dream of doing if they had moved to, say, France.

Language death is the biggest cultural tragedy in the modern world. Perhaps 90 per cent of the world's languages will be dead in 200 years time. So the Welsh are quite right to do everything they can to defend their language against anything that jeopardises its future – including incomers.

But dialect death is also a tragedy; and here in Norfolk we are right to try and defend our dialect against anything which jeopardises its future too – including incomers. Of course, when adults come in gradually, and form a small proportion of the population, their children will acquire our local way of speaking, even if some incoming parents, disgracefully, don't want them to. But if very large numbers of outsiders were to arrive all at once, this would threaten our local culture and speech, because then the children would not be surrounded by a majority of locals to learn from.

It now seems that 30,000 new houses are going to be built in the Norwich area. Quite a lot of them may be built in the unspoilt rural areas east of the city where I used to walk and cycle when I was young. I know there are homeless people in the Norwich area – but surely not, at 2.3 per household, 70,000 of them? No, apparently, this vast amount of new building is because, as a local politician has said, "Norfolk is a beautiful area, and people want to come and live here." Speaking personally, I rather wish they wouldn't.

## LINGUISTIC NOTES

– For more on Brittonic and Welsh, see Section 1. When the language boundary between Brittonic and English had been pushed back so far to the west that Brittonic was confined to Cornwall and Devon, Wales and the Lake District plus neighbouring areas, this had the consequence that the originally continuous Brittonic-speaking area was now divided geographically into three. The forms of Brittonic spoken in the three areas were now cut off from one another, and gradually diverged linguistically. It is usual, therefore, to refer to the early mediaeval Brittonic of Devon and Cornwall as Cornish; the Brittonic of Wales as Welsh; and the Brittonic of northwestern England and southwestern Scotland as Cumbric. The words *Cumbric* and *Cumbria* have the same Brittonic origin as the Welsh word for Wales, *Cymru*.

## 5.9 "The only thing in life is language"

I am jealous of Iwan Roberts.

Not because he was "one of the greatest goal scorers ever to pull on a Norwich City shirt". And not because he played international football as a striker for Wales – I always wanted to be Ken Nethercott.

No, I envy Iwan because he is bilingual. When he is doing football commentaries on Radio Cymru, he speaks Welsh, his native language. When he is being interviewed about Norwich City on Radio Norfolk, he speaks English, his native language. Iwan has two native languages. Like most people from his part of North Wales, he grew up in a bilingual environment, and he acquired two mother tongues effortlessly as a consequence.

Growing up bilingual is a wonderful thing. Learning a new language as an adolescent or adult is a formidable and daunting task. It can take a very long time, and is only very rarely entirely successful. Learning a language as an infant is a doddle. We all do it, easily, and in the space of a few years. Human infants are genetically programmed to learn perfectly any language they are sufficiently exposed to in early childhood; and they can readily learn two or three or even four languages in this way.

I only managed to acquire one language properly. In the environment which I grew up in, everybody spoke Norfolk. I am very happy to have our local dialect as my native tongue, but it would have been nice to be a mother-tongue speaker of another language as well, such as Dutch, like our Deputy Prime Minister, or Welsh, like Iwan.

Being bilingual also seems to have other benefits, in addition to the practical one of being able to communicate with people who speak a particular language. Those who have grown up bilingual learn third and fourth languages better than the rest of us, even as adults, perhaps because they are more sensitised to the nature of language.

And this sensitivity shows itself in other ways as well. Just think of Richard Burton's amazing way with the English language. He was someone else who grew up bilingual in Welsh and English. He famously said that "the only thing in life is language. Not love. Not anything else."

But he also said "I would rather have played for Wales at Cardiff Arms Park than Hamlet at the Old Vic." To be honest, I wouldn't have minded scoring a few goals at Carrow Road, like Iwan, myself.

---

### BACKGROUND NOTES

*Iwan Roberts (b. 1968) is a former professional footballer who played for Norwich City from 1997 to 2004. He writes a column on football in the* EDP. *Ken Nethercott was the Norwich City goalkeeper in the 1950s, and a big hero of mine.*

*The Deputy Prime Minister at the time of the writing of this article was Nick Clegg.*

*Cardiff Arms Park was the name of the rugby union ground where international matches involving the Welsh team were played.*

---

### LINGUISTIC NOTES

– There are a number of studies which show that bilinguals have an advantage over monolinguals when it comes to learning additional languages; see, for example, Ellen Bialystok (1991) *Language Processing in Bilingual Children*, Cambridge University Press.

## 5.10 Gillian Anderson and the critical threshold

Perhaps you saw the BBC drama series *The Fall*, set in Belfast. It will not have been to everyone's taste – it was about a serial murderer – but I enjoyed it, and I was especially impressed by the leading actress, Gillian Anderson.

Many people know Gillian from the American TV series *The X-Files*, where she played the FBI agent Scully. The remarkable thing about her performance in *The*

*Fall*, though, was that she played the part of an Englishwoman, detective Stella Gibson, and she had an absolutely impeccable English English accent. You could not hear anything at all to indicate she was American; and as a linguist, I was listening very hard for clues. Even the most brilliant of actors, Meryl Streep for instance, however good they are at imitating a particular accent, usually give the game away through small phonetic details. But not Gillian. Many people do switch from one accent to another for various reasons, but they very rarely do it so perfectly. How could she manage it?

Apparently her English accent is entirely genuine. She grew up in England and went to school here. Then, when she was 11, her American parents took her to live in the USA, where she also acquired a perfectly genuine American accent. That age – 11 – was crucial. Much older, and she would never have acquired the American accent so perfectly. Much younger, and she would have totally lost her English accent. As it was, she ended up being completely bilingual or, rather, bi-accentual. On YouTube you can see an interview by Jay Leno with an American woman called Gillian Anderson, and another interview by Michael Parkinson of a Gillian Anderson who is obviously English.

Human beings are genetically programmed to learn perfectly any language they are sufficiently exposed to, up to the age of about 8. Equally, they are likely to forget the language completely if exposure stops around that age. From 8 onwards, this innate ability gradually tails off until it disappears completely by about 14: it is a rare person who can learn a language perfectly after that age. Gillian at 11 was probably at exactly the right age to have a brain flexible enough to acquire a new language variety, but mature enough not to lose an old one.

If you want your children to have a Norfolk accent, as I am sure you do, keep them in the county until they are at least 11. And whatever you do, don't send them away to boarding school.

## LINGUISTIC NOTES

- The role of age in language acquisition is discussed in linguistics under the term the *critical period hypothesis*, also known as the *critical threshold hypothesis* and the *critical age hypothesis*, going back to Eric Lenneberg's 1967 book *Biological Foundations of Language* (New York: Wiley). Most of us know from our own experience that when it comes to language learning, "human children indeed seem to have an advantage compared to . . . adult members of their own species" (Östen Dahl, 2004, *The Growth and Maintenance of Linguistic Complexity*, Amsterdam: Benjamins, 294).

## 5.11 Mother tongue

Norwich City football supporters posting on the *Pink'Un* website about the coming season in the Premier League and about our manager Chris Hughton have been calling him, affectionately, Hoots.

Hoots is a nickname which people from other areas might not understand, because they do not go in for the Norfolk speciality which linguists call *yod-dropping*, made famous by Bernard Matthew's catch-phrase "bootiful" (*yod* refers to the "y" sound like the one at the beginning of words like *you*). We do not have a "y" sound after the *b* in *beautiful*, or after the *d* in *due*, which we say the same as *do*; and we pronounce *Hugh* without the "y", the same as *who*.

But there is something else linguistically interesting about Chris. We use the term Cockney rather loosely round these parts to refer to anyone who sounds vaguely like they might come from the Home Counties. But Chris really is a true Londoner; he grew up close to the West Ham football ground in East London, and he quite rightly talks just like that.

It is always worth listening to what Chris has to say, because he speaks very intelligently, articulately and interestingly about football and our football club. But you might just notice that there is one little thing about the way he speaks which is not Cockney. He does not pronounce the word *many* like Londoners or Norfolk people do. We say "menny". He pronounces it "manny", to rhyme with *canny*.

That was the original pronunciation of the word in older forms of English, which is why it's spelt with an *a*. But why would Chris use this older form? You can pick up a clue to this puzzle from someone else associated with the Canaries. If you listen, as you should, to the excellent BBC Radio Norfolk football coverage, you can hear Paul McVeigh using exactly the same pronunciation as Chris. Paul is from Belfast: people from all over Ireland still use this original pronunciation.

Chris is not actually from Ireland, even though he played for the Republic of Ireland national team fifty-three times; but the point is that he qualified to play for them because his mother is Irish, from County Limerick they say.

So here is a fascinating little thing. "Mother tongue" is not a very good label. Children do not speak like their mothers, or fathers. They speak like their peers – the friends they grow up with. But, occasionally, just a little something from the language of the first person you ever heard speaking may stick.

Let's hope Norwich City will be playing football in the Premier League for manny, manny years to come.

## BACKGROUND NOTES

*Chris Hughton became Norwich City manager (coach) in 2012. Sadly, he did not manage to keep Norwich in the Premier League during 2013–14, and left the club at the end of the season.*

*The Pink'Un was originally the local sports newspaper, and continues publication today as a supplement to the EDP. The Norwich City football team are known as the Canaries, and the club emblem has a canary on it. Norwich was famous for the breeding of canaries, which were said to have first been imported by Flemish weavers who liked to have singing canaries to keep them company in their attic weaving workshops (see 1.12).*

*Bernard Matthews (1930–2010) was a Norfolkman who founded a very successful turkey farming business. He appeared in person in a number of TV adverts for his turkeys, which he claimed tasted "beautiful".*

## LINGUISTIC NOTES

– The accent of Norfolk and neighbouring areas to the west has total yod-dropping, i.e. the original /j/ has disappeared not only in words like *rule, lute, Sue, tune, dune* but also in *pew* /pʉː/, *beauty* /bʉtiː/, *music* /mʉːzɪk/, *few* /fʉː/, *view* /vʉː/, *cue* /kʉː/, *Hugh* /hʉː/ etc., where /ʉː/ is a central vowel between /uː/ and /yː/.

## 5.12 Vallée d'Aoste

In July 2014, the Norwich City football squad were involved in a slightly embarrassing situation during their pre-season tour in northern Italy. One of the games they had arranged was called off by the Italian club involved, and a replacement fixture was rapidly arranged against another side.

NCFC reported that the rearranged match was to be played against an Italian Serie D side, Saint-Christophe Vallée d'Aoste. After Norwich had won 13–0, that Italian club complained that the match had not actually involved them at all but a scratch eleven of local non-professionals: Norwich apologised for the misunderstanding.

I wonder if there were some language difficulties in all this, because there is something linguistically rather interesting about that area of Italy. You may have noticed that the name of that local football club is not Italian but French: *vallée* is the French word for 'valley'. This is because French is the official language in the area. The indigenous local language, however, is not French or Italian but

Franco-Provençal, a now endangered language originally spoken all over western Switzerland, eastern France and northwestern Italy.

Monolingual English speakers often assume when we are travelling that language and national boundaries coincide. We travel to Majorca and, thinking that Majorca is in Spain, get ourselves a Spanish phrase book. That's OK – everyone can speak Spanish there; but the local language is not Spanish but Catalan, as spoken for example by Majorcan tennis star Rafa Nadal.

Tourists skiing in St Moritz or Davos may not realise that the local language there is Romansch, not German or Italian. People holidaying in the South Tyrol in northern Italy may not, in spite of the fact that all the place-names there are in German, pick up on the fact that the locals are German rather than Italian speaking.

Most European countries have sizeable indigenous linguistic minorities. Hungarian is the native language of southern Slovakia as well as extensive areas of central Romania. There are large regions of Finland where people speak Swedish. France has citizens whose mother tongue is Dutch, German, Breton, Basque, Catalan or Provençal. In parts of southern Italy, Greek and Albanian are still spoken natively. And Greece has speakers of Albanian, Bulgarian, Turkish, Romany and Rumanian.

It is communities like these that the European Charter for Regional or Minority Languages is intended to help and protect. Sadly, France and Italy have not ratified the Charter yet, and Greece has not even signed it. It's about time they did.

## 5.13 Barriers

It is obvious that languages are barriers to communication. Most of us arriving for the first time in Moldova or Kazakhstan will not be able to communicate at all, unless we can find someone who has learnt English.

It is easy to think, then, that the world would be a much better place if we got rid of our different languages. Surely, if we could all understand and communicate with one another in a single common language, then our planet would enjoy a more harmonious and peaceful future?

Well, it is easy to think that – until you remember the American Civil War, where both sides spoke English. Or the appalling genocide in Rwanda, where the Hutus spoke the same Bantu language, Kinyarwanda, as the Tutsis. Or the carnage in Yugoslavia which involved Croats, Serbs and Bosnians, who all spoke Serbo-Croat. All of the groups involved in these orgies of killing were able understand one another perfectly well, but that did not help.

I prefer to think that barriers to communication are actually a Good Thing. Languages are barriers which can be penetrated – it is perfectly possible, and desirable, to learn foreign languages. But the separation of the world's population into groups speaking different languages does have the very beneficial consequence of helping to promote the growth of cultural diversity. And diversity can lead to the development of alternative possibilities for humankind for making social, political and technological progress: we are not all heading up the same, possibly blind, alley.

A world where everyone spoke the same language would be a less interesting place. But there is also a good chance that it would be a rather stagnant place too. If the entire population of the world consisted of native speakers of English, then we would probably not only all be watching American soap operas on TV and drinking Coca Cola, we would also all tend to have the same values, the same ideas and the same worldview. If diversity does lead to progress, then this would be a disturbing scenario.

It is already clear that English-speaking countries like Britain and Australia are more vulnerable than many others to the infiltration of influence, not all of it beneficial, from American advertising, ideas and values. I don't actually know the answers to the following questions, but: Have high-school leavers in Moldova actually started organising proms yet? And do children in Kazakhstan go trick-or-treating at Halloween?

## BACKGROUND NOTES

*The American-style celebration of Halloween, with trick-or-treating, reached Britain in a major way only in the 1980s and 1990s. Prior to that, Halloween was celebrated in more traditional ways in Scotland, northern England, Wales and the southwest of England, but was completely unknown in southern and eastern Britain. When I was a child in Norwich in the 1950s, we had never heard of Halloween. According to Iona and Peter Opie, in their* The Lore and Language of Schoolchildren *(see 11.3), Halloween was a night when one half of the country had no idea what the other half were doing.*

## LINGUISTIC NOTES

- The Bantu language family consists of languages spoken over nearly all of the southern half of the African continent. Major Bantu languages include Swahili, Shona and Zulu.
- Serbo-Croat is a South Slavic variety which was formally the major official language of Yugoslavia. It is now often considered locally to be four separate languages, although these are extremely similar and have more or less total mutual intelligibility: Serbian, Croatian, Bosnian and Montenegrin.

# 6 Respecting English grammar

In this section, I continue with the descriptive, anti-prescriptivist theme, arguing that all dialects have grammatical rules and structures, and that no one dialect is more "correct" than any other, nor grammatically superior to any other.

## 6.1 You done it, did you?

The word *grammar* has scary associations for many people; but there is really nothing to feel frightened about. We all use grammar all the time. You cannot speak without it. With no grammar, a language would not be a language. Think of the important difference between *Norwich beat Ipswich* and *Ipswich beat Norwich*: that's grammar. All languages and dialects have grammar, and the Norfolk dialect is no exception – we may "do different", but we're not that different!

Most of the grammatical rules of the Norfolk dialect are the same as those in other English dialects. All types of English agree that adjectives come before nouns – unlike in French. There is a grammatical rule of English which allows *the red car* but not *the car red*. Everyone knows that, even if they have never thought about it. That is grammar too. It's not very scary, is it?

But English grammar does vary from place to place. Scottish has *my car needs washed*. American has *I've gotten used to it*. In England we do not say these things, but grammar may differ here too. In Norfolk we can say *he drive very fast, she like that a lot*, without the *s* that many other dialects use. That is one of the ways in which our grammar differs from Standard English.

Standard English is the dialect which is used in books and newspapers, and in the education system, so this sort of difference has led some people to think that Norfolk grammar is "bad grammar". But there is nothing bad about it; it is just different. Local dialects may have lower social status than Standard English, but that does not make them "wrong". They just have their own, different grammars, with their own rules.

Think about the verb *to do*. Standard English often uses past-tense *did* where Norfolk and most other local dialects would use *done: she done lots of work*. But Norfolk uses the form *did* too, according to a specific grammatical rule which Standard English does not have. There are two different verbs *to do*. There is the full verb *do*, which refers to someone actually doing something: *I do my shopping on*

*Mondays.* And then there is the auxiliary verb *do*, which is used for grammatical tasks like making questions – *Do you like it?* – and making negatives – *I do not like it.*

In Norfolk we treat these two verbs differently; we have a grammatical distinction which Standard English does not have. Standard English speakers say *You did it, did you?*, while dialect speakers here say *You done it, did you?* This does not make Norfolk better than Standard English, it's just different. Many Norfolk dialect speakers probably could not tell you what an auxiliary verb is. But they do actually know – because none of them would ever say \*You done it, done you?* That would go against the rules of Norfolk grammar, rules that all dialect speakers learn as small children and know intuitively.

Some features of Norfolk grammar are older language forms which have been lost elsewhere. When we say *Come you on!*, we are using grammar that goes back to the Old English of a thousand years ago. But when Norfolk dialect speakers say *You'd better go to bed now, do you'll be tired tomorrow*, they are using an East Anglian innovation where *do* has turned into a conjunction which means 'otherwise'. My grandparents used this construction, but it has never been part of my natural speech, and it is not heard so much these days. But it did make its way from Norfolk to the southern USA. In her 1948 novel *Seraph*, the Florida writer Zora Neal Hurston has an American character saying *Git this spoon betwixt her teeth do she's liable to bite her tongue off.* So maybe it will survive longer there than here.

It would be a pity if this *do* was lost for ever. If there are any Norfolk dialect features you are particularly fond of, keep you a-usen on 'em, do they might disappear.

### BACKGROUND NOTES

*Linguistic scientists place an asterisk \* before sentences and other forms to indicate that they do not actually occur.*

### LINGUISTIC NOTES

– The French for *the red car* is *la voiture rouge*, literally 'the car red'.
– Most nonstandard dialects of English around the world have the same distinction that we have in Norfolk between past-tense forms of the auxiliary verb *do* and forms of main verb *do*. Some dialects also have a distinction between the present-tense forms, as in *You dos it, do you*?
– For the genesis of the East Anglian conjunction *do*, see Peter Trudgill (1995) "Grammaticalisation and social structure: nonstandard conjunction-formation in East Anglian English", in F. R. Palmer (ed.), *Grammar and Meaning: Papers in Honour of John Lyons*, Cambridge University Press, 136–47. On the American connection, see Peter Trudgill (2002) *Sociolinguistic Variation and Change*, Edinburgh University Press, chapter 1: "British vernacular dialects in the formation of American English: the case of East Anglian *do*".

## 6.2 Long John Hill

There are those who erroneously believe that Norfolk is flat. People who grew up in Norwich know different. You may well know the old city rhyme which goes:

> The cart stood still and the wheels wuz goin round,
> A-goin up o' Long John Hill a-com'n down.

Long John Hill in Lakenham no longer holds the terrors it used to. If you drive up it these days in your car, or whizz up it on a modern lightweight multiple-geared bicycle, it is no kind of challenge; but in the old days, if you wanted to negotiate it with a heavily laden cart pulled by a tired old horse, that was another story.

But what about the words of the rhyme itself? What's all this *a-coming* and *a-going*? Specifically: why is it *a-coming* rather than just *coming*?

This is an ancient grammatical feature which the Norfolk dialect has retained. Linguists call it "*a*-verbing". The Standard English dialect has lost it; but all over the world English speakers are still familiar with it from the words of nursery rhymes like "Cry Baby Bunting, daddy's gone a-hunting"; traditional folk-songs like "Frog went a-courtin"; and even from more recent songs like Bob Dylan's "The times they are a-changin".

The origin of the form lies way back in the history of our language. In *he is hunting*, the *is hunting* part is known technically as a progressive verb. The very earliest forms of English did not have progressives: the languages related to English still don't – in Norwegian *han jakter* means both 'he hunts' and 'he is hunting'.

The English progressive was an innovation which developed about a thousand years ago out of expressions like *he is on hunting*, i.e. 'in the act of hunting', where *hunting* was a noun, as in *The hunting of deer is prohibited*. Speakers would say things like *He was on hunting of the deer*. Over time, however, the unstressed word *on* was reduced in pronunciation, resulting in *a-hunting*; and eventually even that *a-* was lost in the standard dialect. In our dialect, though, we have retained it. And not only that, we have also retained the *of*, albeit in the local form of *on*, so we say *He was a-hunten on 'em*.

That is why, if you see an old fella trying to bike up Long John Hill on a heavy old velocipede, you might find yourself saying: "What on earth d'you think you're a-doin on?"

## LINGUISTIC NOTES

– It has been argued that there is a reason why English has the progressive verbal aspect while other Germanic languages typically do not: this is that it is a feature which is due to language contact. After the arrival of the Anglo-Saxons in Britain,

*cont.*

there was very considerable contact between Old English and Brittonic Celtic, the ancestor of modern Welsh. Brittonic had a grammatical construction similar to the English progressive, as Welsh still does, and the argument is that this was transferred into Old English by speakers who were bilingual in the two languages. Ahlqvist gives a persuasive account, and one informed by a deep knowledge of Celtic linguistics, and suggests that the argument that the English progressive results from influence from a Celtic source is a sound one: Anders Ahlqvist (2010) "Early Celtic and English", *Australian Celtic Journal* 9: 1–17. For a slightly different view, see Kristin Killie (2012) "Old English-Late British language contact and the English progressive", in M. Steenroos, M. Mäkinen & I. Særheim (eds.), *Language Contact and Development around the North Sea*, Amsterdam: Benjamins, 119–40.

## 6.3 *Youse, y'all, together*

There is something very strange about the Standard English pronoun system. The Standard English dialect makes no difference between the second-person singular pronoun, *you,* and the second-person plural pronoun . . . *you.* This is rather odd, and can be confusing. If someone enters a room and says "How are you?", are they talking to me – or to us?

There used to be a difference in older forms of English: *thou* and *thee* referred to one person, and *ye* and *you* to two or more people. But that original difference has been lost, except in some local dialects in the north and west of England. The famous Yorkshire song *On Ilkla Moor baht 'at* begins "Wheear 'ast tha bin sin' ah saw thee?" – 'where hast thou been since I saw thee?' Clearly there was only one person who had been seen on Ilkley Moor without a hat.

However, instead of settling for the confusing Standard English system, many other dialects have restored the difference, for the obvious reason that it is rather inconvenient not to have one. In many dialects of Irish English, and in places which have experienced large-scale Irish immigration, *you* is only used as the singular, with the plural being *yous,* sometimes also spelt *youse.* If you go into a room full of people in Belfast and ask "How are you?", they may well look around to see which one of them you are actually talking to: you are supposed to say "How are yous?" In the southern USA, people say *y'all* if they want to refer to more than one person. In Jamaican Creole English, *you* is singular and the plural is *unu,* a word from the West African language Igbo. And it is becoming increasingly common these days for English speakers everywhere to express the plural by saying *you guys.* You can also say things like *you all, you people, you girls* or *you lot* if that helps. It is useful to have these ways of making it clear what we mean.

Here, in our part of the world, according to the grammar of the Norfolk dialect, we have our own very special way of expressing *you* plural: we use the phrase *you . . . together*. In the singular, we say "Come you on!"; and in the plural, "Come you on, together!" You can also just address a group of people as "together". So "How are you getting on, together?" does not mean the same thing as "How are you getting on together?" You can even say "How are you getting on together, together?"

Have a good day, together.

> **BACKGROUND NOTES**
>
> *"On Ilkla Moor baht 'at"* translates into Standard English as *'On Ilkley Moor without (a) hat'*.

**LINGUISTIC NOTES**

- In earlier forms of English, *thou* was the original singular subject form, and *thee* the object. *Ye* was the plural subject form, and *you* the object.
- For more on the grammar of East Anglian English, see Peter Trudgill (2004) "The dialect of East Anglia: morphology and syntax", in B. Kortmann & E. Schneider (eds.), *Handbook of Varieties of English*, vol. II, Berlin: Mouton de Gruyter, 142–53.

## 6.4 Quadruple negatives

By the end of World War II there were 20,000 courageous Poles in the Royal Air Force, and quite a few of them were here in Norfolk. Probably, though, not many local people have ever learnt much Polish, so here is a little language lesson. I apologise if it is too early in the morning.

The Polish sentence *Nigdy nie mogłem nigdzie żadnego znaleźć* literally means 'Never not could-I nowhere none find'. Or, as we say in Norfolk, *I couldn't never find none nowhere*. The term "double negative" doesn't do it; in Polish and in Norfolk, these are quadruple negatives. In Polish, you have to say it like that: in a negative sentence, everything that can be negative must be negative. This is known as grammatical agreement.

Linguists call this agreement "multiple negation". Multiple negation is very common in the world's languages. You find it in French: *Je ne sais rien* 'I not know nothing'. It has always been normal in English too. King Alfred used it; Chaucer used it; Shakespeare used it. And most modern native English speakers all round the world use it: *You ain't seen nothin' yet; I can't get no satisfaction; Went to Swaffham to do some troshen – din't do nothen*. When that ol' Mrs W. looked after

Aunt Agatha's hens and they laid fewer eggs than usual, the Boy John reported that "Aunt Agatha she dornt suspect nobody o' nuthin". So it's Norfolk dialect all right. But it is not just Norfolk, it is pan-world English.

For the last 250 years, though, it has not been part of Standard English: *I couldn't ever find any anywhere* is the Standard English version; and so people who do not like local dialects have tried to invent reasons for why multiple negation is "wrong". They say that if you could not find none, then you must have been able to find some; and – as if English was algebra – "two negatives make a positive", which is nonsense. If two negatives do not make a positive in French or Polish, they do not make a positive in Norfolk – or America or Australia – either. This is just a desperate attempt to rationalise prejudice against dialects.

Of course, if you are attempting to write Standard English, you should avoid multiple negation. But there is absolutely nothing wrong about it as such, just as there is everything right about it in Polish.

Polish and Norfolk people, though, have a lot more in common than just their grammar, and to this day there is nothing negative about our regard for those brave Poles.

**BACKGROUND NOTES**

*"Troshen" represents the Norfolk dialect pronunciation of the word* threshing *(see also 4.10). "Went to Swaffham to do some troshen, din't do nothen" is a well-known Norfolk saying.*
   *On the "Boy John" letters, see 2.8.*

**LINGUISTICS NOTES**

– For more on multiple negation, see notes to the next article, 6.5.

## 6.5  As you like it

When people are suffering from linguistic pain, they sometimes seek solace by writing to this newspaper in the hope of easing their distress. Since the *EDP* are kind enough to let me write a column on language, I feel I ought to try and help. We have had letter writers bemoaning too many *likes* and *wells* in the speech of others. Now we have a complaint about the phenomenon of "double negatives" which, a correspondent suggests, indicates a need for more education.

Perhaps he might find this helpfully soothing: William Shakespeare was a very educated man. His grammar school education gave him a thorough knowledge of the grammar of Ancient Greek and Latin – much more than the majority of *EDP* readers, including me – and he was very familiar with the works of Ovid, Virgil, Seneca, Plutarch, Cicero, Horace ...

He also wrote the following lines: "You know my father hath no child but I, nor none is like to have" (*As You Like It*); "Nor go neither; but you'll lie like dogs and yet say nothing neither" (*The Tempest*); and "No woman has, nor never none shall be, mistress of it" (*Twelfth Night*).

Sufferers often argue that two negatives make a positive. But that is maths, not language. If you ask for something in a shop and get the reply "We in't got none", you don't hang around waiting for it, you leave the shop. The label "double negative" is wrong, too, because there can easily be more than two negatives – "nor never none shall be" – and if we really were dealing with maths, three negatives would actually make a negative, though complainants don't seem to find this any less painful.

Linguists call grammatical constructions with more than one negative "multiple negation" or "negative concord". Most languages in the world have multiple negation. Just think of French: *Je ne sais pas* = 'I not know not'. All varieties of English used to have it, as the Shakespeare examples show; but over the last few centuries Standard English has gradually lost it, while most other English dialects around the world have kept it. As it is not Standard English, we do not normally use it in writing. But there is nothing wrong or bad about multiple negation as such. You do not have to use it yourself if you do not want to. But if you feel the pain coming on again when others do use it, try relaxing and thinking of the Bard.

## LINGUISTIC NOTES

– English has a number of inherently negative indefinite quantifiers and adverbs such as *nothing, nobody, no one, none, never, nowhere, neither* which in nonstandard varieties of English occur together with negation of the verb by *not*. All dialects of English used to have this multiple negation, as can be seen in Chaucer's "He nevere yet no vileynye ne sayd", but subsequently Standard English lost it. Single negation in Standard English is an oddity which there have been a number of interesting attempts to explain, with accounts of precisely when, how and why it came about; see Terttu Nevalainen (1998) "Social mobility and the decline of multiple negation in Early Modern English", in J. Fisiak & M. Krygier (eds.), *Advances in English Historical Linguistics*, Berlin: Mouton de Gruyter, 263–91.

*cont.*

– Single negation is also an oddity worldwide. Martin Haspelmath shows that single negation is very unusual in the world's languages, and that it is basically a rather restricted areal feature. It is particularly typical of European languages, and then only of a single core geographical area of the continent: single negation is found only in the Germanic languages, Ibero-Romance, Italo-Romance and Albanian. This central zone is then entirely surrounded by areas that have multiple negation, with both negated verbs and negative indefinites: Celtic, Basque, Finnic, Baltic, Slavic, Hungarian, Rumanian, Greek and Turkish. As Haspelmath says, this is also the case with "a clear majority of the world's languages": his figures indicate that only about 12 per cent of the languages of the world have single negation (Martin Haspelmath, 2001, "The European linguistic area: Standard Average European", in M. Haspelmath, E. König, W. Oesterreicher & W. Raible (eds.), *Language Typology and Language Universals*, 1492–1510, Berlin: de Grüyter).

## 6.6 Who knows what an adverb is?

I am sorry to keep going on about Mr Gove, but his less than well-informed views on language really are very tiresome. It would not matter so much if he was not the Secretary of State for Education but, as you have probably noticed, he is.

Mr Gove has got a thing about adverbs. He thinks pupils in our schools do not know what an adverb is. I am not at all sure he knows what an adverb is either. It is a tricky issue. The magnificent 1,800-page *Comprehensive Grammar of the English Language*, which devotes over 200 pages to adverbs, says that "the adverb class is the most nebulous and puzzling of the traditional word classes". I would be very surprised if Mr Gove could help untangle this puzzle.

When we were at school, we were told that an adverb is a word which modifies a verb, as with *quickly* in "she runs quickly". This may be what Mr Gove believes too. But as the *Comprehensive Grammar* suggests, adverbs are a lot more complicated than that: they can also modify adjectives, clauses, sentences and other adverbs. An example of an adverb modifying a sentence is *naturally* in *Naturally the sea's warm – this is August in Lowestoft*; and an example of an adverb modifying another adverb is *very* as in *Lowestoft Town played very well*.

But I think I know what Mr Gove is obsessing about. He is not interested in adverbs like *aboard, about, abroad, afterwards, almost, already, always, anyway, around, aside, away*. He is fixated on adverbs which are derived from adjectives by adding *ly*, such as *accidental-ly, active-ly, annoying-ly*.

This can only be because he has a deep and irrational prejudice against local dialects. He is terribly irritated by the fact that, unlike Standard English, local dialects generally do not construct adverbs from adjectives in this way. English dialect speakers typically use the same form for adjectives and adverbs: *she's a quick runner, she run quick; he's a nice speaker, he speak nice.*

And why shouldn't they? This is not a mistake. It does not mean that dialect speakers do not know what an adverb is. It just means that in the grammar of, say, the Norfolk dialect, we make no formal distinction between this particular type of adverb and the corresponding adjective. And we are not alone: this is exactly what happens in many other languages too, like Dutch, German and Norwegian.

So Norfolk dialect speakers should not fear Mr Gove, even if he do talk very fierce.

> **BACKGROUND NOTES**
>
> *On Michael Gove, see 2.4.*
> *Lowestoft is a town in the northeast of Suffolk.*

## LINGUISTIC NOTES

- The superb English grammar referred to is: Randolph Quirk, Sidney Greenbaum, Geoffrey Leech & Jan Svartvik (1985) *A Comprehensive Grammar of the English Language*, London: Longman.
- It is interesting to note that the contrast between Standard English, which has adverbs in -*ly*, and nonstandard dialects, which often do not, can lead to hyper-correction (see 2.10). For example, it is now rather common for Americans to say that they "feel badly" about something rather than that they "feel bad" about it, as has always been more natural in English. This is because they have been told in school that "adverbs modify verbs", and that "adverbs should end in -*ly*". They then suppose that, since *feel* is a verb, they should say *badly* rather than the more normal *bad*. This shows how the promulgation of invented unnatural "rules" based on faulty analyses can have unfortunate effects. The fact is that in "I feel bad", *bad* modifies not *feel* but *I*. Its function in this sentence is as a complement, not an adverbial, just as it would be in sentences such as "I feel stupid" or "It looks good" or "They sound marvellous."

## 6.7 *Nowt, nought, naught*

Some while ago, we saw in the newspapers that the headteacher of a school in Middlesbrough had taken the extraordinary step of writing to parents urging them to "correct" their children's English. Did she really think that would make any difference? Children quite rightly and naturally speak like their peers, not like their parents, and most certainly not like their teachers.

It is amazing the extent to which people who know nothing about language are willing to believe they are actually authorities: this teacher was clearly someone who did not know very much. She arrogantly informed parents that *"you* is never plural". I'm sorry, but if I bump into Russell Martin and Wes Hoolahan at Thorpe Station and tell them "It's nice to meet you", that IS plural. But what she was referring to was the fact that the Middlesbrough dialect, very intelligently, has followed Wes's Irish English example in distinguishing between singular *you* and plural *yous*.

The headteacher said she was not asking children to change their dialect. But she was. Astonishingly, she instructed parents, even though she must have known most of them say it themselves, that it is wrong to say *nowt*. What on earth makes her think that? *Nowt* is a word which has come down to us over more than a thousand years of English language history; it is the same as *nought* and *naught*. Millions of people in the north of England say it, and will continue to say it however many letters they get from headmistresses. *Nowt* is part of their local dialect.

Her justification was that she did not want her pupils to enter the world of work without knowing about Standard English. Well, of course not. But why would they? She is, we hope, teaching them to read and write the Standard English dialect in her school. It is actually very interesting in the classroom to contrast local dialect grammar with Standard English. What is not interesting for children is to be told that the way they speak is "incorrect". Making children feel insecure about their natural speech is no way to produce articulate adults.

Instead of wasting her time writing interfering letters to parents, this headteacher should inform herself about language structure so that she can talk about it in an analytical, non-judgemental way. Happily, our well-informed Norfolk teachers already do this, as we have learnt in our excellent sessions with FOND in local Norfolk schools. Maybe we should open a branch of FOND in Middlesbrough.

## BACKGROUND NOTES

*At the time of writing, Wesley Hoolahan and Russell Martin are Norwich City footballers. Hoolahan is an Irish international player, and Martin plays for Scotland.*

*FOND is the Friends of Norfolk Dialect organisation.*

## LINGUISTICS NOTES

– The word *nowt* is commonly found not only in northern England but also in parts of Scotland and northern Ireland. It has the same origin as *nought* and *naught*.

## 6.8 Good grammar makes you happy

Mr Gove wants all civil servants to read what a certain Mr Gwynne (the *Daily Telegraph* calls him a "a self-taught schoolteacher") has to say about grammar, in his book *Gwynne's Grammar*.

I quite agree that there is a deficiency of knowledge about grammar in this country. We should all know what nouns, verbs and adjectives are. We should know about subjects and objects. We should even know what adverbs are, although they are rather difficult to define. And everybody, including Mr Gove, should know what complements, aspects, copulas and conjuncts are too. I wonder if he actually does.

Mr Gwynne – I heard him on the radio – wants people to be able to write clearly, and of course we all have to agree. But knowing what a noun is will not actually help you with that very much. Knowing about grammar is important; and writing coherently is important. But they are very different things, and the one will not assist you much with the other.

Mr Gwynne is one of those people who link what they call "good grammar" to "clear thinking". I heard him say that unless you get your grammar right and make the right grammatical distinctions, you will not be able to think straight, you will not make the right decisions, and you will end up being, er, unhappy. (I have probably omitted some stages in his argument, but not many.)

So I have a proposal to make to the two Mr Gs. In English there is an important difference between subject pronouns such as *I, he, she, we, they* and object pronouns such as *me, him, her, us, them*. We say "I like him, he likes me, we like them, they like us". But most English speakers have a problem here. They – carelessly, it could be argued – don't bother to make this subject–object distinction with the third-person singular neuter pronoun. They say "I like it – it tastes good". Two *its*! No distinction! Is there some potential unhappiness lurking here?

In Norfolk we are given to thinking much more clearly than that. We say "I like it", but "That taste good". What a superb, elegant and very precise grammatical distinction between the subject *that* and the object *it*! So here is how Mr Gove could achieve greater happiness. Next time he looks out of the window and sees a little precipitation, he could try saying, as we do in this part of the world, "That's raining!"

### LINGUISTIC NOTES

– Professor Geoffrey Pullum of Edinburgh University, one of the leading linguists in the world and co-author of the award-winning 1,800-page *Cambridge Grammar of the English Language*, was quoted in the *Daily Telegraph* on 19 March 2014 as saying of *Gwynne's Grammar* that "I've never seen a book so bad on my subject. It's the familiar old nonsense, modified through 200 years of rubbish, from teachers who didn't quite understand it to students who understood it less."

*cont.*

- Strictly speaking *me, him, her, us* and *them* are oblique pronouns rather than object pronouns, as they occur in many constructions where they are not objects, as in "It wasn't me" (see also 2.9).
- The use of *that* rather than *it* as the subject form of the third-person singular neuter pronoun is very common in Norfolk, Suffolk and (at least) northern Essex, and is found even in relatively non-dialectal speech (see Peter Trudgill, 2004, "The dialect of East Anglia: morphology and syntax", in B. Kortmann & E. Schneider (eds.), *Handbook of Varieties of English*, vol. II, Berlin: Mouton de Gruyter, 142–53).
- I am of course not being serious when I use the words "problem" and "carelessly".

## 6.9 Bad English causes crime

Norman (Lord) Tebbit, the former Tory government minister, once said: "If you allow standards to slip to the stage where good English is no better than bad English, where people turn up filthy at school – those things cause people to have no standards at all, and once you lose standards, then there's no imperative to stay out of crime."

So there you are, then: "bad English" causes crime.

And we know what Norman means by "bad English", don't we. He means saying *that go* instead of *it goes*. He means saying *Hair that be!* instead of *Here it is!* He means saying *I done it yisty* instead of *I did it yesterday*.

So that is very good news: all we have to do now is to persuade everybody in Norfolk to abandon our native dialect grammar and use the Standard English dialect instead, and then the crime rate in our county, already low, will plummet even further.

In the meantime, though, it would be fun to know which particular crimes are caused by which particular aspects of "bad English". It is hard to imagine that the absence from the Norfolk dialect of third-person singular *s* has been directly responsible for any terribly serious criminal activity. In fact, it is almost certain that the nation was swindled out of millions through the mis-selling of PPIs by people who were saying *This product works really well*, not *This product work rarely good*.

The whole thing is, of course, complete nonsense, but notice the effortless self-confidence with which Norman used the word "standards". That is what people in positions of wealth and power do. They define the way they themselves speak as being of a "high standard", and their English as "good": cultured, elegant and "correct". Any other way of speaking, as used by ordinary people with less power and wealth, is self-evidently inferior, and not just inferior but "bad".

That would all be OK – we could just leave them alone to get on with their delusions – if it was not for the fact that they try very hard to persuade the rest of us that their language really is the only "good" English there is; and since they have always had the power to control our media and education, they have been rather successful.

But we must not let ourselves be fooled. All dialects are equally good, correct, systematic and of a high standard, including ours. Next time a policeman stops you for cycling without lights, tell him that in't nothing to do with your grammar, just your battery.

**BACKGROUND NOTES**

*The PPI scandal involved British banks who were very aggressively selling highly profitable "payment protection insurance" to their customers which was expensive, ineffective, inefficient and very often totally unnecessary.*

**LINGUISTIC NOTES**

- The spellings <hair> and <rarely> for *here* and *really* are intended to indicate the local accent merger of the vowels of NEAR and SQUARE and the usage of the vowel /ɛ:/ in all words of these sets; see also 13.4.
- *Here that be*: the Norfolk dialect has a grammatical phenomenon unknown in Standard English which is called "presentative be". The verb *to be* has forms no different from those of Standard English *I am, you are, she is* etc. except when the speaker is announcing the presence (location, arrival, discovery etc.) of something or somebody, in which case the invariant form *be* is used for all persons: *Here that be! Here I be! There she be!*

## 6.10 Ministry circular

When I become Minister of Education, I am going to issue a circular to all the schools in our country which will read as follows:

It is the duty of teachers to show great respect for children's spoken language, and they should ensure that children feel and understand this. Teachers should help and encourage children to speak their local dialect and accent clearly, mellifluously and well. They should not attempt to have children abandon their native accent and dialect or have them speak the standard language in school. The school head must immediately intervene against any action of this type and instruct the individual concerned to adhere to this clear legal regulation.

What this means is that, under my Ministry, teachers will not be allowed to tell Norfolk children that it is "wrong" to say *I'm now a-comen* and *He play very good*. On the contrary, children must be encouraged to say precisely those things if they are part of their local dialect. If Norfolk children pronounce *hair* and *here*, and *pure* and *purr*, the same, that will also be fine and to be encouraged. If they pronounce *few* as "foo", teachers will be required to permit them to carry on doing so.

Do you think this is absurd? If so, you need not worry because I am not ever going to be Minister of Education. But this is not a ludicrous fantasy I am having. This is not just a scenario I have imagined. The above words are not my own. This "edict" of mine is a direct translation of a circular which was issued by the Norwegian Ministry of Church and Education to all the schools in Norway on 27 February 1923.

Under my Ministry, just like in Norway, writing would be different from speaking. Teachers would be required to explain to pupils that in writing, the forms to use will be *I'm just coming* and *He plays very well*. This is not because these forms are "right" as opposed to "wrong", but because they are part of Standard English, the dialect which is conventionally used in formal writing in the English-speaking world.

Norway is a country which is to be admired not just for its mountains and fiords, and for the role of its government as a mediator in international disputes. It is also to be admired for being a place where common sense about language, dialect and accent are more prevalent than ignorance, prejudice and unreason.

## LINGUISTIC NOTES

- For those wanting to find out more about the linguistic situation in Norway and its history, see Ernst Håkon Jahr (2014) *Language Planning as a Sociolinguistic Experiment: The Case of Modern Norwegian*, Edinburgh University Press; and see also 2.12.

# 7 Respecting ordinary language

This section again argues for the legitimacy and value of vernacular language, as the previous section did with respect to grammar, but here I attempt to do this with respect to the normal everyday usage of words and phrases. In particular, I argue against the use of the form of business-school terminology which is intended to commodify more or less everything. And I attempt to point out the value of discourse markers such as *well* and *like*. One problem that English-speaking people have is that most of us know very little about our language because we have not been taught very much about it at school; but we are particularly ill-informed about the nature of our spoken language. So much more attention is focussed on written English that many essential features of the spoken language can easily be thought of as aberrations. In fact, we spend so very much more of our lives speaking than writing that, if anything, it is the written form of the language which is aberrant.

## 7.1 *Well*

When we were about 6 years old, there was a joke which we thought was very funny: "Have you heard about the three deep holes? Well, well, well ... ".

I agree it is not very amusing, but a correspondent to the *EDP* seems not even to have heard of it. He is "irritated beyond bounds", poor chap, by the continuous use of the word *well* at the start of "almost every report on the news". He wants the word to be banned, unless it applies to a person's state of health, or a hole in the ground which supplies water. He does not say how he will set about enforcing this ban; I suppose a short prison-sentence for any offending journalist might work.

But he has completely missed the point about the important role words like *well* play in English, or in any language. They are called discourse markers, and they have very important functions. There are rules about how to use them which we all know, even if we do not know we know them. You can sometimes hear foreigners using *well* incorrectly because they do not know what the rules are.

An American linguist called Deborah Schiffrin has written a whole book called *Discourse Markers* which is devoted to a study of the rules involved in the usage of *well, oh, so, y'know, now, then, I mean.* One of the jobs that *well* does is to act as a warning that a response to what another person has said is going to be less than satisfactory. If someone asks the time, you don't reply "Well, it's four o'clock." But you might say "Well, I'm not sure – my watch is slow."

*Well* can warn that a reply will be unsatisfactory because it expresses disagreement. If someone says "Norwich City have a got a great team", you might agree; but someone else might reply "Well, I'm not so sure about that." *Well* can also show reluctance – "Well, I don't really want to"; resignation – "Well, all right then"; or uncertainty – "Well, yes, I suppose that's right."

Imagine you are a radio reporter for the BBC Radio 4 *Today* programme. You are sheltering from the bombs in Damascus. The studio in London asks for your analysis of the current Syrian situation. You feel that any 60-second answer you could possibly give will be utterly unsatisfactory for conveying the total complexity, uncertainty and horror of it all. Don't you think you might begin by saying "Well, John ... "?

## BACKGROUND NOTES

*The BBC* Today *programme is broadcast every Monday to Saturday from early in the morning until 9 a.m. One of its best-known regular presenters and interviewers is John Humphrys.*

## LINGUISTIC NOTES

– The reference is to Deborah Schiffrin (1988) *Discourse Markers*, Cambridge University Press.

## 7.2 Like *like* like

Oh dear. Readers of the nation's largest-selling regional morning daily newspaper seem to be in a bad way, some of them. First, on the Letters pages, we had the gentleman who was badly afflicted by too many *wells*. Now we have a lady who is clearly suffering terribly from too many *likes*.

These correspondents are part of our great Complaint Tradition: the tradition of older people complaining about the way the language is changing. It is interesting, however, to wonder what it is that is making them want to complain in this way. I think, with *like*, that I might know where their dislike comes from.

The word *like* in "He was like just standing there" and *well* in "Well, I'm not sure" are called discourse markers or discourse particles. These are words which have little actual meaning as such, but do have an important function. They are found in all languages. We all use them. Even if you do not use *like* in this way, I promise you that you do use *I mean* or *sort of* or *you know* or (if you're an academic) *as it were*: try listening to yourself sometime. It is so automatic we do not even notice we are doing it.

*Like* has a long history of being used as a downtoner: "He was just standing there, like." This means more or less the same as "He was just sort of standing there." Downtoners have the job of, well, toning down the force of what you are saying. That might be because you are not quite sure about it; or because you do not want to sound too assertive. Using downtoners is a way of signalling that you are part of the group and that you are not trying to come across as over-confident and superior. It is a way of showing solidarity.

There are two main reasons why older people today are complaining about younger people saying *like*. One is that, although *like* has been used as a downtoner in English for many generations, it is more conspicuous now because it has become more common during our lifetimes; and it is being used in new grammatical contexts, not just at the end of a sentence.

The other is that younger people always use more downtoners than older people. Teenagers tend to be less confident, less assertive, more group-oriented and more concerned about their friends' reactions than older people. When I was at school, my mother spent several years encouraging me not to say "it was sorta kinda like . . . ". I did stop, but I don't think it was because of Mum's kind efforts. It was because I got older.

## LINGUISTIC NOTES

– On the Complaint Tradition and its history, see James Milroy & Lesley Milroy (2012) *Authority in Language: Investigating Standard English*, 4th edn, Oxford: Routledge.

## 7.3  A sexist outrage

Everybody who lives in my part of Norwich agrees that we have a truly wonderful, helpful, popular and very efficient postman. Her name is Kelly.

Can I call her the *postman*? She calls herself our "post-lady", which is very reasonable since she is, obviously, not a man. But these words ending in *man* are very interesting. Can they apply to women? Does it feel OK to you to say *She's a postman*? I don't find it too bad. After all, we don't say "post-man". We say "postm'n". *She's a milkman* does sound odd to me, though. Is that just because there are not many female milkmen around? *Postwoman* sounds OK, but *milkwoman* doesn't, does it?

In the 1970s, there was a lot of fuss about *chairman*. Feminists argued that it made no sense to call a woman a "chair-man": it was an outrage to imply that only men were suitable for such a position. Some people said a woman should be called a *chairwoman*. Others preferred *chair*. Yet others did not want to be called after a piece of furniture.

Personally, I thought *She's the chairm'n* sounded all right. Arguing that *chairman* meant 'chair-man' was, I reckoned, an example of "the etymological fallacy", which holds that the current meaning of a word should be the same as its etymology, its historical meaning. This is not so. Obviously a chairman was originally a man in a chair. But a *cupboard* was equally obviously originally a board for cups; and a *saucer* was obviously originally something for serving sauces in. A word means what it means now, not what it used to mean.

But a real sexist outrage did, in a way, occur, even if it happened very many centuries ago. The word *man* originally meant 'human being' or 'person', as in *mankind* or *Man is destroying the planet*. But then there was a gradual shift of meaning so that *man* mostly ended up meaning 'male person', as if men were normal as human beings and women less so.

Nobody seems to find the word *woman* sexist, even though it ends in *man* too. It comes originally from the Anglo-Saxon *wif-mann*, where *wif* (modern *wife*) meant 'woman', and *mann* meant 'person'. (The old Anglo-Saxon word for 'male person' was *wer*.)

There was no such thing as posting letters in early Anglo-Saxon Norwich but, if there had been and we had been alive then, everyone round this way would most certainly have wanted Kelly to be our *post-mann*.

## LINGUISTIC NOTES

- A well-known example of the etymological fallacy as this is sometimes applied to English can be seen in arguments about the word *aggravate*. *Aggravate* comes from Latin *aggravare* which meant 'to make heavy' and, subsequently, 'to make worse', which is what it also means in English, as in *that just aggravated the situation*. Perhaps the most common English meaning, however, is 'to annoy, to exasperate', a usage which English speakers have been employing for over 400 years. The etymological fallacy holds that this latter meaning is "incorrect" because of the lack of relationship with the original Latin meaning. But it is in fact the etymological fallacy which is fallacious: *aggravate* does mean 'annoy', as all English speakers know.
- On the sociolinguistics of sexist language, see Peter Trudgill (2000) *Sociolinguistics: An Introduction to Language and Society*, Harmondsworth: Penguin, chapter 4.

## 7.4 Tomatoes and girls

Words mean what they mean. Not what they used to mean. And not what someone thinks they ought to mean.

When I was about 8 years old, in those non-paranoid days when small children were free to walk around on their own, my mother sent me to the grocers on Plumstead Road in Thorpe to do some shopping for her. The grocer, Mr Goldsmith, was a very nice man, and I liked him. "Good morning, Peter", he said as I walked in. "It's not morning, Mr Goldsmith", I replied cockily. "It's after 12 o'clock." We had just been taught at school what the word *noon* meant. The word is common enough in North America, but it is not one that English people use much, and we didn't know it. The teacher told us that it meant the same as *midday*, and that it was the origin of the word *afternoon*.

Mr Goldsmith smiled at me and answered, with great authority: "That's not afternoon until you've had your dinner." I was rather embarrassed, because I knew he was right. Dinner was the meal you had in the middle of the day – one o'clock in our house – and afternoon began once it was over.

English speakers know what *afternoon* means. It does not mean 'after noon'. If someone tells you they will visit you tomorrow afternoon, you would be most surprised if they turned up the next day at 12:15.

English speakers also know what the word *fruit* means. If you say to your hostess that, yes please, you would like some fruit for dessert, you would be most surprised to be served tomatoes rather than peaches or pears. Everyone knows that tomatoes are not fruit except, of course, for botanists, who tell us that, technically, they are; but that does not make any difference to what the word means in normal usage.

In my line of business, there are academics who tell their colleagues that they are wrong if they refer to their female students as *girls*. The students are adult human beings, they say, and should be accorded the respect of being called *women*. I see what they mean. But if you and I were together in my office and I told you that a woman was about to come and see me, you would, I think, be just a little taken aback if the person who walked in turned out to be 18 years old.

Words mean what they mean. And not what someone thinks they ought to mean.

---

## BACKGROUND NOTES

*Predictably, when it was first published, this column produced some negative comments from (male) academic colleagues who repeated that 18-year-old female persons "ought not to be" referred to as girls. Maybe so; there are good arguments in favour of this point of view. But to refer to such people as women, say, on Norwich market would only cause confusion, since in normal everyday vernacular English usage they are universally referred to as girls, including by themselves. This fact is recognised by the Oxford English Dictionary, where part of the definition of girl is "young or relatively young woman". In fact the 'relatively young woman' meaning may actually be the most common one in everyday English speech, since in spoken English we often naturally observe some other subtle distinctions, with little girl being used of a small or smallish children, and young girl of youngish teenagers. I also note that most of the academics concerned cannot actually bring themselves to use the word woman of their students, saying young woman instead, which seems to work for them as a kind of translation of girl.*

## LINGUISTIC NOTES

- *Afternoon* has always had some connection with mealtimes. The *OED* tells us that *afternoon* originally meant "the part of the day between the midday meal and the evening meal" and subsequently came to mean "the part of the day from noon or lunchtime to evening".
- The word *girl* is first attested in English in the 1300s, where it seems to have meant a child of either sex. Its etymology is not known with any degree of certainty – something which is also true of *lass* and *lad*: *girl* is not obviously related to any word in any other Germanic language.

## 7.5 The euphemism treadmill

In the 1940s and 1950s, if I remember rightly, schoolchildren in England who were seriously intellectually handicapped by difficulties with learning and understanding were labelled *retarded* and, perhaps, given special help. This term was an originally innocent word which simply meant 'delayed': the development of these children was somewhat delayed compared to the average. *To retard* was, and still is, a normal verb which English-speaking people use to refer to holding back or impeding something, as in *fire retardant*, for example.

Unfortunately, though, elements in our society were prejudiced against people who were handicapped in this way, and so the word *retarded* gradually took on very negative connotations. It was even used by spiteful children, and adults who should have known better, as an insult which they used for denigrating and abusing others.

In view of this abuse, it was natural that responsible people involved in education saw the need for another descriptive word to use instead, and *educationally subnormal* began to be employed. This was once again meant to be a neutral, descriptive term with no malice attached to it: *subnormal* simply meant 'below normal'.

But then this term, too, sadly began to acquire negative overtones, and so quite naturally it began to fall out of favour as well, and new words started appearing. In the last few decades, different terms have been used, including the description of certain children as having *special needs*. But now this phrase itself, it seems, is also beginning to be used maliciously for hurling insults at others. We have to wonder how long we will be able to persevere with it as a designation.

It is not my place as a linguist to intervene in this issue, but one thing is clear to linguistic scientists, because of what we know about the way in which the meanings of words change: this cycle of stigmatisation and replacement – it is sometimes called the "euphemism treadmill" – is bound to continue until attitudes change. We must of course be sensitive to the problem, refer to minority groups as they wish to be referred to, and abandon words which are used to demean people. But these words are a symptom of this disease of prejudice, not the disease itself. When a patient is ill, it is no good just removing their symptoms, you have to treat the sickness itself.

You can get rid of words, but unless you can get rid of the sick underlying prejudice, you will have to change those words again and again – and again.

### LINGUISTIC NOTES

– The term "euphemism treadmill" is due to Stephen Pinker (2003) *The Blank Slate: The Modern Denial of Human Nature*, London: Penguin.

## 7.6 Visions

Words are dangerous things. Sometimes you have to choose them carefully. They can change their meaning through time, and so mean different things to people of different ages. To my mother *cute* meant 'too clever by half', but for young people it means 'good looking'. In the old Norfolk dialect, *gays* meant 'pictures, illustrations in magazines and books', but that is not what it means nowadays.

Words also vary in their meaning from place to place. When Americans say *homely* they mean 'not very good looking', the opposite of *cute*, but that is not what it means to us. In Norfolk *linen* means 'washing, laundry' – many people still have linen lines and linen pegs – but in other places it just refers to textiles made from flax.

And many words have several different meanings, so *funny* means 'peculiar' but also 'amusing'. For all these reasons misunderstandings can occur if we are not careful.

I recently got an appointment letter from the hospital which had, at the top, a small logo (a word that most of us had never heard of fifty years ago), together with a slogan (originally a Scottish Gaelic word, rather older than that). This read "Our vision: to provide every patient with the care we want for those we love the most". Well, 'ass a rumm'n! Who would have thought our NNUH would have wanted to give everybody the best possible medical treatment!

Like most people, I have every reason to be extremely grateful to our National Health Service. But you can't help wondering how much the NNUH paid someone to come up with this sentimental drivel and have it printed on all their stationery and plastered all over their website.

I wonder, too, if whoever it was who took the money should have thought a bit more carefully about the word *vision*. Whatever this word meant to them, I am not sure the rest of us will share the same understanding. Obviously they did not mean 'the faculty of sight' or 'hallucination'. Probably it was something more along the lines of 'the act of anticipating that which will or may come to be'. But it actually seems to be business-speak. On a leading "Human Resources" website, I find that for HR-types, *vision* has a rather special significance. It means 'the skill of visualizing and thinking beyond the obvious'.

Well, as I say, if there is something which is not obvious about providing top-level medical care in a hospital, 'ass a rumm'n.

---

**BACKGROUND NOTES**

The NNUH is the Norfolk and Norwich University Hospital, formerly the Norfolk & Norwich Hospital. It is universally known locally as "the N and N".

The British National Health Service provides all resident citizens with totally free health care for life: I am by no means alone in being grateful.

'Ass a rumm'n *is the local dialect form of* That's a rum one = *'That's strange'; see 1.10.*

---

**LINGUISTIC NOTES**

– The American equivalent of British *homely* is "homey".
– The word *logo* first started being used in English in non-technical contexts in the 1960s: the *OED* has a citation from the *Guardian* newspaper from 1969. I do not remember hearing the word myself until the mid 1970s.
– *Slogan* comes from Scottish Gaelic *sluagh-ghairm* 'battle cry', where *sluagh* meant 'host' or 'army' and *gairm* meant 'cry' or 'shout'. *Slogan* first appeared in English in the 1500s in the form *slogorne*. The spelling <slogan> appears to date only from the 1800s. The change from *g-* to *gh-* as between *gairm* and *ghairm* is due to the fact that Celtic languages often signal grammatical relations at the beginning of words rather than at the end, as we do in English. These alternations in Celtic are known as "word-initial mutations". For example, in Welsh, 'dog' is *ci* but 'my dog' is *fy nghi*.

## 7.7 Customers

How do Norwich people feel about being "customers" in their very own City Hall? Citizens of our Fine City entering the seat of our government these days are greeted with a sign directing them to the Customer Service Centre. That feels wrong. Surely no one who lives in Norwich is a customer of the City Council? Doesn't that word suggest the wrong kind of relationship?

We have already watched with some bemusement as our railways have fallen victim to the language of the Business School graduates who run them. They do not want us to think we are passengers anymore. They too want us to think we are customers.

We do not think that, of course: we still refer to ourselves as passengers; and no real railwayman or woman who has worked their way up through the ranks would normally say *customers* either. They only say that because they have been instructed to do so when making public announcements, presumably on pain of whatever it is that business school-educated managers do to you if you do not say exactly what they want you to say.

When the friendly, experienced railway people who actually meet the public are talking to you face to face, they always say *passengers*, and they are quite right, because this use of *customer* is very odd. It is not what *customer* means. In normal everyday English, the word is used of people buying things in shops or, these days, on line. People attending the doctor's surgery are not customers, they are patients. People at the solicitor's are not customers, they are clients. People staying at a hotel are guests. People visiting museums are visitors. People at Carrow Road are spectators.

And people travelling on trains are passengers. Everybody knows that. Why don't the railway managers know it? We cannot blame it on our local railway currently being run by a Dutch company. The managers were trying to persuade us that we were not passengers even before the Dutch took over.

And why don't the City Council know we are not customers? Surely we are Norwich, and Norwich is us? Do we not elect the City Council? Are we not all in this together?

I am afraid it is beginning to look as if we are not all in this together anymore. Not only are our elected officials using this strange, alienating vocabulary about us, the citizens of Norwich – we are not even allowed to use the toilets in the City Hall anymore, even though it does belong to us.

## BACKGROUND NOTES

*Visitors entering Norwich by road are greeted by signs saying "Welcome to Norwich, a Fine City". This is a partial quotation from George Borrow (see 1.10), who referred to Norwich as "a fine old city".*

Norwich City Hall

## 7.8 *Alight*

I overheard this conversation on the 8:30 Norwich to Liverpool Street train the other week: "I'm not alighting at Liverpool Street today – change of routine, I'm alighting at Diss." "Bit different for me too this time, I'm alighting at Stratford – a lot of people will be alighting there today."

Well of course I did not overhear that at all. Any reader of this column can tell immediately that I made that up. Normal people do not go around alighting from trains. They get off. Nobody ever uses the verb *alight*. Never. Nobody, that is, except the people who make the announcements on trains. It is not their fault, I know. They do not normally say it either. They are just reading out what they have been told to read out by their bosses.

But I wonder why their bosses tell them to say that? Do they really think visiting businessmen from Japan or tourists from Germany or even 5-year-old children from eastern England are going to understand what *alight* means? And why don't they care that people will not understand?

It is for the same reason that airline staff are made to tell passengers that "we are about to commence our descent". Do you ever commence anything? I don't think I do. I reckon I normally start or begin something. And that is not just because I am from Norfolk. English speakers all round the world avoid the word *commence* in normal speech.

What is going on here is all part of a let's-try-hard-to-be-impressive syndrome. These people seem to think it is more important to impress the general public with how you say something than to help them to understand what you are saying by using simple, straightforward, everyday language.

It is rather important for foreign visitors who are not very good at English to know that they have to get off the train at Stratford if they want to change onto the Jubilee Line. But none of that matters to these bosses. They think there is something a bit *infra dig* about using the word *get*. They don't get at all bothered that people get confused and don't get the message and get into a muddle if you don't get your language right.

The rest of us know that it is much more important for listeners to get what you are saying, rather than get a good impression of how clever you are. But I doubt if these bosses will ever get that.

### BACKGROUND NOTES

*Liverpool Street railway station is the London terminus which trains from Norwich arrive at. Diss is the south Norfolk town which is the first stop on the Norwich–London line; and Stratford is the last station on the line before Liverpool Street.*

## 7.9 *Mate*

Our *EDP* colleague Steve Downes wrote in his column that he does not like being called "mate", and does not want anyone to call him that unless they really are his mate. Now I am not actually Steve's mate. I have not met him, though I would like to sometime; but I do rather think that if I accidentally bumped into him on The Walk, I might just say "Sorry, mate" by way of an apology.

I respect the way Steve feels about this, but I think he is missing the point. There are two different usages of this word. Yes, *mate* can be a noun meaning 'friend', as in *they are good mates*. (It comes from the Hamburg-area Low German word *ge-mate*, meaning a person one shares food with – the *mate* part is the same as English *meat*, which originally meant 'food'.)

But *mate* can also be a term of address. All languages have words which speakers use to address other people, like Norfolk *bor*. These words are employed according to specific rules, very often to be polite or friendly, and do not necessarily have much meaning of their own.

Think about the rules for using *mate* as a way of addressing someone. First, you can only say it to a man; and it is used much more by men than by women. Most address terms are gendered in some way like this: the word *dear* is not used in Norfolk by men to men. It is used by women, and by men to women.

Then, *mate* is also rather informal. It implies some kind of equality. You would probably not call your doctor 'mate'.

And *mate* is very helpful, the way many of us use it, as a means of addressing men if we do not know their name. It is good to have something to call out to people to attract their attention. Americans would say "Sir!" We are often reduced to a cough or an embarrassed "Excuse me!" *Mate* can work much better. In the BBC film footage from the scene of that shocking accident by Vauxhall Station in London when a helicopter crashed into a crane, a man can be heard shouting to another man "Mate! Mate! Your car's on fire!" Those two men were not mates. And that was the point. If he had been his mate, he would have shouted his name.

Many of us reserve the word *mate*, as a term of address, for precisely those people who are not our mates.

> **BACKGROUND NOTES**
>
> *On "the Walk", see 14.13.*
>   *On the helicopter accident,* www.bbc.com/news/uk-england-21040410.

## LINGUISTIC NOTES

- The *Oxford English Dictionary* says of *mate* that it is "used as a form of address to a person, especially a man, regarded as an equal".
- Low German, known in German as *Niederdeutsch* or *Plattdeutsch*, is the language of the northern part of Germany, and was formerly the written language used by the powerful Hanseatic League. It is a good deal more similar to Dutch and English than *Hochdeutsch* (High German) is. The future of the language is not at all secure: many people in northern Germany are no longer able to speak it, and it is widely regarded as a "dialect" of German; see Charles Russ (ed.) (1994) *The Dialects of Modern German: A Linguistic Survey*, London: Routledge.
- The traditional and now moribund Norfolk-dialect term of address *bor* probably has an origin in the same root as the *bour* of *neighbour* (see also 11.2).

## 7.10 Viability

Norfolk is falling into the sea. We are losing large bits of the eastern part of our county to erosion every winter.

Unfortunately, our national leaders do not seem to care much about this. They have singled out Norfolk as a place they are not committed to defending. Our county may be collapsing into the North Sea as a result of winter storms; but that is just too bad.

I wonder if their attitude has something to do with the words they use. Tony Blair and David Cameron were both very keen to defend what they called our "nation" by sending troops to Iraq and Afghanistan. They spent vast sums on these expeditions because, they said, they made our nation safer – even if it was not necessarily obvious to everybody exactly how it did that.

Tragically, however, they and most other politicians in government seem to have no interest at all in defending the actual material fabric of this place where we live, right here. Maybe it would help if governments would start thinking of this as our "country" – instead of this abstraction "the nation". They might then be more focussed on defending us here at home. In fact, it might be even better if, instead of using either of these originally French words, they could go back to Old English and start thinking of this place as our "land".

Interestingly, one spokesman told us why the government did not want to try and save eastern Norfolk. It was another word: saving us would lack "viability". *Viability* is rather a new word, but it comes from the older form *viable*, which was originally a French word derived from *vie* 'life'. It was initially used of newborn infants, meaning 'capable of life'; and it started being used in a more generalised sense in the nineteenth century. Well, obviously coastal Norfolk will not be 'capable of life' if the government choose not to spend any money to help us – because what our leaders seem to mean by "lacking in viability" is "not worth spending money on".

If the Dutch had not wanted to defend Holland because it was not viable, they would not have any land left by now, and therefore no country, let alone a nation. But they are defending it; and our politicians could certainly protect us in the same way if they wanted to. But apparently Norfolk is not important enough.

I wonder how viable Bayswater and Charlbury would be if they were on the edge of a cliff.

---

**BACKGROUND NOTES**

*Bayswater, London, is where Tony Blair (b. 1953), the Prime Minister of the United Kingdom from 1997 to 2007, has a house. Charlbury, Oxfordshire, is about 2 miles / 3 kms from the small village where David Cameron (b. 1966), who became Prime Minister of the United Kingdom in 2010, has a house.*

---

## 7.11 Seagulls

I have quite a few friends who are birdwatchers.

Some of them have taken to calling themselves *birders*. This an Americanism, though not a particularly ancient one: in 1962 the *Boston Globe* reported that an assembly of Audubon enthusiasts "had rejected the term 'bird watchers' by which they had been commonly known, and adopted the designation 'birders'". This was rather unfortunate, as the original meaning of *birder* was 'one who catches or hunts birds' – but of course it is up to them what they call themselves.

My bird-watching friends are all extremely nice people, but they do have this annoying habit, as soon as anyone utters the word *seagull*, of chanting the mantra "There's no such thing as a seagull."

What can we say? Of course there are seagulls! Millions of them! As it happens, I can see one from where I am sitting right now.

But actually, of course, it is the actual word *seagull* which birdwatchers object to, for some reason. Their objections, though, are in vain. *Seagull* is so well established as an English word that a Google search produces 25 million hits. Our famous writer and poet John Milton used the word. Our famous novelist Charles Dickens used it. The name of Chekhov's famous play is always *The Seagull* in English-language productions. And if saying *seagull* is some kind of mistake, as certain ornithologists would have us believe, it is a pretty venerable mistake: the first recorded usage of *seagull* was in 1542!

Birdwatchers reckon we should say *gull*. Well, people do say that too, including me – *gull* and *seagull* basically mean the same thing – but it is probable that *seagull* came to be the most common term in everyday usage in order to avoid confusion with one of the several other meanings of *gull*, especially the word *gull* meaning 'fool', as in *gullible*.

*Gull* was not originally an English word. The first recorded usage was not until the 1400s, and it is thought to have come into English from Welsh – the modern Welsh form is *gwylan*.

The original English word was *mew*, which is related to German *Möwe* and Dutch *meeuw*. Birdwatchers will hardly be pleased to know that the forms *sea-mew*, *Seemöwe* and *zeemeeuw* also occur. In Norse-influenced regions of Britain you can also find *maw* or *sea-maw*, with the old Norfolk form of this being *mow*, as reported by Sydney Cozens-Hardy in his 1893 book *Broad Norfolk*. And, yes, I am sorry, there is also *sea-mow*.

---

**BACKGROUND NOTES**

*The* Oxford English Dictionary *shows that* birder *was used in English in the sense of 'a bird-catcher, a fowler' at least from the 1400s; and it also shows it being used in the nineteenth century with the meaning of 'breeder of birds'. The first British citation of the word in the sense of 'birdwatcher' which appears without quotation marks or the qualification "American" comes from the specialist journal* Birds, *from 1985.*

*The Audubon Society is an American naturalist organisation devoted to conservation. It is named after Jean-Jacques Audubon, a nineteenth-century American ornithologist who emigrated to the USA from France at the age of 18. He catalogued and painted North American birds in his famous book called* Birds of America.

---

## 7.12 Is language really for communication?

I was on the market in Norwich waiting to buy something at a stall with lots of other customers at it. The man who was doing his best to serve everybody was joined by a woman coming to help him. She looked, half at us customers and half at him, and said "Who's next?" He pointed to me and said "He was, and them next", indicating the couple next to me, so I moved forward to get served. But then I saw that the couple were moving forward as well, and the woman who was serving was looking a bit cross. "No, you're not next", she said to me. It emerged, after a brief and amiable discussion, that what the man had really said was "He wasn't, them next."

You can see how that could happen. My hearing is not as good as it used to be when I was younger – nobody's is. But against the background noise of the busy market, I think quite a few people might have heard "he wasn't them next" as "he was 'n' them next". The only difference was the microsecond-long presence of the *t* sound.

That made me think about an important question for linguistics. Is language really for speaking? Is it really for communicating information? Obviously we do use it for that. But surely if the original function of language was for communication, we could have come up with something better than this flawed system which fails to work properly quite so often?

Miscommunication is not always due to mishearing either. It can also have to do with the ambiguity of many words. And with misinterpretation – how often do we find ourselves saying "That's not what I meant"?

Some specialists think that maybe the original purpose of language was not for speaking at all, but for cognition, for thinking with. Perhaps speaking to each other was just a kind of secondary benefit? We certainly use the categories set up for us by our language to classify and think about the world.

For Norwegians, for example, the word *hus* does not just mean 'house', it also means 'building'; so if they are speaking English, they may tell you the University Library is "in that house over there". Obviously they are not dividing the world up exactly like we are.

And you can still, back on Norwich market, buy milches and roes at the fish stalls. When people from elsewhere call milches "soft roes", we think that is very strange. They are not roes at all. They're milches.

## BACKGROUND NOTES

*Soft (male) herring roes are called* milches *in Norwich, but elsewhere they are more generally known as* milts. *Roes* are the hard *roes, i.e. the eggs of the female herring.*

## LINGUISTIC NOTES

- I misheard [hi: wɒzn? ðɛm nɛkst] as [hi: wɒzn ðɛm nɛkst].
- The way in which we use the categories set up for us by our language to classify and think about the world is often discussed under the heading of *linguistic relativity* or the *Sapir–Whorf hypothesis*, after the two linguists who the topic is most closely associated with, Edward Sapir and Benjamin Lee Whorf (see Peter Trudgill, 2000, *Sociolinguistics: An Introduction to Language and Society*, London: Penguin, chapter 1). Sapir and Whorf were particularly influenced by their work on the indigenous languages of North America, which they found to be remarkably different from the European languages they were more familiar with. One aspect of this had to do with the use of *evidentials* (see 10.1).

## 7.13 The lexical bar

I was once briefly taken ill with a condition caused by medication I was taking. The condition was called *hyponatraemia*. "Blimey", said alarmed English friends when I told them, "that sounds really serious – what on earth is it?"

Greek friends had a very different reaction, when I mentioned it to them. "Oh yes," they said calmly, "not enough salt".

Hyponatraemia is a condition where there is too little sodium in the blood. Greeks who have never heard this medical term before nevertheless have no trouble working out what it means. The Greek word for blood is *aema, natrio* means 'sodium', *ypo* means 'under or sub' (*subtitle* in Greek is *ypotitlos*); so for them the meaning of the word is totally transparent.

Talking of transparency, *Undurchsichtigkeit* is a long German word which is nevertheless totally transparent to German speakers. Translating it bit by bit, the different parts of *Un-durch-sicht-ig-keit* are equivalent to English 'un-through-sight-y-hood', so: 'unseethroughableness'.

The normal English word for unseethroughableness is *opacity*, a word which is itself opaque: English-speaking children hearing this originally Latin word for the first time cannot work out from its structure what it means, while a German child can do so easily with their version.

This aspect of English has been called "the lexical bar" by some educationists. English-speaking children are at a disadvantage because of the way English expanded its vocabulary over the last few centuries, not by creating new words from its own resources so they are easy to understand and learn, like many other languages, but by borrowing words from Greek and Latin.

We have the word *omnivorous*; Norwegian has *altetende* 'all-eating'. English has *ambidextrous*; the German is *beidhändig* 'both-handed'. We have *incoherent*; Dutch has *onsamenhangend* 'un-together-hanging'. Our usage of alien sources is a barrier which, it is argued, has kept an important area of English vocabulary out of the reach of large parts of the population, hence the feared elitist category of "long words". But, as German shows, it is not the length of words which is the problem, but the unseethroughableness.

It is a problem which could have been avoided. Unlike with many other languages, the English-speaking men who carried out the important work of expanding our vocabulary in the 1600s and 1700s, introducing all sorts of new scientific, philosophical and cultural terms, looked to Latin and Greek for help because they thought their own vernacular language was inadequate and inferior. They were wrong.

## LINGUISTIC NOTES

- On the notion of the lexical bar, see David Corson (1985) *The Lexical Bar*, Oxford: Pergamon Press.
- *Opacity*, *omnivorous*, *omnivorous*, *incoherent* all started being used regularly in English in the seventeenth century. In the sixteenth and seventeenth centuries, there was considerable controversy in England about the use of "inkhorn terms", by which was meant words which were borrowed from other languages, especially Latin and Greek, which were considered to be pretentious and unnecessary. "It was the growing tendency to borrow merely for the sake of magniloquence that gave rise to the Inkhorn Controversy in the latter half of the sixteenth and early part of the seventeenth century. What came to be seen as superfluous learned borrowings from Latin were heavily criticised", Terttu Nevalainen (2000) "Early Modern English lexis and semantics", in Roger Lass (ed.), *The Cambridge History of the English Language*, vol. III, Cambridge University Press, 332–458.
- One writer who introduced many new coinages based on the classical languages into English was the polymath Sir Thomas Browne, who lived in Norwich from 1637 to 1682. *Ambidextrous* seems to have been one of his words.
- William Barnes, the nineteenth-century Dorset poet and philologist, was one of a number of writers who have tried to restore or introduce Germanic-origin words into English, in an attempt to reduce the amount of Latin and Greek vocabulary. Some of these writers were undoubtedly motivated by ideas of linguistic "purity" rather than by a desire to improve comprehensibility. Amongst Barnes's Germanic words were the very nice *bendsome* instead of *flexible*, and *wortlore* rather than *botany*.

# 8 Sounds and fury

This section is concerned with pronunciation. Linguistic scientists discuss the subject of pronunciation using the terms phonetics, which is the study of the way in which human beings produce speech sounds, and phonology, which is the study of the way in which speech sounds are organised and used in different languages to make the contrasts which distinguish between one word and another. This section, then, is necessarily occupied with the topic of accents. Everybody has an accent, because your accent is the way you pronounce your language, and you cannot speak without pronouncing!

Your accent normally goes together with your dialect – where dialect consists not only of your pronunciation but also of the words and grammatical forms you use – so if you speak Norfolk dialect, you naturally speak it with a Norfolk accent. But it is also possible and normal to speak the Standard English dialect with a local accent, which is what I do when I am giving a university lecture – I use Standard English grammar, but I speak in my native local Norfolk accent.

There is a small minority of people in Britain, however – especially in England – who do not have a local accent. These people are not only native speakers of Standard English, but also speak with what is called the RP accent – which is the topic of the first article. My main message in this section is that all accents are worthy of respect, and that no accents are lazy, inferior, wrong or ugly.

## 8.1 Well-spoken?

There are a few people in England who are not fortunate enough to have a regional accent. They include many of the men who are currently in charge of the nation. David William Donald Cameron, George Gideon Oliver Osborne, Nicholas William Peter Clegg and Alexander Boris de Pfeffel Johnson all have the misfortune of not seeming to come from anywhere in particular at all when they speak English. You can tell they hail from England, rather than Ireland or Canada or New Zealand. But that's about it. They are nowhere men.

This is because their parents paid large sums of money – £30,000 a year for Eton, currently – for them to go to schools for deracinated upper-class people where they, quite naturally, came to speak like all the other deracinated upper-class pupils. There are about 220 of these so-called public schools in England, out of a total of around 4,000 secondary schools, so little more than 5 per cent of the total.

The upper-class accent which is transmitted from one generation to another in these schools goes by different names. Linguistic scientists call it RP. This stands for "Received Pronunciation", an old-fashioned Victorian/Edwardian term meaning 'accepted in the "best" social circles'. Linguists do not much like this term, but we seem to be stuck with it now. Other people have called it the BBC accent, or Oxford English, or the Queen's English.

The accent is non-regional because the public schools were traditionally boarding schools. Upper-class children, originally mostly boys, were first taken from their homes at a young age and sent to board at preparatory schools. Then, at the age of 13 or so, they were sent to spend most of their adolescence at a public school, again away from their family home. So the RP accent tells listeners very little about where its speakers come from geographically, but a lot about their social background.

This is very odd. On a worldwide scale, the RP accent is a freak – just about everybody else in the world betrays their geographical origins to a greater or lesser extent when they speak.

Speakers of this freakish accent are sometimes said to be "well-spoken". This is, if you think about it, outrageous. Why should "speaking well" mean sounding like George Osborne? Why can't it mean speaking clearly and articulately; and being able to say exactly what you want to say?

You can do that in any local accent.

## BACKGROUND NOTES

*In Britain, and particularly in England, the term* public school *generally refers to a group of long-established and very expensive private schools. They are, or at least were originally, socially exclusive single-sex boarding schools which accept pupils aged from 13 to 18.*

*At the time of the writing of this piece, David Cameron was the Prime Minister of the United Kingdom, George Osborne was the Chancellor of the Exchequer, Nick Clegg the Deputy Prime Minister and Boris Johnson the Mayor of London.*

## LINGUISTIC NOTES

– There is no standard accent for English, and it is possible to speak Standard English with any regional or social accent. The RP accent, on the other hand, only occurs together with Standard English. RP is, as indicated above, the English English

*cont.*

accent which developed largely in the English public schools, and which was until relatively recently required of all BBC announcers. It is still the accent taught to non-native speakers learning so-called "British" pronunciation. RP is unusual in that the relatively very small numbers of speakers who use it do not identify themselves as coming from any particular geographical region. RP is largely confined to England, although it also has, or used to have, prestige in the rest of the British Isles, and, to a decreasing extent, in Australia, New Zealand and South Africa. (It is also favoured by American film directors for the portrayal of sinister characters.) As far as England is concerned, though, RP is a non-localized accent.

- The label "British" is entirely inappropriate with reference to pronunciation since Britain consists of England, Scotland and Wales, and there is nothing at all Welsh or Scottish about the RP accent, which historically has a southeast of England origin: there is no bigger difference in the English-speaking world between accents than between those of Scotland and the English southeast.

- Like all accents, RP changes through time. Some of the changes are internally generated, but others involve the incorporation into RP of formerly regional (English southeastern) features such as HAPPY-tensing (the term is due to J. C. Wells, 1982, *Accents of English*, Cambridge University Press). This is the replacement in word-final unstressed syllables in words like *happy*, *money*, *city* of the KIT vowel (which still occurs in such words in the north of England) by the FLEECE vowel, so that words like *seedy* have the same vowel in both syllables; see Peter Trudgill (2008) "The historical sociolinguistics of elite accent change: on why RP is not disappearing", *Studia Anglica Posnaniensia* 44: 1–12. For a map of the distribution of HAPPY-tensing in England, see Peter Trudgill (1999) *The Dialects of England*, Oxford: Blackwell.

## 8.2 Prejudice holds us back

The *EDP* received a wonderfully revealing letter about my piece on the term "well-spoken" (see above, 8.1). The correspondent wrote that it is "difficult enough to make one's way in the world without encumbering oneself with a local accent".

This is, apparently, because speaking with a Norfolk accent makes him, or at least certain other people, think that we sound "slow of brain". This tells us a lot about what is going on in the minds of these certain people: *they* think we sound "slow". So the problem is not with us, but with the people who brazenly indulge in this ... well, doesn't it feel rather like racism to you?

The only possible reason for thinking that a Norfolk accent makes someone sound stupid is because you believe that Norfolk people *are* stupid. Which we are not.

It is horrible to recall, but it is quite true that the nineteenth-century conventional wisdom in Britain was that non-white people – and women – were "slow of brain" too, compared to white men. Which they were not, either. What we need to do is not remove local accents, but rid our land of the highly unappealing mind-set this letter exemplifies, just as we have tried to rid the country of racism and sexism. People are not "encumbered" by their accents, but rather by irrational prejudices against these accents which hide behind false judgements about "slowness" and incomprehensibility.

The correspondent offers what he thinks is a solution: it is "better not to acquire the accent in the first place" – just as it would have been better not to have been born black or female, I suppose?

Apart from the 4 or 5 per cent of the UK population who speak RP, everybody grows up with a local accent, like normal people everywhere else in the world. We all grow up speaking like the people around us. The only way to ensure a child will not acquire a local accent is to keep a check on who the people around them are – to segregate them from the locally accented majority of the population.

The most efficient form of segregation is to send children to "pukka" (the correspondent's word) schools, which of course most people cannot afford to do. Which is the point. This apartheid-type "solution" will work only for the small minority it already works for. It can't work for everybody.

What we must try to do is get rid of the prejudice. You cannot abolish racism by turning everybody white.

---

**BACKGROUND NOTES**

*In nineteenth-century Britain, people who advocated university education for women were widely ridiculed; a certain Henry Maudsley in 1874 wrote in his book* Sex in Mind and Education *that women would suffer enormous harm to their mental and physical health if they were allowed to study. Even as the idea of higher education for women gradually gained acceptance, it was still considered that there were some subjects, such as mathematics, which women would not be able to cope with.*

---

## 8.3 I don't have an accent

A number of people have written letters to the *EDP* in which they claim, or mention in passing, that they "don't have an accent".

They are not alone: there are many people in the world who think that only other people have accents. "You have an accent!" people in America exclaim when they meet an English person. They do not mean anything bad by it – they are just being friendly and are intrigued by the way you speak; but they clearly do not think they have an accent themselves. Which of course they do – an American accent, as everyone here will agree.

I have not met any of the letter writers "without an accent", but I am happy to say that I am quite sure that, like the Americans, they are not correct in what they say. The fact is that everybody has an accent, including you and me and Her Majesty the Queen. There are no exceptions.

The term "accent" refers to pronunciation, and you cannot speak without pronouncing. Your accent is simply the way you pronounce the vowels and consonants of your language, and the intonation patterns you use. Accents are mostly acquired in early childhood, and in England they are always simultaneously both social and regional. The higher up the social scale your origin, the fewer regional clues your accent normally contains.

Some local people sound like they come from Norfolk, some like they come from somewhere in East Anglia, some just like they come from somewhere in the English southeast. And you cannot tell from his accent where Stephen Fry comes from at all, except somewhere in England – though you can tell a lot about his social background.

Sometimes when people say "I don't have an accent", they mean they speak with Stephen's regionless upper-class accent – but they are wrong because it is still an accent.

Other people may mean that they have a mixed accent, because they moved a lot in their childhood and so "come from" several different places: their accents are not regional in any straightforward sense, though a linguist will often be able to point to the different regional sources of the mixture. But these people do still have an accent like the rest of us do, even if it may be unique to themselves.

The accents which we all have are part of ourselves and of our identity; and we have no reason to be anything but happy about them, whatever our background.

---

### BACKGROUND NOTES

*Stephen Fry (b. 1957) is a very well-known comedian, actor, writer and presenter: see* http://en.wikipedia.org/wiki/Stephen_Fry. *The point about citing him as an example here is that he does come from Norfolk – but you cannot tell this from his accent.*

---

## 8.4 Droppin your *g*'s is lazy

I was talking to someone the other day who strongly objected to people saying "runnin" for *running*. She said she did not like it because "dropping your *g*'s is lazy".

"Lazy" is a pretty odd word to use in this context. It means 'disinclined to work', and it applies to people who cannot be bothered to make an effort to do things they are supposed to do. But where did the idea come from that you are "supposed to" say *running* rather than *runnin*? And is it really more of an effort to say one rather than the other? Is it easier to say *goblin* than *gobbling*, or *robin* than *robbing*? No, of course it isn't.

It is not true, either, to say that the pronunciation of *running* as "runnin" involves dropping a *g*: there was no *g* sound there to drop in the first place! The two letters *ng* stand for a single nasal sound which bears the same relationship to *n* that *g* does to *d*. (Try saying *bang*, *ban* and then *bag*, *bad*, and you'll see what I mean.) It is unfortunate that we do not have a single letter in our alphabet to represent it so we have to use two, as we also do with *sh*, *ch* and *th*. Saying *sip* rather than *ship* doesn't involve leaving out an *h*, and saying *robin* rather than *robbing* doesn't involve leaving out a *g*.

In Norfolk and Suffolk we do not actually say "walkin" anyway; we say "walken". We pronounce *baking* the same as *bacon*, and *lighting* the same as *lighten*. And we are quite right to do so.

Modern English *ing* does two different grammatical jobs. It is used to turn verbs like *walk* into nouns, as in "Walking is good for you" – these nouns are called gerunds. Secondly, it produces present participles, as in "She's walking down the road." In mediaeval English, the gerunds had the same *ing* ending that they have today, but the present participles had *end* (*walkend*).

Eventually, the Standard English dialect lost the distinction between the gerund and the participle, and finished up using *ing* for both. In Norfolk we also lost the distinction, but we "did different" and went the other way, using *end* for both instead.

So when we say "walken", it's true that there was a *d* there that went missen, many hundreds of years ago. But no one here is droppen any *g*'s. And no one is be-en lazy.

## LINGUISTIC NOTES

- The phonetic symbol representing the velar nasal *ng* sound in *bang* is [ŋ], so *bang*, *ban*, *bag*, *bad* are /bæŋ, bæn, bæg, bæd/.
- Most English speakers are capable of sometimes saying *walking* with the velar nasal *ng* and sometimes with the *n*: *-ing* is a well-known linguistic variable which tends to correlate with the social background of the speaker and the social situation they are speaking in.
- The East Anglian pronunciation of *ing* is typically not /-ɪŋ/ or /-ɪn/ but /-ən/ or /-n/: *walking, baking, missing, dropping, being* /wɔːkən, beɪkən, mɪsn, drɒpən, biːən/. This also applies to place-names like *Docking* and *Walsingham*.

## 8.5 Phonotactics, or chimleys and goalkeepers

A letter-writer to the *EDP* has wondered why people in Norfolk say "chimley" instead of "chimney".

I don't know. But I can make what I hope is an intelligent guess.

The question is: why should an *l* have been substituted for the *n* in *chimney*? (And it is not just in Norfolk that people say "chimley": this pronunciation occurs in vernacular speech all over Britain and Ireland.) The word *chimney* came into English from Old French *cheminée*, perhaps as a consequence of the greater architectural sophistication of the Normans, so there was an *n* there originally.

My guess is that it has to do with what linguistic scientists call "phonotactics". This just means rules about what sequences of vowels and consonants can and cannot occur in particular languages. English has a *d* sound and a *v* sound; but we can't put them together at the beginning of a word, as the Czechs can, to make words like the name of the composer Dvorak.

English has *b* and *n* and *l* sounds. You can start a word with *bl*: there is no word *blick*, but there could be. But you can't start a word with *bn*: there is no word *bnick*, and there could not ever be.

Not so very long ago, Norwich City scored a goal against Arsenal because of a mistake by their Polish goalkeeper Szczesny. *Sz* and *cz* are just the Polish ways of writing two sounds we also have in English, *sh* and *ch*. But in the English language you can't start a word with *shch*. In Polish you can. That is phonotactics.

I think there is something similar going on here with *mn*. It is true, of course, that in English you can actually have an "m" sound followed by an "n" sound, but think about the words, apart from *chimney*, where this happens: *alumnus, amnesty, amniocentesis, calumny, hymnal, insomnia, limnetic, omnivorous, somnolent*. These are not ordinary words. They all come from Latin or Greek, and they are rather rare and learned. We normally say *hymn book*, not *hymnal*, and *sleepy* rather than *somnolent*; and I don't know what *limnetic* means, though perhaps you do. So the combination *mn* is rather marginal in English.

The combination *ml*, on the other hand, is much more usual and occurs in several everyday English words: *harmless, hemline, farmland, aimless, streamline, hamlet, seemly, calmly, firmly*. And since the consonants *n* and *l* are very similar sounds, it is not at all surprising if Norfolk and other dialect speakers have replaced something abnormal (*mn*) with something normal (*ml*). People here in Norfolk may not know all the terminology of linguistics, but they do know their English phonotactics.

**LINGUISTIC NOTES**

- In Polish, the goalkeeper's name is actually spelt Szczęsny, with the letter ę representing a nasalised vowel. The letter y stands for a close central vowel. The correct pronunciation is therefore approximately /ʃʧɛ̃snɨ/. The name derives from an old Polish word meaning 'cheerful', so it corresponds exactly to the common Norfolk surname Blyth.
- "The consonants n and l are very similar sounds": they have the same place of articulation. They are both alveolar consonants, pronounced with the front part of the tongue making contact with the alveolar ridge behind the top teeth.

## 8.6 Dropping your aitches

I recently published a column in the *EDP* where I mentioned the beautiful, Norfolk-accented BBC broadcasts by the late John Taylor (see 9.2). His son, our well-known novelist and biographer D. J. Taylor, then wrote to me to say that he reckoned John had actually spoken with a Norwich accent, not a Norfolk one.

Many people will understand perfectly well what David Taylor means. The urban Norwich and rural Norfolk accents really are rather different, even if less so now than they used to be. In the old days, it was common for the country people of Norfolk to look down on the city people of Norwich because of their accents – and vice versa! The Dumpling and Canary mascots at Carrow Road, and in Banger's weekly cartoons in the Saturday evening *Pink'Un*, represented realities everyone recognised.

This accent rivalry was a common topic of conversation in my childhood home. My mother grew up in the country, in the north Norfolk villages around Holt; and my father grew up in the city, in a terraced house in New Catton. When my parents first met in the 1930s, my city grandparents' family used to tease my mother because she pronounced *hundred* "hundret" and *naked* "naket", rural pronunciations they did not use. And, though she was too polite a young woman to tease them back, she actually looked down on them for the way they spoke too.

One feature she often mentioned in talking about this was that Norwich people "dropped their aitches". Mostly when you hear people using this phrase, they seem to be implying that there is something rather reprehensible about the whole thing, as if aitches were catches in cricket. It must be wrong, they claim, to say "ammer" because *hammer* is spelt with an *h*.

But if you think about it, that does not make sense. Writing is a way of representing speech. If speech and writing do not match, it is because the writing system is inadequate. Our English spelling system is notorious for being a good representation of fifteenth-century pronunciation, and hopeless as a way of indicating modern speech.

But the truth is that arguments about "correct" pronunciations are rationalisations for prejudices against accents with low status. This is obvious from the fact that no one suggests it's "wrong" to drop the *h* in *hour* or *honour*, because not even posh speakers pronounce the *h*'s in these words. Nor does anybody claim that the *h* in words like *night* and *thought* should be pronounced. Lowland Scots do still pronounce the *h* in these words, using a pronunciation usually shown as *nicht, thocht*; but their accents do not have high prestige, and "thocht" as a pronunciation actually has lower status than the more widespread version without an *h*.

It is quite true that during the twentieth century, *h*-dropping was not heard out in the Norfolk countryside. It was a feature which was typical of the Norwich accent: in the city you might well be called "Arbo" if your name was Herbert. The reason for this rural–urban difference is well understood by linguists and geographers. Languages change all the time, and changes which begin life in urban areas jump from one town to another, and only later move out into the countryside. *H*-dropping is an innovation in English which started in London some centuries ago. It then spread out gradually from there – it has not reached Tyneside or Scotland yet – arriving in the more important cities first.

So these days it is much less common for the Dumpling to look down on the Canary about *h*-lessness because, predictably, some Dumplings have now started to drop their aitches too, although none of us, urban or rural, do it nearly so often as the Cockneys.

Fascinatingly, we have also recently been presented with the phenomenon of younger people – are they all under 40? – who are so worried about making the "mistake" of dropping their aitches that they have started calling the letter *h* "haitch" [see also 4.14].

## BACKGROUND NOTES

*D. J. Taylor (b. 1960) won an award for his biography of George Orwell, and has published many other works, including* Bright Young People: The Rise and Fall of a Generation 1918–1940 *(2007) and novels such as* Real Life *(1992) and* Derby Day *(2011).*

*The Norwich City football team are known as the Canaries, and the club emblem has a canary on it. Norfolk dumplings are the stereotypical traditional local dish. E. H. 'Harry' Banger was a comic-book writer, artist, illustrator and cartoonist who was born in Norwich and supported Norwich City. On the* Pink'Un, *the local sports paper, see 5.11.*

*On New Catton, see 1.11.*

*Tyneside is the area around Newcastle in the far northeast of England, south of the Scottish border.*

**LINGUISTIC NOTES**

- The spelling *thocht* is intended to indicate the Scottish pronunciation of *thought* as [θɔxt]. In Scots, [x] and [h] are best analysed as two allophones of the same phoneme, /h/, where [h] appears in syllable-initial position and [x] elsewhere.
- On the geographical diffusion of linguistic innovations, and the role played by urban areas in this kind of spread, see J. K. Chambers & Peter Trudgill (1998) *Dialectology*, Cambridge University Press.

## 8.7 Glottal stops

Most people in this country know what a glottal stop is. Our schools do not teach much about phonetics, the scientific study of speech sounds, which is a great pity because they really ought to. But the glottal stop is famous because there are many people in this country who say, rather loudly, that they do not like it, even though they use it themselves. They hate it particularly in words like *better* and *city* – "be'er, ci'y". If you say "Po'er Heigham", they call that "dropping your *t*'s".

The glottal stop is actually a perfectly normal consonant. Lots of the world's languages have it: Arabic, Danish, Persian, Mohawk, Hebrew, Maltese, Tahitian . . . There is no letter for it in the Latin alphabet because Latin did not have the sound, so in Polynesian languages it is written as an apostrophe, as in Hawai'i.

In phonetics, a "stop" is a consonant made by totally blocking off the flow of air out of the mouth: *p* is a bilabial stop because the block is formed by the two lips. The glottal stop goes by that name because in this case the block is made by closing the vocal cords in the larynx, and the larynx is part of the glottis.

In English, the glottal stop is not a consonant in its own right. It is a way of pronouncing the consonant *t*, though according to rather strict rules. In Norfolk we use it as the way of pronouncing *t* before another consonant, as in *Scotland* – try saying it! But you cannot use it at the beginning of a word, unless the first syllable is unstressed. So you cannot pronounce *cup of tea* with a glottal stop for the *t*, but you can say "see you 'omorra!" (tomorrow).

In the English of England, the glottal stop pronunciation of *t* is becoming increasingly common when the *t* occurs before a vowel, as in "abou' eleven". It is quite wrong, however, to claim that that is "dropping your *t*'s". If you drop the *t* from *beating*, you get *being*, not "bea'ing"!

It is not "lazy" either – it probably actually requires more energy.

So what's to dislike? Nothing, actually. But languages change all the time, especially their phonetics; and there are always people around who do not like anything new. The glottal stop as a way of pronouncing *t* is an innovation dating back about 150 years. It probably started in Norfolk; studies of rural dialects spoken by people born in the 1870s showed that it was more prevalent here than anywhere else.

This change from using the tip of the tongue to using the glottis in order to pronounce a *t* is a fascinating development for linguistic scientists to observe – and here Norfolk is in the vanguard! So much for the idea that our region's way of speaking is "a bi' yesterday"!

---

### BACKGROUND NOTES

*When I wrote "this country" I was thinking of England, but it would be equally true of Scotland.*

*Potter Heigham is a village in eastern Norfolk. Norfolk people pronounce Heigham with the original pronunciation "hay-um" – it often sounds like "ham" to outsiders (as does the same name in Norwich) and it is often spelt* Ham *in informal and jocular writing, including on the internet. There is also an incorrect newer pronunciation "High-um" which has become quite common. See also 14.1, 14.4, 14.10, 14.11.*

---

### LINGUISTIC NOTES

– By "a way of pronouncing the consonant *t*", I mean that [ʔ] (this is the phonetic symbol for the glottal stop) is an allophone of /t/. The technical term for this phenomenon, as introduced by J. C. Wells in his 1982 book *Accents of English*, is T-glottalling. The pronunciations I have been trying to indicate by use of the apostrophe ' are: *better* [bɛʔə], *city* [sɪʔiː], *Scotland* [skɒʔlənd], *tomorrow* [ʔəmɒrə], *beating* [biːʔɪn].

## 8.8 *Snarl, sneer, sneeze, snicker, sniff*

Most people probably do not know what the old Norfolk dialect word *snurle* means. I had never heard of it myself until I came across it in John Greaves Nall's *Glossary of the Dialect and Provincialisms of East Anglia*, which was originally published in 1866. It is, though, an interesting fact about the English language that you might perhaps be able to have a stab at guessing something of what it means from how the word sounds.

Vowels and consonants usually have no meaning of their own. We can put them together to make words which do mean something, like *house*, or to make grammatical sub-parts of words which linguists call "morphemes", like the *es* in *houses* which means 'more than one'. But sounds like "e" and "s" don't have any meaning on their own.

There is also generally no connection between how a word sounds and what it means – the link is totally arbitrary. There is no reason why, as Shakespeare implied, a rose should be called *a rose* or, as he did not imply, why a dwile should be called *a dwile*. A book can equally well be called a *llyfr* (Welsh) or a *vivlio* (Greek) or *książka* (Polish). The word *mark* means 'mark' in English, 'marrow' in German, and 'worm' in Norwegian.

However, sometimes we come across combinations of sounds in English (and other languages) which do seem to have some kind of significance of their own. Think about words like *lump, bump, dump, thump, jump, crump*. Doesn't it seem as if these "ump" words all have something, rather heavy, in common? And what about *glare, gleam, glimmer, glint, glisten, glitter, gloss, glow*? The "gl" combination at the beginning of these words seems to indicate something to do with being shiny.

Linguists call this "sound symbolism". Maybe "ump" does have a rather heavy sound to it. But there doesn't seem to be any obvious reason why "gl" should have anything to do with luminescence; in English, it just does.

This, then, gives us our clue about *snurle*. Think of words like *snarl, sneer, sneeze, snicker, sniff, sniffle, snigger, snitch, snivel, snob, snoop, snooty, snooze, snore, snort, snot, snout, snuff* and *snuffle*. It is not too far fetched, I think, to say that they all seem to have some connection with the nose; and so it is not too much of a surprise to find that in Norfolk, *snurle* as a noun means 'a cold in the head' and, as a verb, 'to talk through the nose'.

## LINGUISTIC NOTES

– Phonological sequences such as /-ʌmp/, /gl-/ and /sn-/ are referred to by linguists as *phonaesthemes*, a term introduced by J. R. Firth in his 1930 [1964] book *The Tongues of Men, and Speech*, Oxford University Press. Other phonaesthemes in English include /fl-/ as in *flap, flare, flicker, flitter, flurry*; /-ʌtə/ as in *stutter, sputter, splutter*; /-æk/ as in *crack, clack, hack, smack, thwack, whack*; and /-æʃ/ as in *bash, brash, crash, clash, gash, gnash, lash, mash, smash, slash, thrash*. *Flash* can be interpreted as consisting of two phonaesthemes, one after the other, and so can *flutter*. For more on phonaesthemes, see Laurie Bauer (2004) *A Glossary of Morphology*, Edinburgh University Press.

# 9 Respecting local speech

In the section that follows, I write about various ways in which our society would be a better place if there was more respect than is currently the case, on the part of metropolitan, social and educational elites, for local habits of speaking and local ways of using language.

## 9.1 He in't watchen on the marshes

When he was conducting his 2012 anti-Norfolk dialect campaign from the safety of the other side of the Suffolk border, one thing Ken Hurst did was to contrast the Norfolk dialect with the dialect of North Yorkshire. He quoted the famous Lyke Wake Dirge:

> When thoo frae hence away art passed, ivvery neet an' all ...

"There, Norfolk dialect lovers," he wrote gleefully, "is proper dialect for you!"

You can see what he means. The language is impressively different. But Ken was being provocative – and I am provoked into saying that he was being unfair. The Lyke Wake Dirge dates from the 1500s, so it is bound to look very different from modern English. (The word *lyke*, by the way, means 'body'. We still have it in Norfolk in the form of *lych*, as in the lychgate to churchyards, where the first part of funeral services used to be held.)

North of England dialects do seem more "dialectal" than southern dialects like ours because Standard English originated in London, with some input from Oxford and Cambridge – and from Norfolk. Norwich was the second largest city in the realm, and there was a lot of immigration into London from Norfolk; so it is not so much the case that Norfolk dialect is quite like Standard English as that Standard English is quite like the Norfolk dialect!

Today, dialects north of the River Humber are more conservative than English dialects anywhere else in the world. Linguistic changes in England normally begin in London and spread outwards from there, so the far-northern dialects still have mediaeval pronunciations like "hoose, moose, oot" rather than modern "house, mouse, out". The London-based change from the one vowel to the other, which reached Norfolk centuries ago, hasn't arrived there yet.

But you do not have to go to Yorkshire to find dialect poetry which is moving and lyrical. You need look no further, I reckon, than the poem by our own dialect writer, the late John Kett, which was written in 1974 on the passing of his friend Dick Bagnall Oakeley. Dick – a naturalist, teacher, writer and all-round Norfolk Renaissance man – was a great speaker, friend and defender of our dialect. John Kett's poem begins:

> This arternune I see the swallers flyin by the pond;
> They'a come agin, a-glidin trew the air.
> An baads in thousans there mus' be,
> A-comin in acrorst the sea.
> But he int watchen on the marshes there . . .

That's proper dialect for you.

## BACKGROUND NOTES

*I started writing columns on language for the* Eastern Daily Press *as a result of the public reaction to an article in the newspaper which had been written by the journalist Ken Hurst, which aroused much local hostility. He claimed, in this and other columns, that our local dialect was backward and mangled jabbering, and proclaimed that he was glad he did not speak it himself, suggesting that the sooner we got rid of it the better. I was urged by many local people to write a response in our local paper, and the editor agreed that I could. The response appears as the* Postscript *at the end of this book. One reader then wrote to the* EDP *asking that I be allowed to write more columns – which I started doing.*

*"When thoo frae hence away art passed, ivvery neet an' all" is 'When thou from hence away art passed, every night and all'.*

## LINGUISTIC NOTES

- Dialects in the far north of England, and in Scotland, still have the pre-Great Vowel Shift vowel /u:/ in words such as *house, mouse, out*.
- The spellings <arternune> 'afternoon' and <acrorst> 'across' in the Norfolk poem are not intended to indicate any kind of /r/. They are rather intended to indicate the long vowels /a:/ and /ɔ:/ respectively. Similarly, the spelling <swaller> is simply intended to indicate word-final /ə/. *Trew* is 'through', *baads* is 'birds'.

## 9.2 The news in dialect

I am lucky enough to have a part-time job teaching at the University of Agder in Kristiansand. That is how I know that an important national prize is awarded annually in Norway. The prize has been awarded every year since 1978, and it is presented to a person who, on Norwegian TV or radio, "distinguishes themselves through their good use of language and employment of dialect". Last time, the prize-winner was Trude Teige. Trude is a kind of Norwegian Jeremy Paxman. She presents a prime-time TV news programme four times a week on the Norwegian equivalent of BBC 2. The committee who awarded her the prize congratulated her on using her dialect in a clear and natural way. At the award ceremony, Trude told journalists that she believed it was important in broadcasting to speak your own dialect, and to speak it in a modern, clear and comprehensible way. In that way, you can concentrate on what you are saying and not, self-consciously, on how you are saying it.

Wouldn't it be nice if we had such a prize here in this country? At the moment this is unthinkable. Ms Teige comes from a rather out-of-the-way place on the west coast of Norway called Sunnmøre – a sort of Norwegian Norfolk – and she started her broadcasting career presenting the news on local TV there in her local dialect. Can we imagine that here?

It is only relatively recently that we have had radio and TV presenters in England who use any kind of local accent at all, let alone local dialect. Older people remember when, if you wanted to be a newsreader, you needed two qualities: you had to be able to read – and you had to have a public school accent. So BBC Radio Norfolk must take credit for employing some presenters and other broadcasters who do speak in a Norfolk way: what a joy it was to hear John Taylor's vivid reports of local football matches – local events reported in the local media in a local form of English. And Radio Norfolk does give lots of airtime to locally accented people who phone in, take part in interviews, or make other types of contribution – and it is very good that they do.

But how long will it be before we actually have the news presented in a Norfolk accent? We get to listen to people with local accents from elsewhere – who do not always know how to pronounce local place-names correctly – but not with Norfolk accents. In Scotland it is expected that presenters will have Scottish accents. But here we have learnt not to have any such expectation.

If the BBC did start using locally accented presenters to read the local news, there would be people who would protest. Some of them, sadly, would be local people. They would feel, perhaps, that it was "inappropriate" to use local speech in this way. One of the tasks that the Friends of Norfolk Dialect organisation has set itself is to help people get over this kind of embarrassment – to encourage people to feel that local speech can always be appropriate in local settings.

Too often, when the local dialect is used in the printed media here, this is done for comic effect. But a dialect which is used only for jokes is suffering rather badly from an inferiority complex. Perhaps this is not surprising when outsiders keep telling us that our local speech is "mangled" and that we "struggle" with our language – both words which have been used in this newspaper recently. The fact is that no one dialect or accent is in itself better or worse than any other. It is only attitudes towards them which differ. We can make a beginning locally in producing more positive attitudes towards our local speech by deciding that we are all going to start feeling positive, here in Norfolk, about speaking in a distinctively Norfolk way.

---

**BACKGROUND NOTES**

*Jeremy Paxman is a well-known English TV presenter and writer. On John Taylor, see also 8.6.*

---

## 9.3 In the USA

This summer, my wife and I spent the 4th of July in the USA, celebrating American independence with her family (well, I was not actually celebrating, of course). As usual, I had a series of pleasant experiences over there which I never have here. In America I always get complimented on the way I speak.

"I just love your accent!" shop assistants exclaim. "You sound so authoritative when you speak," say academic colleagues. "That's a beautiful voice you have," students tell me. This is, sadly, not something which happens very much to those of us with a Norfolk accent in this country. On the contrary, there are people here who find our accent so unpleasant that they write to the *EDP* asserting virulently that it is ugly and makes us sound stupid.

Why do we get these totally different reactions on the two sides of the Atlantic? Beauty is in the eye the beholder. So is ugliness. And this is particularly true of accents – although here it is the ear that is involved, of course. Linguists have carried out research into American, Canadian and Irish listeners' reactions to English accents which shows this very clearly.

If people in this country find a Birmingham accent "ugly", or a Highland Scottish accent "attractive", they are not making aesthetic judgements about speech sounds as such. A Cockney saying "paint" ('ugly') sounds just like a toff saying "pint" ('nice'). What British people are responding to are the associations which different accents have for them.

If you take away the knowledge about where an accent is from, you also take away the associations, and you do not get the same reactions. Can you imagine finding different dialects of Vietnamese especially ugly or beautiful? We do not react like that to Vietnamese because we have no idea what we are listening to. All we are hearing is sounds – and, as sounds, they are not ugly or beautiful. They are just sounds. That is the position Americans are in when they listen to British accents. They have never heard most of them before, and they may not even recognise them as mother-tongue accents – a Scottish friend was once complimented in Indiana on his excellent English and asked how long he had been learning it!

Mostly, though, Americans just identify our accents as "British" – and they have favourable reactions to all of them. It is those associations again. For Americans, Britain is a beautiful country, with Her Majesty the Queen, Shakespeare and red double-decker buses. It is a place to go on vacation. They have no awareness of the significance of different social accents, and cannot tell the rural from the urban. For them, our accents are just accents.

So the people who react most negatively to British accents are the British themselves. If some British people harbour negative feelings about the Norfolk accent, that is because in some important sense they feel negative about us. We are right to be offended by this. But it is their problem, and we should not let it be ours. There is nothing worse than feeling ashamed of the way you speak.

Americans think people with a Norfolk accent sound intelligent and sophisticated. That makes Norfolk people like me feel good, but we should not have to go to America to get this kind of boost. All we have to do is to tell ourselves that the way we speak is something that, as Norfolk people, we can feel proud about. The Norfolk accent is the splendid, legitimate result of centuries of development in this part of the world of the ancient Anglo-Saxon language spoken by our ancestors. Those of us who have a Norfolk accent should feel good about using it in all situations, everywhere we go – not just in the USA.

---

### BACKGROUND NOTES

*The 4th of July is the national holiday in the United States which commemorates the declaration of independence from Great Britain in 1776.*

---

### LINGUISTIC NOTES

- Cockney *paint* and RP *pint* can both be pronounced [paɪnt]. The research on the differential reactions to British accents by North Americans and British people can be consulted in Peter Trudgill (1983) *On Dialect: Social and Geographical Perspectives*, Oxford: Blackwell, chapter 12: "Sociolinguistics and linguistic value judgements: correctness, adequacy and aesthetics".

## 9.4 Hypocrisy and intelligence

Yesterday was an interesting day for me linguistically.

I am on the West Coast of the USA. About 9 p.m. last night, at a party, an American woman came up to me and said "I just love your accent – it's beautiful!" Then, about an hour later, I downloaded the iPad edition of today's *EDP* – Oregon time is 8 hours behind Norwich time – and found columnist Steve Downes also talking about my accent (and his). But Steve was taking a very different line. "Our regional accent", asserted Steve, "can make us sound a bit slow. Just ask people from outside Norfolk."

"Sometimes", reckons Steve, "the truth hurts." But, Steve, it is not the truth! That woman was from outside Norfolk, and she did not think my Norfolk accent made me sound "a bit slow". She thought it made me sound intelligent and authoritative.

I do not agree with Steve either that, as he also claimed in his column, it is hypocritical to alter the way you speak according to context. Most people do that quite naturally and spontaneously. But I do agree with Steve that we must hope for a future where it is what we say that matters, not the accent we say it in. Steve, though, is not helping matters at all if he believes that, when he speaks in his native local accent, he comes across as "slow". He has got to stop believing that. I don't believe it. But I acknowledge that Steve is not alone. Sadly, many people in Norfolk do feel that way. They have been brainwashed by the ignorant attitudes of "people from outside Norfolk".

We should not waste our time asking such people what they think, as Steve suggests. On the contrary, we should work on what we think about our accent ourselves. There is nothing inherently stupid-sounding about our accent at all. Such judgements are, as Steve rightly says, lazy stereotypes; and they are based on perceptions about particular places.

Let us remind ourselves that Norwich is a famous city, with a distinguished history, a high-level university, a cutting-edge research park, a lively cultural scene, a population of a quarter of a million and, some years, a Premier League football team. It is also one of only eleven UNESCO "Cities of Literature" in the world. We have no need to feel inferior to anyone about the accent that belongs to our city, or anything else.

I just love your accent, Steve. The USA is full of people who think it makes you sound intelligent and authoritative. Why don't you decide you feel the same way about it yourself?

**BACKGROUND NOTES**

*Of the eleven UNESCO Cities of Literature worldwide, Norwich is the only one in England. There are two others in the British Isles, Dublin and Edinburgh.*

*For more on negative attitudes to language varieties, see 8.2.*

## 9.5 Prejudice in art and business

The Norwich Twenty Group is seventy years old; and their anniversary exhibition, "The story of a unique group of artists in Norfolk", is being hosted by the Bridewell Museum in Norwich.

The original Twenty Group were a collection of radical, forward-looking local artists who, in the last months of World War II, got together to promote better understanding of contemporary art and to counter widespread hostility and prejudice against it. My father was one of the original members. He moved, we can say, in distinguished artistic circles.

He also came to move in elevated business circles, as the manager of Jarrolds Publication department, and he mixed with all sorts of nationally known figures; but he had grown up in a working-class family and originally spoken with a real Norwich accent, as his parents did all their lives. He did not speak like that in later life, though; you could tell he came from Norwich, but he had modified his accent considerably.

That modification came at a cost. Dad knew that some people in business circles would look down on him if he spoke in the way that came most naturally to a young man from a terraced house in New Catton, and that opportunities might be denied to him. So throughout his adult life, on important and formal occasions, he suffered the anxiety that goes with having to think, not only about what you are saying, but about how you are pronouncing it.

No one should have to do that. No one should have to feel, because of the bigotry of others, that they can make progress in life only if they abandon their native dialect. We are doing our best in our society to stamp out the scourges of racism and sexism: we do not tell non-white people and women that it is their fault if they are discriminated against. Equally, if people with truly local accents are dismissed as not being worthy, we should not say it is their fault, but do our best to stamp out this scourge of linguicism – which is even now often overtly and shamelessly expressed.

People are at their most relaxed and articulate and expressive when they are speaking in their own natural accent. In creating his paintings, my father felt free to express himself as he wished, in spite of the prejudice that existed against modern art in the 1940s. It is a pity he could not do the same thing when he was speaking.

At the Bridewell exhibition, I shall have two reasons for thinking about combatting prejudice.

## BACKGROUND NOTES

*The Norwich Twenty Group celebrated its seventieth anniversary in 2014. On the Twenty Group, see http://en.wikipedia.org/wiki/Norwich_Twenty_Group.*

*On Jarrolds, see the Foreword to this book. Jarrolds was very much a local company, and the Jarrold family are very much a local family, so my father never experienced anything other than encouragement from them.*

*On New Catton, see 1.11.*

*For more on linguicism, see 9.8.*

Bridewell doorway

## 9.6 Offensive

Some while ago I wrote about how, sixty years ago, my father felt he had to modify his Norwich accent to avoid being discriminated against in his working life. He was manager of the publishing department at Jarrolds for very many years, here in the city, and he had no problems there – Jarrolds was very much a local firm. It was out in the wider world of East Anglian and British business generally that he felt there were problems.

My column was republished in the *EDP24* online edition, and a number of people posted interesting and sympathetic comments. One lady wrote that she was deeply saddened when she heard about how others are judged by their accents: "We should be applauding their rich variety, not condemning or making judgements." Of course I agree with this.

She then reported that someone she knew had said that they would remove their children from a particular local school in our area if the children started speaking with a regional accent. "As a person born and bred in Norfolk", she continued, "I find this kind of ignorance deeply offensive."

So do I. It was ignorant. And it was offensive.

It was ignorant because everybody in the world grows up with a regional accent of some kind. This is because young children quite naturally learn to speak like the people around them. It is part of our heritage as primates that we are social animals. Humans are genetically programmed to engage in "behavioural coordination" with the other human beings we associate with. We talk like the others talk. That is how we learn our language in the first place; and the particular form of the language we learn will almost always be the dialect and accent of those around us. If children speak like the rest of the pupils they go to school with, that is a good sign. It is normal. When young children do not speak like everybody else at their school, it indicates that something is wrong – that somehow they do not belong, and are not properly integrated into the community they should be part of.

And the comment was offensive because the person whose remarks were reported was objecting specifically to *our* local accent. If you live in Norfolk and are pleased about that, then you should expect your children to sound like they grew up in Norfolk, and be pleased about that too! If you want them to grow up sounding like they come from London, you should move to London. Please.

## 9.7 *R*'s where they don't belong

In February 2011, BBC Radio 4 broadcast a play in the *Afternoon Drama* slot which was called *Children's Crusade: Memoirs of a Teenage Radical*. It was widely thought to be a good play; and it was set in Norwich.

Afterwards, however, the BBC was inundated with complaints sent in by Norfolk listeners. These complaints found their way to the office of the excellent Radio 4 programme *Feedback*, and they decided to do an item on it. They contacted that well-known Norfolk spokesman, our very own Keith Skipper, who then referred them to me. They sent me a recording of the play, and I was invited to go down to the BBC studios at the Forum in Norwich and record a segment for the programme.

I was interviewed from London by the amiable presenter, Roger Bolton, who was very sympathetic to the Norfolk complainers' case. Their objections, as you will have guessed by now, were to the accents the actors had used. Roger asked me what I thought – had they got the Norfolk accent right? I said that not only did the actors not get the accents right – they didn't even seem to be trying. If they had tried and got it wrong, at least we could have given them credit for that. But anyone turning on the play half-way through would have been absolutely certain that it was set at least 200 miles away from Norwich, probably in Dorset. The actors did a good job of reproducing West Country accents.

At the end of the segment, Roger read out a statement from the BBC saying: "We are keen to vary the settings of our dramas, and some accents are more difficult to find than others. There are numerous considerations when going through the casting process, but we always start by looking for authentic accents. We know we didn't get it right this time, but hope this did not spoil listeners' enjoyment of the play." Roger concluded: "Good grief! That's a *Feedback* rarity – a BBC apology!"

But of course it did spoil Norfolk listeners' enjoyment. And we have to wonder why this sort of thing keeps happening on the BBC and ITV. Roger asked me if perhaps there was something especially difficult about the Norfolk accent. But there isn't. Trained, professional actors can master any accent they set their mind to, with the help of trained, professional dialect coaches. Just think of Meryl Streep.

The fact is that when it comes to imitating East Anglian speech, most actors – or, more likely, their producers – just don't care. They say to themselves that the accent is not Scottish or Welsh. It is not Northern. It is not Midlands. So it must be some kind of southern accent. And since it is not Cockney, then any old thing that sounds southern and "rural" will do. They think that the Norwich accent is "rural", even though there are 250,000 of us living in this urban area. The actors then try and signal "ruralness" by things like rolling their *r*'s in words like *cart* and *farm* and *yard*. If you listen to *The Archers*, you can hear actors doing the same thing and trying so hard to sound "rural" that they put in *r*'s even where they don't belong – "Erlizerrberrth", for instance.

I put this carelessness down to a lack of respect. If the BBC drama department had more respect for regional accents, then they would try harder to get things right. But I suppose we should not be surprised if they do not try, because this is part of a general pattern of lack of respect in England for local cultures and local ways of speaking. I have more than once heard people who have moved to our county from elsewhere say that they love living here, in our beautiful countryside, but if their children come home from school speaking with a Norfolk accent, they will be horrified. How are those of us who have a Norfolk accent supposed to feel about that?

---

**BACKGROUND NOTES**

---

The Archers *is a very popular 15-minute BBC radio soap opera, set in a fictional area in the west of England, which has been broadcast daily since 1951. It purports to be "an everyday story of country folk".*

---

**LINGUISTIC NOTES**

---

– The East Anglian accent is non-rhotic, i.e. non-prevocalic /r/ in words like *car* and *cart* is not pronounced. Accents from the southwest of England typically are rhotic, and it is these accents that actors often mistakenly use even when playing Norfolk and Suffolk roles. *The Archers'* setting appears to be somewhere on the borders of the southern West Midlands and the northern West Country, and many of the actors try for rhotic accents. There is, however, much hyperadaptation of the hyperdialectism type: actors attempt to achieve dialect authenticity but overdo it, in this case by inserting non-prevocalic /r/s in inappropriate places, as in *Elizabeth* /əlɪzəbərθ/.

## 9.8 Casual linguicism

Social commentators sometimes write about "everyday sexism" and "casual racism". By this they are referring to situations where people who do not want to be – and do not believe that they are – sexist or racist still behave in ways that are. The commentators are thinking about situations such as where the office manager unthinkingly always asks one of the female staff to get the coffee; or where someone naively expresses surprise that an Afro-Caribbean friend is no good at dancing.

This same sort of heedlessness can also be seen in the case of linguicism, when people are unthinkingly stereotyped or discriminated against on the grounds of their accent, dialect or language. Casual, everyday linguicism appears in many guises. For example, the casual use of the term "well-spoken" in this country to refer only to the small minority of English speakers who have public school accents implies that the rest of us, the vast majority, do not "speak well", which of course is not true.

There is also often an unthinking assumption that people with certain local accents are stupid or uncivilised, or not fit to hold positions of responsibility and authority or to make public announcements. When was the last time you heard someone with a Norfolk accent announcing departures at Thorpe railway station? Or reading the news on any of our local radio and TV stations?

The BBC TV *Breakfast* presenter Steph McGovern has recently suffered from this same kind of attitude. No matter that she is an award-winning journalist; that as a teenager she won the Young Engineer for Britain award; that she has a degree in science communication and policy; or that she has had ten years of experience in top-level financial journalism. None of this seems to be of any significance to the people who have complained about her Middlesbrough accent. One gentleman even sent her £20 to put towards what he astonishingly called "correction therapy" for her accent; he said it was a terrible affliction.

I can see only one thing which needs correction here, and that is this gentleman's attitude. And I can see only one person who is suffering from a terrible affliction: him. He is the one who is very badly afflicted – by a form of linguicism which in this case, come to think of it, is so deliberate that it is not even casual.

> **BACKGROUND NOTES**
>
> *Happily, you can actually hear people with local accents making public announcements at Carrow Road, the Norwich City football ground.*

## 9.9   The elephant in the room

When I was at the City of Norwich School in the 1950s and 1960s, 30 out of the 32 boys in my class had been born in the Norwich area. Of their 60 parents, something like 50 had grown up in the Norwich area too. Things are not like that anymore.

Nearly all of those 30 also spoke with a local accent, to a greater or lesser extent. Things are not like that anymore either.

"To a greater or lesser extent". Yes, some of us were more "Norwich" than others. The elephant in this room is social class. Discussions of local dialects often ignore the importance of social background. Unlike in more egalitarian nations, the higher up the social scale you go in this country, the fewer regional features there are in people's accents – until you get to the top, where there are no regional features at all. You can tell our Prime Minister was educated at a so-called public school, but you can't tell where he is from.

When the CNS – or as it's now called, CNS – took part in the nationwide BBC radio quiz show *Top of the Form*, we were as puzzled by the team selection as we were many decades later by some of Glenn Roeder's Norwich City elevens. Were these really the four cleverest boys in the school? And why did the headmaster select this boy to be School Captain rather than that one?

Now I am older and wiser, I realise what was going on. Speaking with a local accent disqualified you from selection. You were not even on the bench. The headmaster used to talk about his "better boys". If you came from Norwich, and sounded like it when you spoke, you were not one of those.

The good news is that people are not quite that bigoted anymore, though we still have a long way to go to get rid of prejudice against local accents altogether. But the bad news is that our headmaster would have had a bigger squad to select from these days. Many fewer people in Norwich have a local accent.

East Anglian speech is on the defensive. It is gradually receding geographically. Essex used to be East Anglian. Now most of it isn't. But our speech is receding socially too. In modern Norwich, if you want to be absolutely sure of hearing local accents, it is no good going to Waitrose. You have to go on the market and buy yourself some chips.

---

**BACKGROUND NOTES**

Top of the Form *was a very popular BBC programme on the radio, or wireless as it was called in those days, in which teams from different schools around the country competed in a general knowledge quiz. Each team had four members ranging in age from 13 to 18.*
  *Glenn Roeder was the manager of Norwich City Football Club during he period 2007–9. Football players are said to be "on the bench" if they are not in the starting line-up for a particular match but have been named as substitutes.*
  *Waitrose is a somewhat upmarket chain of British supermarkets.*

---

## 9.10 Dialects and hitch-hiking

There is a place by the side of Ipswich Road, just after the junction with Hall Road in Norwich, which has a special importance for certain local people of my age. At one time, it was our gateway to the world.

These days, it seems that jetting off with your children to foreign holidays in the sun is a basic human right that no one should be denied, least of all by petty annoyances like the kids having to go to school.

In the 1960s, things were very different. Our only way to go on foreign trips, as teenagers, was to pack a rucksack and stand by the side of the road with our thumbs out. And that is what we did; hitch-hiking was a brilliant and exciting way to travel and explore the European continent. From that Ipswich Road starting point, we found our way to Paris, Berlin, Vienna, Venice, Rome – even Athens and Belgrade. Our route lay through Ipswich, Colchester, Brentwood, the Tilbury ferry across the Thames east of London, along the A2 trunk road to Dover, and then by cross-channel ferry to Boulogne or Calais or Dunkirk in France or Ostend in Belgium.

It was a fascinating and educational series of experiences we had, and as Norfolk youngsters encountering the world on the other side of the North Sea, we were on a series of steep learning curves. Not the least of these curves was linguistic. We would make terrible gaffes, like getting off the ferry in Ostend and speaking French to everyone, and then wondering why they did not reply. It is embarrassing to think of how little we knew about the language situation on the European continent. Shouldn't it have been obvious that a place with a name like Oostende was Dutch speaking?

It was fascinating to observe the changes in the language situation as we travelled. As hitch-hikers, it was important in Belgium to know that Liege was called Luik in Dutch and Lüttich in German; and that Mons and Bergen were the same place.

Stopping at the passport control between Holland and Germany, in those pre-Schengen days, we watched the German and Dutch border officials talking. How did they understand one another? Which language were they speaking? We gradually realised that they were speaking their local dialects, and that the dialects on either side of the border were so similar that communication was no problem at all.

If they had been speaking Standard German and Standard Dutch, communication would have been much more problematical.

Often, speaking your local dialect is the best thing to do.

> **BACKGROUND NOTES**
>
> *Many European countries today have signed the Schengen Agreement, which enables their citizens to pass from one country to another without any passport control.*

**LINGUISTIC NOTES**

- The Dutch–German border dialects are part of the large West Germanic dialect continuum which stretches from Ostend on the North Sea coast in the west to Vienna in the east, and from the Danish–German border in the north to the north of Italy in the south. The dialects on the continuum are linked to each other by a chain of mutual intelligibility, with geographically neighbouring dialects always being mutually comprehensible, but with the dialects at one end of the continuum not being intelligible to speakers of dialects at the other. For more on dialect continua, see J. K. Chambers & Peter Trudgill (1998) *Dialectology*, Cambridge University Press.

## 9.11 Like what I done here

Until a couple of hundred years ago, no one in Norfolk would have thought about writing in their local dialect. What I mean is: they wouldn't have thought about it because they would have just gone ahead and done it. That wasn't so very long ago that Lord Nelson was writing in his log that "Captain Lambert have been very fortunate". That was what everybody done in them days.

Speech come before writing. All the languages in the world was spoken long before they was written; and most on 'em still in't written down. Children learn to speak before they learn to write. And many people in the world never learn to read and write at all. For nearly all of human history, there weren't no such thing as writing. Human language developed about 200,000 year ago, and writing weren't invented until 195,000 year later.

When writing did first develop, what people naturally done was to write like what they spoke. What else was they a-going to do? Writing is just the representation of speech in a more permanent medium, and so they writ down what they would've said if they had-a been a-talking.

But now a different practice have evolved: people are encouraged *not* to write like what they speak – unless they come from the upper social classes. The upper classes speak Standard English as their native dialect; and the rest on us are encouraged to write in *their* dialect, not in our own. The idea seem to be that uniformity is a good thing. But this is a very new idea, and that in't totally obvious that that's a good one. That make for problems for children who have to learn to read and write in a kind of language that in't their own.

Of course, there are still writers what use their native dialect. But we have a long way to go before we get to the level of dialect use reached in Norway, where that's not unusual for serious novels and poetry to be in dialect. The problem is that local dialects are often looked down on as inferior – even though from a linguistic point of view they definitely in't. And writing in a local dialect is often considered to be eccentric – even though from a historical point of view that most certainly in't.

Whatever can be written in Standard English can be written in dialect too, like what I done here.

## BACKGROUND NOTES

*This piece is written in the Norfolk dialect: I have used Norfolk grammatical forms throughout. This is how English would have been written if, some centuries ago, the Norfolk dialect, rather than the dialect of the metropolitan ruling classes, had formed the basis of modern Standard English. There are no specifically Norfolk dialect words in the piece because the topic is a rather technical one whose vocabulary is shared by all English dialects. And I have not changed any spellings in an attempt to represent the Norfolk accent. That would have been pointless because it would have made the piece difficult to read for many readers, and our usual English spelling is in any case accent neutral. A Times editorial can just as well be read aloud in a Cockney accent or a Glaswegian accent or a Norfolk accent as any other. An American will see a word like* path *written down and read it out aloud in one way, someone from the North of England in another way, a speaker from the South of England in another, and so on.*

*The point of writing an article in the Norfolk dialect is simply to show that anything which can be written in one dialect of English, including Standard English, can be written, if writers want to do this, in any other.*

## 9.12  So you can tell 'em apart

The sense of humour that goes along with the Norfolk dialect is not a bit like the Cockney humour of London, or the Scouse of Liverpool. Norfolk humour is dry, slow, deadpan, sardonic, understated, ironic. The fact is that outsiders don't always get it – which is part of the point. In October 2014, the London *Times* ran a leader called "Land of laughter" in which they used the phrase "even in Norfolk", implying that our county is a humourless place. They *clearly* don't get it!

In his book *In Search of England*, H. V. Morton wrote about the car trip he took around the country in the 1920s. After he had travelled from Lincolnshire into Norfolk, he wrote: "I was lost in a Norfolk lane, so I stopped a man and said to him: Good morning! Can you tell me if I am right for Norwich? The Norfolkman replied: 'What d' ye want to know for?'"

You and I can see that was a joke. The old Norfolk boy was having him on. But Morton didn't get it. He continued: "I might have been annoyed, but putting on an affable expression, I said: My dear old bor, I want to know because I want to get to Norwich." Then, patronisingly: "The ghost of a smile flitted over the man's rustic face, and he replied after some deep thought, rather reluctantly, and looking away from me: Well, you're right!"

Morton thought this was because of a distrust of outsiders: the Norfolkman behaved "in an uneasy, suspicious way". But of course Morton was quite wrong. Here was a posh, supercilious outsider – driving a car in the 1920s no less! – being the victim of Norfolk humour and not realising it.

Norfolk humour, of course, is not just country people poking fun at sophisticates from the Sheres. The Boy John's Aunt Agatha came up with many an amusing, laconic and wise Norfolk aphorism: "All husbands are alike, only they have different faces so you can tell 'em apart" is a good one.

And city people are pretty sharp too. I was once walking out of the doorway of a shop in Norwich as another man was coming in. When I stepped to my left to let him pass, he simultaneously moved to his right to let me out, and blocked my exit. So I moved quickly back to my right – but at the same time he stepped in the same direction. And then the same thing happened again. And again – and again. The frustrating dance ended when we both stopped, with me still inside and him outside, looking at each other. Then he said, without cracking his face: "Jus' one more time, then I gotta go hoom."

## BACKGROUND NOTES

*H. V. Morton (1892–1979) was a very successful English journalist and travel writer. His best-selling book* In Search of England *was first published in 1927. A 2004 biography of Morton by Michael Bartholomew suggests that he was vain, cynical and misanthropic.*
  *On "the Sheres" = Shires, see 1.5.*
  *On the Boy John and his Aunt Agatha, see* Themes *and 2.8.*
  *On the term of address* bor, *see 7.9 and 11.2.*

## LINGUISTIC NOTES

– The usual Norfolk pronunciation of *home* is /hʊm/ or, in more formal speech, /huːm/. The vernacular Norwich pronunciation is /ʊm/.

# 10 Grammar: the wonder of it all

This section continues the discussion of grammar, but concentrates more on grammatical processes and categories, and how they differ between different language varieties.

## 10.1 What is your evidence?

What a pity that some people in this country think that grammar is something to get worried or indignant about. Grammar is a magnificent and exciting and wonderful thing. To see it reduced to the mundane level of letters to the press complaining that people say *sat* rather than *sitting* is depressing, as is Mr Gove testing our children by instructing them to "Complete the sentence below using either I or me: My team and ____ are playing next week." Obviously he thinks the "correct" answer is *I*, which I agree is not wrong; but it is certainly not so common in that context as the equally correct *me*.

All languages and dialects have their own special grammars. Over the millennia, human minds and societies have produced a range of amazing grammatical phenomena. I wonder if Mr Gove knows that many languages have two different pronouns corresponding to English *we*? This is very sensible, because *we* is ambiguous. If I tell you that "We've got great tickets for Carrow Road for Saturday", you might get excited until it turns out that the "we" is me and my wife, and not me and you. (Mr Gove would mark me wrong for that last sentence.)

And what about verbs? English verbs are not particularly interesting. If you start from the basic form *move*, you can use the grammatical endings we call morphemes to produce the forms *moving*, *moved* and *moves* (except in Norfolk, where we don't even trouble ourselves about the latter). And that's it.

But in other languages there are verb morphemes which do all sorts of fascinating things. In the Californian language Pomo, there is a grammatical prefix *f-* which means 'with the side of a long object'. It would be rather fun, I think, to be able to say "I fmoved it" in English.

And many languages have morphemes we call *evidentials*. These are compulsorily attached to verbs to show what your evidence is for saying something.

They mean things like 'I know because someone told me' or 'I saw it' or 'I assume'. In the Amazonian language Tariana, *Wes irida di-manika-mahka* means 'Wes played football (we heard him)' whereas *Wes irida di-manika-nihka* means 'Wes played football (we infer that from visual evidence, e.g. his boots are dirty)'.

If Mr Gove was speaking Tariana, he would never be able to just say *"My team and me are playing" is wrong*. People would accuse him of using bad grammar and would want to know what his evidence was.

> **BACKGROUND NOTES**
>
> *For Mr Gove, the Minister of Education, see 2.4.*
> *"Wes" is a reference to the very popular Irish-international professional football player Wes Hoolahan (b. 1982), who joined Norwich City in 2008; see also 6.7.*

**LINGUISTIC NOTES**

- Many varieties of English English have *he was sat at the table* rather than *he was sitting at the table*, and the former has been spreading at the expense of the latter over the last forty years. Some people do not like this.
- The distinction between inclusive and exclusive first-person plural pronouns is discussed in Anna Siewierska (2004) *Person*, Cambridge University Press.
- The Pomo example is taken from Julius Moshinsky (1974) *A Grammar of Southeastern Pomo*, Berkeley: University of California Press. Moshinsky's grammar lists a large number of instrumentals consisting of bound morphemes such as /q-/ 'with biting or scratching', /ʔ-/ 'with the hand', /ʃ-/ 'with a long, flexible object' and /f-/ 'with the side of a long object'. Two of the original seven Pomoan languages of Northern California are extinct, and the others are all highly endangered.
- The Tariana example is based on Alexandra Aikhenvald (2003) *A Grammar of Tariana from Northwest Amazonia*, Cambridge University Press. The best book-length treatment of evidentials is Alexandra Aikhenvald (2004) *Evidentiality*, Oxford University Press.

## 10.2 *He* and *she*

I was recently reading Donna Tartt's novel *The Goldfinch*. I can't have been reading it very carefully, because it took me a couple of chapters before I realised that the narrator – the *I* – was a man and not a woman.

If the book had been written in Polish – not that I can actually read Polish – I would have twigged much sooner. The first phrase in the whole book is "While

I was . . . ". In Polish, a female narrator would have written 'I was' as *byłam*, while a man would have written *byłem*. In Polish, past-tense verbs, even for first-person *I* forms, differ according to whether they refer to males or females.

In English we mark this kind of gender difference only for third-person pronouns: *he* is for males and *she* for females. How else, you might ask, could it possibly be? But it does not have to be like that. In Finnish, there is no distinction at all between 'he' and 'she' – *hän* means both. The same is true of Turkish, where the word for s/he is *o*, and in Hungarian, where it is *ő*.

How do they manage? How do people understand what a Finnish speaker means? Well, maybe French-speaking people would like to know how we manage without their two different words for 'they': *ils* for males, and *elles* for females. And Spanish speakers might like to know how English speakers manage without two different words for 'plural you': they have *vosotros* (male) and *vosotras* (female). They even have different words for 'we' – *nosotros* and *nosotras* – and they probably find it rather odd that we don't. And Polish speakers would certainly want to know how we can tell what sex a fictional first-person narrator is supposed to be (clearly, some of us can't!).

But to go back to the question: if a Finnish speaker says *hän*, how do listeners know if they're talking about a man or a woman? Well, sometimes they don't. But usually it is rather obvious, because pronouns like *he*, *she* and *they* refer to people who have already been mentioned, or whose identity is clear.

When my Norwich schoolmates and I had summer jobs fruit-picking out in the country, we sometimes noticed how local women, arriving first thing in the morning, might address their fellow villagers by saying things like: "Know what he say to me last night?" They didn't have to specify who *he* was. Even we could work that out.

## LINGUISTIC NOTES

- The usage of gender-marking on personal pronouns in the languages of the world does not appear to be random. Some languages, as we have seen, do not have it at all, like Finnish. But if a language does have it, then this is most likely to be in the third-person singular, as in English. The next most likely location is in the third-person plural; and the next most likely after that is the second person, followed by the first person. The least likely of all is the first-person singular. There is also an implicational hierarchy here: if a language has gender-marking in the third-person plural, one can predict with more or less total certainty that it will also have it in the third-person singular, and so on.
- A very good source for more information on the manifestation of gender in the world's languages in general is Greville Corbett (1991) *Gender,* Cambridge University Press.

## 10.3  I'm going (to see them win)

When I was about 5 years old, my mother told me that we were going to go out, it was raining, and I should go and get my mackintosh. I returned, saying that I had found my mack but I could not find my tosh.

I can still remember her laughing.

But what had happened there was actually very revealing linguistically. The original full version of *mackintosh* was often used in those days, as well as the abbreviation *mack*, and so I was familiar with both words. I had made the mistake, on the basis of my knowledge of *mack*, of interpreting what my mother said as "mack and tosh". I owned a matching sou'wester, and I had assumed that was my "tosh".

The way we say *mackintosh* in Norfolk is identical with how we would say *mack and tosh*, if there was such a thing: "mack'n'tosh". (This would not have happened in London, where people say "mack-in-tosh".) My interpretation of what my mother had said made good sense, and was actually very clever, if I may say so myself. It just happened to be completely wrong.

This is an example of what linguists call *reanalysis*. Children hear and learn what older people say, but they may analyse it in their heads in a different way. The new analysis will be perfectly consistent with the sounds that have been uttered, but the exact interpretation will be different.

This tendency to reanalyse what we hear, if there is more than one possible interpretation, can have permanent consequences for languages. *An apron* was *a napron* in older forms of English; and *an adder* was originally *a nadder*, while *a nickname* was originally *an eke-name* (where *eke*, a word that has now been lost from the language, meant 'also').

Reanalysis can be responsible, too, for more far-reaching changes, such as the modern English use of *going to* to indicate the future. If I'm going [somewhere in order] to see John, then seeing John will happen at some later time, and so *I'm going to see John* can be reanalysed as expressing a future event. *Going to* can now therefore be ambiguous. If you say you are *going to win*, does that mean that you are travelling somewhere in order to try your best to be victorious, or that you are unreasonably confident about your abilities?

You can see both of these different meanings of *going to* in the totally reasonable and frequently used sentence *I'm going to Carrow Road where Norwich City are going to win.*

### BACKGROUND NOTES

*A mackintosh is a raincoat. The word is not now widely used in American English, although it was in the past.*

## LINGUISTIC NOTES

- The word *mackintosh*, originally *Mackintosh*, first started being used in English in the 1830s, following on from the invention by Charles Mackintosh of the waterproof material from which these coats were first made in the 1820s. The first records cited by the *OED* of everyday usage of the abbreviated forms *mack/mac* date from the 1920s, which certainly tallies with my recollections of both *mack* and *mackintosh* still being common in England c. 1949.
- On "mack'n'tosh" /mækəntɒʃ/ versus "mack-in-tosh" /mækɪntɒʃ/: the Norfolk accent is one of many English accents around the world which have the "weak vowel merger" (J. C. Wells, 1982, *Accents of English*, vol. I, Cambridge University Press) in which *Lenin* and *Lennon*, *roses* and *Rosa's* are pronounced identically. Others include Irish English and Australian English.
- The word *eke* seems not to have been very current in English much after 1600. It is related to modern Dutch *ook* and German *auch* 'also'; and to Danish and Norwegian *og*, Swedish *och* 'and'.
- The *going to* future is not unique to English: precisely the same development has happened in French, where *ils vont gagner* = 'they are going to win'.
- The two senses of *going to* in English can be phonologically different, with the more grammaticalised future variant being reduced in a way that is not so readily possible with *going to* as the original verb of motion: *I'm going to Carrow Road where Norwich are gonna win.*

## 10.4  Eat shoot and leave

Lynne Truss is a well-known English author and journalist. She has been described as a "professional pedant". And she has made a lot of money out of writing a book which is based on the observation that the phrase "it eats shoots and leaves" is ambiguous. She says, quite rightly, that the phrase represents a very good example of how important punctuation can be for making meaning clear in the written language. *A panda eats shoots and leaves* means something very different from *A panda eats, shoots, and leaves.*

This is a joke, of course. It is quite a good joke, I suppose. But there is no way this phrase would actually have led to any ambiguity or misunderstanding in real life, even without any punctuation. The particular scenario conjured up by Truss as the background for her sentence involves a café, and a talking panda in possession of a firearm – not something one would expect to encounter in real life, even in the United States.

As readers of this column will know, I agree very much with Lynne Truss that punctuation is vitally important in writing. But notice that there is something very interesting for Norfolk and Suffolk people about the ambiguity of her sentence.

It is the grammar. We are often told that grammar is very important for making meaning clear. It is. But it does not have to be the grammar of Standard English, as some pedants would have us believe. All dialects have their own grammatical structures and rules, and it is precisely the grammar of Standard English which makes Lynne's sentence ambiguous. Her illustrative phrase represents a case where the grammar of the Standard English dialect is not as clear as the grammar of the Norfolk dialect.

In Norfolk, even without punctuation, there would be absolutely no ambiguity. This is because we would have different sentences for each of the meanings. In fact, we can translate Lynne's sentence in as many as three different ways.

Of any normal real-life, unarmed panda in the wild, we would say *That eat shoots and leaves*. If a particular one of these wild animals was known for its frequent departures, we could say *That eat shoots and leave*. But of the rather scary, even if imaginary, armed panda in the café, we would have to say *That eat shoot and leave*.

Three chairs for our Norfolk dialect!

---

### BACKGROUND NOTES

The book referred to is: Lynne Truss (2003) *Eats, Shoots and Leaves: The Zero Tolerance Approach to Punctuation, London: Profile Books.*

For more on punctuation, see 2.8.

---

### LINGUISTIC NOTES

– In Standard English, *s* is both the third-person singular present-tense verbal suffix and the plural noun suffix. This is what makes for the ambiguity in Lynne Truss's example. There is no ambiguity in the Norfolk dialect because it lacks third-person *s*.

– The spelling <chairs> refers to the merger in the Norfolk dialect of the lexical sets of NEAR and SQUARE, such that *cheers* is pronounced identically with *chairs* /tʃɛːz/ (see 13.4).

## 10.5 *Known* and *thrown*

All languages work by analogy. If they didn't, we would not be able to learn them. Once small children have learnt that the plural of *boot* is *boots* and the plural of *shoot* is *shoots*, then by analogy they can work out that the plural of *root* is *roots*, and so on. Occasionally this gives them the wrong result, since the plural of *foot* is not *foots*; but languages can only tolerate a certain amount of that kind of irregularity or they would be unlearnable.

Sometimes when languages change, they change as a result of analogy. The past tense of the verb *to snow* in the Norfolk dialect is not *snowed*, as it used to be, but *snew*. This is an innovation we developed through analogy with *blow–blew* and *know–knew*.

This is probably the same kind of thing that has happened with Professor Robert Bartlett's pronunciation of words like *thrown, mown* and *known*. Correspondents to the *EDP* who have watched his BBC TV programme *The Plantagenets* have wondered why he says "throwen", "mowen" and "knowen".

One correspondent's suggestion was that Robert was speaking Middle English. Middle English was the form of our language as it was spoken from about 1150 to 1500; and if Robert had been clever enough to speak fluent Middle English, we would have had a very hard job understanding him. If you have ever heard somebody read Chaucer in the original fourteenth-century pronunciation, you will know what I mean. (If you haven't, there are plenty of linguistic scientists about who would be glad to demonstrate. And there are recordings on the internet, though unfortunately they were not actually made by Chaucer himself.)

So, no, Robert Bartlett was not speaking Middle English, though it is true that the past participle of *know* in Middle English could be "knowen". Some dialects of English which have this pronunciation may therefore, possibly, have preserved it from earlier stages of the language – some Norfolk speakers say "knowen". But the "knowen, throwen" pronunciation is particularly common in modern Australia and New Zealand English; and I think the most likely reason is that this is, once again, an innovation that is due to analogy. If people have started saying "knowen" and "throwen", this is as a result of them drawing an analogy with words like *given, chosen,* and *ridden*.

If the past participle of *fall* is *fallen*, and the past participle of *rise* is *risen*, why shouldn't the past participle of *mow* be "mowen"?

## BACKGROUND NOTES

*Professor Robert Bartlett is an English academic historian who is currently Professor of Mediaeval History at the University of St Andrews in Scotland. His 2014 TV documentary series for the BBC about the English Plantagenet royal dynasty aroused much favourable comment from viewers, but also queries about the pronunciation of his past participles.*

## 10.6 On *on*

A letter-writer to the *EDP* tells us that she overheard someone on a bus saying "I was only told on it yesterday – I suppose you heard on it ages ago." She asked why *on* was used here instead of *about*.

One answer to this question is: why not? It is what people say in these parts. You might as well ask: why do Americans say *elevator* instead of *lift*? Well, they just do. That's what Americans say.

I also think we should be careful with the phrase "instead of", which makes it seem like there is something strange or wrong about using *on* in these contexts. There isn't. It is entirely normal in Norfolk and Suffolk to say "What do you think on it?", or "There were two on 'em", or "What are you a-doin' on?"

These examples make it clear that the word *on* was not being used on that bus as the equivalent of *about*. Our local usage of *on* corresponds to the usage elsewhere of *of*. Older people may remember hearing the request, when someone wanted a cigarette: "Any on yuh any on yuh?" = "[Have] any of you any on you?"

But the question this correspondent asked really is a very interesting one: how did it come about that in our part of the world we use *on* in this way?

The answer lies in the common linguistic process of reinterpretation or reanalysis. There is a clue to this in another question the correspondent also posed in the same letter: why did someone else she overheard say "He reckoned he could get a-top of that there hill"? Well, here, *a-top* is being used rather than *on top*; and in fact *atop* is a perfectly good English word, where the *a* is historically derived from *on*, as in many other words like *alive, asleep, abroad, afoot*. The full form *on* has been reduced to the weakened, unstressed form *a*.

Now, it so happens that the same reduction to *a* occurs with *of*. We do not normally say "a cup ovv tea" but "a cupp a-tea". So *a* can be a weak form corresponding both to *of* and to *on*. Because of that, the *a* in "what do you think a-that?" became reinterpreted as the weak form of *on* rather than the weak form of *of*.

At some stage in our language history, when a full form was called for, *on* started being used where *of* had been used before.

And that's what I think a-that.

**LINGUISTIC NOTES**

– I am using <*a*-> here as a way of representing the unstressed vowel shwa /ə/. (For more on shwa, see 13.2.) *Any on yuh any on yuh* = /ɛnɪɒnjərɛnɪɒnjə/.

*cont.*

– The same process of reanalysis can be seen at work in the way some people write, and many people are increasingly saying, "I could of done it" rather than "I could have done it." The weak form of *have* is also shwa, as in *I could a-done it*, and so /ə/ has been reinterpreted as being *of* rather than *have*. On reanalysis as a factor in linguistic change, see Lyle Campbell (2013) *Historical Linguistics*, 3rd edn, Edinburgh University Press.

## 10.7 Dual

The idea behind the grammatical distinction between singular and plural number seems straightforward enough: singular refers to one entity, and plural to more than one. With English nouns, we generally indicate this through the absence versus the presence of the plural suffix *s*: one book, ten books. And with pronouns we have singular forms like *me* versus plural forms like *us*.

Things are a bit more complicated than that, though. Think about the word *both*. This does refer to 'more than one' – but it is not just any old more-than-one: it refers specifically to two, and only two. You cannot say "How are you both?" if you're enquiring about a family of five people. And you cannot ask a couple "How are you all?"

At this point in English grammar, there is a three-way distinction: one–both–all. *All* is plural, of course, but in this case plural does not mean 'more than one': it means 'more than two'.

The word *both* is an example of the grammatical category which linguistic scientists refer to as *dual*. English has several other words which express dual rather than plural number. Just as dual *both* corresponds to plural *all*, so *either* is the dual equivalent of plural *any*, and *neither* is the dual form corresponding to plural *none*. If you were asked which one of two books you wanted, you could not reply "I don't want any of them"; you would have to say "I don't want either of them." And you could not answer "None of them"; you would need to say "Neither of them." (Note that in spite of what pedants want us to believe, the word *none* really can be plural: it is perfectly grammatical to say "None of them are very interesting".)

Many other languages in the world have a much more fully developed dual number system than we have. It is true that Old English used to have special dual pronouns – *wit* meant 'we two' while *we* meant 'we three or more' – but we have lost that in the modern language.

In Slovenian, *si* means 'you (singular) are', *ste* is 'you (two) are' and *sta* means 'you (plural, i.e. three or more) are'. Some languages even have a category of trial number, which relates specifically to three items. In Fijian, *taru* means 'we two' and *tou* means 'we three', so the plural pronoun *eta* can only mean 'we four (or more)'.

Amazing things, languages.

---

**LINGUISTIC NOTES**

– Sursurunga, an Austronesian language spoken in Papua New Guinea, has been reported to have five number categories: singular, dual, trial, quadral and plural, where plural therefore means 'five or more' (Don Hutchisson, 1986, "Sursurunga pronouns and the special uses of quadral number", in U. Wiesemann (ed.), *Pronominal Systems*, Tübingen: Narr). Corbett, however, suggests that quadral number is not truly quadral, referring to four entities, but is actually paucal, referring to 'a few' (Greville Corbett, 2000, *Number*, Cambridge University Press).

---

## 10.8 *Went, goed, went*

I have written before about grammatical rules, and how we all speak according to a set of rules of grammar which we learnt, without being taught them, as small children. We were clever enough, as all human beings are, to analyse the language we heard spoken around us, work out what its rules are and start using them ourselves – without any conscious awareness of what we were doing.

As far as English is concerned, these rules are nothing to do with the so-called rules that certain English language "experts" want to foist on us, such as: "You shouldn't end a sentence with a preposition", and "The word *between* can only be used of two entities, otherwise it should be *among*."

The existence of the real rules I am talking about can very clearly be seen by observing the way in which small children acquire them as they are learning their language or languages. Linguistic scientists who are experts on child language acquisition point out that when small children are first learning to speak English, they employ irregular past-tense forms correctly: they say *Mummy went* and *Daddy fell down*.

Later on, they start getting things wrong. They begin to say things like *Mummy goed* and *Daddy falled down*. These are fascinating mistakes because they show that children have now worked out what the rule is for the formation of past-tense verbs. The rule is not totally straightforward: you take the basic form of the verb and add to it one of three suffixes: *ed* as in *wanted; t* as in *walked* (pronounced "walkt"); and *d* as in *filled* (pronounced "filld") – with the suffix being determined by the final consonant of the basic word form.

But, having learnt this rule, children then very reasonably start applying it to all verbs: if the present tense is *hit*, then the past tense must be *hitted*. This is wrong, but it shows that they have learnt the rule entirely correctly.

It is only later that children then reach a third stage, where they realise that though the rule for past-tense formation is as they have correctly analysed it, there are also exceptions: there are irregular verbs which you can only use correctly by learning and remembering them individually.

Chronological sequences in children's language development such as *went* > *goed* > *went* tell us a lot about how human infants acquire their mother tongue.

## LINGUISTIC NOTES

- Child language acquisition is a fascinating and important subject. For readers wanting to learn more, see Paul Fletcher (2005) *Child Language Acquisition*, London: Hodder.

## 10.9 Why not *goodest*?

Have you ever wondered why the past tense of *I go* is *I went*? OK, so you haven't – but I bet plenty of people studying English as a foreign language have, because it causes them problems. The normal way to make past-tense verb forms in English is to add *ed* to the basic form of the verb: *want, wanted. Went* is not even remotely normal. Even with irregular verbs like *ring*, you can see a connection between *ring, rang, rung*. But there is nothing obvious about *go* and *went* – a nice illustration of how languages are not necessarily particularly logical systems. They have to have regularity, or infants would not be able to learn them, but they can tolerate a certain amount of irregularity of this kind.

The illogical *go–went* situation came about because the modern verb was originally two separate words. *Went* used to be the past tense of *wend*, and only came to function as the past tense of *go* in about 1500. *Wend* then had to acquire a new past-tense form *wended*, as in "he wended his way".

We can see the same pattern with the adjective *good*. If we say *nice, nicer, nicest* and *warm, warmer, warmest*, why on earth don't we say *good, gooder, goodest*? We can ask the same question for all the Germanic languages: Dutch has *goed, beter, best*, Norwegian *god, bedre, best*, German *gut, besser, best* – the pattern must have been present millennia ago in our parent Proto-Germanic language. So although it is obvious that we are again dealing with two originally different words here, the peculiarity in this case is so ancient that we do not know what the words were.

When it comes to the adjective *bad*, we know a little bit more, though we do not actually know where *bad* came from – it appears to be a word peculiar to English. Mediaeval English speakers said *bad, badder, baddest*; but gradually speakers started instead to use *worse, worst* – and this is actually an old Germanic word: in Danish *worst* is *værst*.

When unrelated forms are used as different versions of a single word like this, linguistic scientists call it "suppletion". You can see the same thing happening with the noun *person*. We say *one person* and, while it is possible to say *two persons*, the normal plural is *people*, so we usually say *two people*.

A good question at this point would be: why? Why do languages have suppletion?

As I say, that's good question.

## LINGUISTIC NOTES

– For more on *wend*, see 12.3.

# 11 More about words

In this section, I look at various Norfolk-area dialect words and their histories, and consider the implications that these words can have for the study of our language way beyond our region.

## 11.1 Yes

It may surprise some people to learn that quite a lot of languages do not have words for 'yes' and 'no'. How could they possibly manage without them? But they do. Latin managed it; Gaelic manages it. It's easy: "Are you ready? – I am." "Did they see it? – They did." "Has he arrived? – He has not."

Some languages, though, go the other way and have not one but two words for 'yes'. In German, *ja* means 'yes' – but not if you are disagreeing with something. If someone says the German equivalent of "It isn't raining, is it?", and you think it is, you will reply *Doch!*, meaning 'Yes [it is raining, you're wrong]'.

This was also true of earlier forms of English, from Anglo-Saxon up to Elizabethan times. *Yea* corresponded to German *ja*, and *yes* to *doch*. But we went even further than this in English and had two words for 'no' as well: "You're ready? – Nay [I'm not]"; "You're not ready? – No [you're right, I'm not]."

There are also a number of different words for 'yes' and 'no' in various English local dialects. In the north of Britain, 'yes' is *aye* – you hear it all the time in Scotland. In the traditional dialects of the West Country they said "iss". And of course in this part of the world, too, we naturally have our own word for 'yes'.

I remember extremely vividly one occasion when I heard it used. One summer Sunday in the early 1950s, when I was about 10, my grandfather took my cousin and me for a walk in the country, as he sometimes did. Around midday we found ourselves in Swardeston, and ready for a rest. Grandad got talking to an old boy who was sitting on a bench on the village green, leaning on his stick.

After a while, Grandad asked him a question which absolutely astonished me: had the old gentleman, Grandad asked, known Edith Cavell? What a question, I thought! Of course he couldn't have! Edith Cavell was a heroine from history; she was a revered and legendary and almost mythical figure from long, long ago. I knew she came from Swardeston, of course, but she was someone from our history lessons: how could we possibly be talking about her, as a real person, on the village green now?

But then the old fella's reply astonished me even more. He sighed and nodded. "Ah," he said in very matter of fact way. "Ah. I remember the gal Edie."

---

**BACKGROUND NOTES**

*Swardeston is a village 4 miles / 6 kms southwest of Norwich. The name of the village is pronounced with two syllables, and the "d" is optional.*

*Edith Cavell – her surname is pronounced with the stress on the first syllable – was a nurse who was executed by the Germans in Belgium during World War I for helping British soldiers to escape; see* http://en.wikipedia.org/wiki/Edith_Cavell.

---

**LINGUISTIC NOTES**

- Other languages have forms corresponding to German *doch*: for example, French has *si*; Norwegian and Swedish have *jo*; and Arabic has *mbala*.
- It is possible that Norfolk *ah* is related to the much more widespread northern *aye* 'yes'. Interestingly, the etymology of *aye* is not known. The *OED* tells us that it "appeared suddenly in 1575" and suggests that it might perhaps be related to *ay*, an archaic word meaning 'ever, always'. This is an old Germanic word – the English form comes from Old Norse – but the connection is difficult because the pronunciations are different: *aye* is /aɪ/ and *ay* is /eɪ/.

## 11.2 Donkeys

There is a phrase, well known to older Norfolk people, which is supposed to be exchanged, when in foreign parts, with any new acquaintance you suspect of also being from our area. You have to say: "Ha' your far gotta a dicka, bor?" The other person then establishes their East Anglian credentials by giving the correct reply to this question. Do you know what it is?

The question translates into Standard English as: "Has your father got a donkey, mate?" *Dicky* is simply our local dialect word for a donkey, and the *English Dialect Dictionary* shows this word as occurring only in Norfolk, Suffolk, Essex and Cambridgeshire.

But where did *dicky* come from? We all know that men and boys who are called *Dicky* are officially named Richard. But why would donkeys be referred to by the familiar form of a male first name? Well, there is another similar example: a widely used children's word for a donkey is "neddy" – children read books with names like *Neddy the Donkey*. That too is a familiar form of a man's name – Edward.

In Scotland, Northumberland and Cumberland, there is yet another local word for a donkey derived from a male name: *cuddy*, from Cuthbert. And, according to the *English Dialect Dictionary*, eastern Suffolk also had the word *jeremiah* for a donkey, though I have never heard that.

This is all a bit puzzling, until we start to examine the origin of the word *donkey* itself. Where did that come from? We are not entirely sure. But the *Oxford English Dictionary* has a suggestion which I like because it fits in very nicely with Richard, Edward, Cuthbert and Jeremiah. This is that *donkey* derives from the man's name *Duncan*. This supposition is strengthened by the fact that we know that *donkey* used to be pronounced "dunky", to rhyme with *monkey*.

So what is going on here exactly? Why have all these familiar forms of men's names been used to refer to a donkey? The answer is that they are all jocular nicknames which were used to avoid saying something else. I am not going to spell it out: this is a family newspaper, and some readers might be having their breakfast. But *donkey* is first recorded as having been used in the late 1700s; before that the usual word was *ass*.

And, by the way, the correct response to the Norfolk question is: "Yes, and he want a fool to ride 'im – will you come?"

---

**BACKGROUND NOTES**

*The word* bor *in the first paragraph is an East Anglian term of address, now obsolescent, used most often but not exclusively to males. It is not, as is sometimes thought, a form of the word* boy.

---

**LINGUISTIC NOTES**

– "Ha' your far gotta a dicka, bor?" is [hæ jɔ: fa: gɑʔə dɪkʔə bɔ:]. In the traditional dialect of Norfolk, the vowel of LOT is unrounded, as also in North America.
– A possible etymology for *bor* is as in the second element of *neighbour*: Old English (Anglian) *nehebur* from *neah* 'near' and *(ge)bur* 'dweller' (see also 7.9).

---

## 11.3 Truce words

English dialects in this country are holding up pretty well, but we are sadly seeing quite a lot of what dialectologists call "lexical attrition". This simply means that there is a tendency for local dialect words to disappear in favour of more wide-spread, nationally recognised vocabulary. Local words, though, are still surviving, and they tend to endure most strongly when they apply to informal and domestic areas of life which are less subject to influence from the written language, the education system and the media.

Nobody much, I think, actually uses the Norfolk word *mawther* ('girl') very often anymore. But when it comes to humble, everyday objects and activities, we do tend to still stick to the local words we learnt here in our own part of the world when we were children. Norfolk people may still have their *troughings* repaired, rather than the *guttering* around their house. And many of us still talk about the *linen* – and linen lines, linen cupboards, linen pegs – rather than the *washing* or the *laundry*.

But perhaps the area of life where local words survive most strongly, because they do so in a subterranean kind of way, is in children's games and activities. One well-known example has to do with truce words: terms children use when they are playing so they can be deemed to be out of a game for a short time in order, for example, to do their shoes up. In 1959, a fascinating book came out which was called *The Lore and Language of Schoolchildren*, by Iona and Peter Opie; it was republished in 2000. One of the children's oral subculture topics which Peter and Iona researched was truce words, and their book contains a map showing which terms were used by children in different parts of the country.

Do you remember what you used to say when you were playing games when you were a kid? In London children say – or said – *fainites*. In the northwest of England, the word was *barley*, probably from *parlay*. Other terms in different parts of the country included *kings*, *keys*, *skinch*, *cree*, *scribs* and *crosses*. The Opies reported that in the Ipswich and Norwich areas, the term used was one which seemed to be connected to the form *crosses*, namely *exes*; and that is more or less what I remember. If you had a stitch in your side and needed to stop playing for a moment, you crossed your fingers and shouted "Exies!"

### LINGUISTIC NOTES

– Lexical attrition in England is discussed as "vocabulary loss" in Peter Trudgill (1999) *The Dialects of England*, Oxford: Blackwell, chapter 5: "Dialect words".

## 11.4 Samphire and swad

My maternal grandparents came from north Norfolk, so our family knew all about coastal foods like *samphire*. We knew it was pronounced "sanfer" – not "sam-fire", as less fortunate people call it; and we knew you served it with malt vinegar and white pepper, not melted butter like posh people. But we did not know the word came from French *Saint Pierre*, which is short for *herbe de Saint Pierre*, 'Saint Peter's herb' – Peter was the patron saint of fishermen.

My paternal grandparents were city people, and they knew about other foods. One of these was what people elsewhere call *brawn* or *pork cheese*; my American wife calls it *head cheese,* a literal translation of German *Kopfkäse.*

We got it from the butcher's. It consisted of bits of meat from the head and other parts of a pig, in aspic, with onion, pepper and other spices. We would eat it cold with vinegar and mustard. But my Norwich grandparents had a special, very ancient word for it. I do not really know how to spell it. Norfolk has a special vowel which dialect speakers use in words like *church* and *first.* Sidney Grapes couldn't decide how to write it. In the "Boy John" letters he spells *church* both <chuch> and <chatch>, even though it doesn't rhyme with *much* or *match* – it is somewhere in between. My grandparents' word had this vowel, so I'll write it *swad,* even though it doesn't rhyme with *bad* (or *bud* or *pod*).

*Swad* is not in any normal dictionaries, but I did find it in the *English Dialect Dictionary,* spelt <sward>. The *EDD* shows the word as being used all over the North and Midlands of England. The Norfolk variant is cited as *swerd, swad, schwad,* meaning 'the hard, outer rind of bacon'. But there are two subsidiary meanings for Norfolk, from Sydney Cozens-Hardy's 1893 book *Broad Norfolk*: 'a Norfolk dish composed of the rind of pork, seasoned, rolled up tight, boiled and eaten in slices' and 'a kind of brawn, pork-cheese'.

Norfolk people have had this word for 1,500 years; it comes from Anglo-Saxon *sweard,* 'bacon rind', and it obviously goes back to the days when our Germanic ancestors were still living on the continent: the German word is *Schwarte,* and in Dutch it is *zwoerd.* In the West Frisian language of northern Holland, the language which is most closely related to English, the word is *swaard* – which, come to think of it, sounds pretty much like "swad".

---

**BACKGROUND NOTES**

*Samphire,* salicornia europaea, *is a kind of glasswort which grows on the salt marshes of northern Norfolk, as well as in other tidal areas. It is sometimes referred to as "poor man's asparagus".*

*On Sidney Grapes and the "Boy John" letters, see 2.8.*

---

**LINGUISTICS NOTES**

– The extra vowel in the traditional Norfolk dialect is [ɐ], a low central vowel more open than [ɜ]. This gives contrasts such as *tan* /tæn/, *turn* /tɐn/, *ton* /tʌn/. For more on East Anglian short vowels, see Peter Trudgill (2004) "The dialect of East Anglia: phonology", in B. Kortmann & E. Schneider (eds.), *Handbook of Varieties of English,* vol. I, Berlin: Mouton de Gruyter, 163–77.

*cont.*

> – The *sward* part of the poetic word *greensward*, meaning 'grass-covered ground, turf', has the same origin as *swad*: just as bacon rind is a covering layer of skin, so *greensward* is a covering layer of grass.

## 11.5 Isoglosses and swingletrees

I used to have no idea what a *swingletree* was – there wasn't much use for one of those in post-World War II Thorpe – but then dialectology taught me that it is the loose horizontal bar that goes between the cart-horse and the cart.

The *Survey of English Dialects*, in its 1950s research, studied words for *swingletree* in different parts of England, including thirteen Norfolk localities. They discovered that there were getting on for twenty different words for it. In southern Lincolnshire it was *horsetree*. In Suffolk it was *whippletree*. And what about Norfolk? In the far east of the county – Blickling, Ludham, Reedham – there actually was a truly Norfolk word, *hampletree*. But in the centre and west – Docking, Gooderstone, Snoring, Grimston, North Elmham, Shipdham, Outwell – the Lincolnshire term also occurred across the border here as *hoss-tree*. In the south – Ashwellthorpe, Pulham, Garboldisham – speakers were part of a large area including Suffolk and the whole of southeastern England right down to Hampshire which called it a *whippletree*.

It is fascinating to think that between southern and central England there was an isogloss – a dialect boundary – which ran right through the middle of Norfolk, somewhere between Garboldisham and Shipdham. I wonder where it was – somewhere around Great Hockham perhaps?

We can see a similar pattern, with a different boundary line which must run across the A47 at some point, from responses to the *Survey*'s question about words for 'aftermath' in the agricultural sense: "What do you call it when you let the grass grow again for a second crop?" In the northwest – Docking, Grimston, Gooderstone – they said *eddish*, which was shared with Lincolnshire, Leicestershire, Rutland, Huntingdonshire and Cambridge. (Nobody knows where this word comes from, by the way.) But in the rest of the county, people said *second-cut*, which was also the Suffolk term.

There was yet another dialect boundary which crossed Norfolk. The word for an orphaned, bottle-fed lamb was *pet-lamb*, except in the far south – Garboldisham, Pulham and Reedham – where it was *cosset*. This extended into northern Suffolk – Tuddenham and Yoxford – and the northwestern corner of Essex.

It is quite legitimate to talk about "the Norfolk dialect", but we have to understand that it is not a uniform monolith; and it does not suddenly stop at the county boundary. It does, though, necessarily stop at the North Sea coast. My great-great-grandmother came from Somerton, so perhaps I am biased when I reckon it is not surprising if it is the distant eastern *hampletree* part of the county where Norfolk people do most different.

---

**BACKGROUND NOTES**

*The* OED *definition of* swingletree *is: "In a plough, harrow, carriage, etc., a crossbar, pivoted at the middle, to which the traces are fastened, giving freedom of movement to the shoulders of the horse or other draught-animal."*

*Thorpe is the eastern suburb of Norwich where I grew up; see* Themes.

*Garboldisham is pronounced "Garbls'm".*

*The A47 is a west–east main road which starts in Birmingham and travels across England, entering Norfolk by Wisbech and continuing eastward as far as the coast at Yarmouth.*

*Somerton is about 8 miles / 14 km north of Yarmouth, and just over a mile / c. 2 km inland from the east-coast village of Winterton. It is a parish which consists of two villages, East Somerton and West Somerton.*

---

**LINGUISTICS NOTES**

– *Isogloss* is a term from dialectology for a line drawn on a dialect map marking off an area which has one particular variant of a linguistic form from another neighbouring area which has a different variant. An additional term, *isophone*, is available in strict usage for referring to lines drawn between areas which have different phonetic or phonological variants, leaving *isogloss* to refer to lexical differences. In practice, however, most writers use *isogloss* to apply to phonetic, phonological, grammatical *and* lexical boundaries. Well-known isoglosses include the *maken–machen* line in Germany, the *path* /pæθ/–/pa:θ/ line in England, and the *greasy* /s/–/z/ line in the USA. For a fuller discussion of isoglosses and their status, see J. K. Chambers & Peter Trudgill (1998) *Dialectology*, Cambridge University Press.

## 11.6 Local words?

The *EDP* recently published a letter in which the writer wondered, rather regretfully, if there really was any such a thing as a truly Norfolk word.

It depends what you mean, I suppose, but if we are looking for words which are used in Norfolk and nowhere else, then the answer is probably "no". Many of our local words are shared with Suffolk, especially northeastern Suffolk, as well as with the old Essex dialect.

But it also turns out that some of "our" words are also shared with other more distant parts of the country. The *English Dialect Dictionary*, which was published by Oxford University Press between 1898 and 1905, is a remarkable record of nineteenth-century English. It has about 70,000 entries.

Look at what it says about that well-known Norfolk dialect word *mawther*. The *EDD* definition seems entirely correct to us: 'a girl just growing into womanhood, especially a great rough awkward wench; a little girl; an unmarried woman'. But look, too, at one of the examples the dictionary gives: *a gret stawgin' mawther*. What's this word *stawgin*? We do not know what that means in these parts because this example comes from North Yorkshire (where *stawging* apparently means 'simple, foolish, half-witted'). The dictionary also reports that *mawther* was used in Gloucestershire and Wiltshire. Happily, it does cite the usage of *mawther* in East Anglia; but in the 1890s that included Hertfordshire, Cambridgeshire and Essex as well as Norfolk and Suffolk.

And what about that other famous Norfolk word *squit*, beloved of Keith Skipper? The *EDD* gives a definition we can all agree with: 'silly talk, nonsense'; and the examples it cites are familiar to us – *your talk's all squit*. But it is a bit of a shock to see that last example came from . . . Warwickshire; and the dictionary shows the word as being used in Hampshire as well.

Some words we think of as being part of our local dialect were once in much wider use in the country, but their usage has gradually receded geographically under the influence of London-based usage until they have become confined to the more peripheral (even if more important!) parts of England.

But some good news for our correspondent: that good old Dutch/Norfolk word *dwile* 'floorcloth, dishcloth' is listed in the *EDD* as being purely East Anglian. According to the Dictionary, it is found only in Norfolk, Cambridgeshire and Suffolk. Probably that's the best we can hope for.

## LINGUISTIC NOTES

– It is very common for people in England to think of traditional dialects in terms of counties. We talk of the "Yorkshire dialect", the "Lancashire dialect", the "Somerset dialect" and so on. But in modern times county boundaries have not provided any kind of barrier to communication, so there is no reason why dialect boundaries should coincide with county boundaries, and for the most part they do not. (The same is true of American states.) The dialects of the far western Fenland part of Norfolk, for instance, are rather different from those in the rest of the county, while there is no real dialect boundary at all between the dialects of

*cont.*

Norfolk and those of the northeastern Suffolk area around Lowestoft. The biggest dialect boundary of all in England runs right through Yorkshire and Lancashire: this is the so-called Humber–Lune line which starts at the mouth of the River Humber on the east coast of England in Yorkshire and travels in a northwesterly direction until it reaches the west coast by the estuary of the River Lune in Lancashire. It is north of this line, for example, that dialect speakers still pronounce *out, house, cow* as /uːt, huːs, kuː/ "oot, hoose, coo".

– For more on *dwile*, see 1.11 and 1.12.

## 11.7 *Punt* and *quant*

*Quant* is one of our local dialect words. As you will know if you grew up in a Norfolk family – especially in the Fens or the Broads – a *quant* is a long pole for propelling a punt or a wherry; and *to quant* is a verb meaning to push a boat along using a quant.

The *English Dialect Dictionary* shows the word *quant* as occurring only in East Anglia, Kent and Sussex. It gives a number of quotations, including one from the 1890 book *Noah's Ark: A Tale of the Norfolk Broads* by Darley Dale (who was in reality the author Francesca Maria Steele): "The man, seizing the quant, worked away with a will, supplementing the wind by poling her along." Another comes from the 1895 book *Birds, Beasts and Fishes of the Norfolk Broadland* by Peter Henry Emerson, who was an author and photographer specialising in marsh and fen scenes: "If a good quanter goes in after the pike, he will soon 'muddle' him up."

The etymology of *quant* seems to be difficult, but Walter Skeat (1835–1912), who was Professor of Anglo-Saxon at Cambridge and President of the English Dialect Society, had an interesting idea about it. He suggested in his etymological dictionary that *punt* and *quant* might originally have had the same Indo-European origin. *Quant* could go back to Ancient Celtic *quonto*, which was related to Latin *contos* and Ancient Greek *kontos* 'punting-pole'; and that *punt* came from Latin *ponto* 'punt', which was borrowed by the Romans from Gaulish, the pre-Roman Celtic language of France. Skeat reckoned that *ponto* also went back to *quonto*, which is a definite possibility since Ancient Celtic *qu* did change to *p* in Gaulish – as well as in Brittonic Celtic, the ancestor of Welsh, Cornish and Breton. Irish and Scottish Gaelic, which did not undergo this change, are often referred to as "Q-Celtic", while the Brittonic languages are known as "P-Celtic".

The Gaelic word for 'son' is *mac* (with the original *kw* sound represented by *qu* now having changed to the *k* sound represented by *c*), while in mediaeval Welsh 'son' was *map*. Gaelic surnames, of course, often begin with *Mac*; and Welsh names like *Pritchard* come from *Ap-Richard*, where the *ap* derives from *map*.

I would like to think that, back here in Norfolk, our two words *punt* and *quant* were originally the same word. And maybe they really were.

## BACKGROUND NOTES

*The Fens of the far west of Norfolk and neighbouring areas of Cambridgeshire and Lincolnshire are an extensive area of low-lying marshy terrain. The Norfolk Broads form a large wetland area of eastern Norfolk and northeastern Suffolk which has an extensive network of rivers, and associated lakes called "broads". In modern times it has become understood that the broads themselves are the result of the flooding of mediaeval peat diggings.*

## LINGUISTIC NOTES

– The Proto-Celtic word for son was *mak$^w$o-*. The linguistic change /kw/ > /p/ which differentiates between the Goidelic/Gaelic Celtic languages of Ireland and Scotland, on the one hand, and the Brittonic languages Welsh, Cornish and Breton, on the other, is an innovation which is not uncommon in the world's languages. The same change has happened in Rumanian, in some phonological environments: *apă* 'water' comes from Latin *aqua*, and *patru* 'four' comes from Latin *quattor*. The sound change itself involves a form of assimilation, where voiceless velar /k/ followed by voiced bilabial /w/ turns into the voiceless bilabial /p/: the /p/ retains the bilabial place of articulation of /w/ and the voiceless stop manner of articulation of /k/.

# 12 Origins

This section of the book looks at the historical linguistic origins of different types of name associated with East Anglia, and attempts to draw from them conclusions of wider historical and linguistic significance

## 12.1 Anne Boleyn

It is rather well known that French-speaking people do not call our national capital London, they call it *Londres*. It is perhaps not so well known that the Greeks call it *Londino*, the Italians *Londra*, and the Poles *Londyn*. In Albanian it is called *Londer*, in Finnish *Lontoo*, in Lithuanian *Londonas* and, in the original language of this country, Welsh, it is *Llundain*.

There is a common tendency for places which have been of historical importance to have different names in different languages. We call München *Munich*, the Italians call it *Monaco*, the Poles say *Monachium*, and the Czech name is *Mnichov*.

It is not like that for humble settlements, of course. A place such as, say, the Norfolk village of Blickling is not going to be called anything other than Blickling in other languages. And, sadly, even our local capital city has not had foreign-language names in modern times, apart from the Latinised version *Norvic*, though it was formerly called *Noordwijk* in Dutch (Yarmouth was *Jarmuiden*). That is a pity, because having different names in other languages is a sign of fame and distinction.

We ourselves have many English-language names for important centres which are different from their local names: Rome, Athens, Venice, Gothenburg, Florence, Brussels, The Hague, Belgrade, Prague, Lisbon, Cologne, Copenhagen, Naples, Warsaw, Moscow, Vienna are just a few such names. Copenhagen is *København* in the local language, Vienna is *Wien*, Prague is *Praha*, Florence is *Firenze*.

But some of the English names we used to have for important foreign places have been forgotten. The German city of Trier used to be *Treves* in English. We originally called Leipzig *Leipsic*, but most people do not know that anymore. Other names are now in the process of being forgotten. The English for Basel is *Basle* (pronounced "Bahl"), but Ryanair don't seem to know that. It is probably more common to write Lyon than *Lyons* these days. Chania in Crete was *Canea* in English until quite recently. And some Americans talked about *Torino* during that city's winter Olympics because they did not know that the English name is Turin.

And who now remembers that Calais – which was actually part of England for a couple of centuries – and Boulogne used to have English-language names? Calais was called *Callis*. And the English name for Boulogne was *Bullen*.

Bullen is also a surname, of course. This is not a coincidence. The family name is probably derived from the English word for Boulogne. It is also a surname which is much more common in Norfolk than almost anywhere else in Britain; and there is a special resonance for us about this name because of the one very famous Norfolk person, born at Blickling, who bore it – our tragic queen Anne Boleyn.

---

**BACKGROUND NOTES**

*Blickling is a village about 12 miles / 20 kms north of Norwich.*

*Anne Boleyn [Bullen], second wife of Henry VIII, was Queen of England from 1533 until 1536, when she was executed. She was born in Norfolk at Blickling Hall, which had been built by Sir John Fastolf, widely believed to be the prototype for Shakespeare's Falstaff, in the fifteenth century. The present Hall is a seventeenth-century construction on the same site.*

*Calais was under English control from 1347 to 1558 and had representation in the English parliament.*

---

**LINGUISTIC NOTES**

- On Welsh as the original language of the country, see 5.8.
- The local names of the other cities mentioned are Roma, Athina, Venezia, Göteborg, Brussel/Bruxelles, Den Haag, Beograd, Lisboa, Köln, Napoli, Warszawa and Moskva.

## 12.2 Back-formation: Thetford and the Germans

Have you ever wondered what the connection is between Thetford and the Germans? You probably haven't. But there is one.

It is obvious that Thetford is called Thetford because there was a ford there across the River Thet. It is obvious, but it is totally wrong: the naming was the other way round. The River Thet is called the River Thet because there was a ford across it which was in Thetford.

This way of forming river names is called "back-formation". The name of the River Glaven has the same sort of origin. The Glaven is called after the village of Glandford which it flows through, not vice versa. The oldest recorded forms of the name of the village, which lies between Letheringsett and Wiveton, are Glamford and Glanford. Experts think that the original form was probably Gleam-ford, where *gleam* was an Old English word for 'merriment', so it was a 'ford where sports were held'.

Exactly the same thing is true of the River Nar. Narford is not named after the river, the river is named after Narford. The *nar* part of the name meant 'narrow', so it was a ford in a pass or a narrow place. The River Thurne and the River Stiffkey are also named after villages on their banks.

But then the question arises: where does the *thet* bit of Thetford come from? The answer is that the original Anglo-Saxon name for the settlement was Theodford. *Theod* was an Old English word which meant 'people', so Theodford was 'the people's ford'. *Theod* went back to an ancient Proto-Germanic word *thiud*, which also had a related form *thiudiskaz* meaning 'of the people'. That word came down into Old English as *theodisc*, which no longer exists in the modern language. But the corresponding word in Old High German, the name we give to the language which was spoken in central and southern Germany up until about AD 1050, took the form of *diutisc*, which has made it into modern German as *Deutsch*. This word now refers, not just to people generally, but to the German people specifically, and to their language. In English we use the same word, but in the form of *Dutch*, with reference to the closely related language of Holland and northern Belgium, and to the people of the Netherlands.

So the *thet* in Thetford, the *dut* in Dutch and the *deut* in Deutsch were all originally the same word. Strange but true.

And that's the connection between Thetford and the Germans.

| BACKGROUND NOTES |
| --- |
| *The rivers, towns and villages named here are all in the county of Norfolk.* |

**LINGUISTIC NOTES**

– Back-formation is a process whereby a new word is formed by removing an affix, usually a suffix – or something which has been reanalysed as a suffix – from an existing word. A well-known English example of a back-formation is the verb *to burgle*, which is derived from the noun *burglar*. The English verbs *to edit* and *to enthuse* have similarly been formed through back-formation from the nouns *editor* and *enthusiasm*.

## 12.3 Anglo-Saxon dialects: the River Wensum

The river that flows through the middle of Norwich is called the Wensum. It is an interesting name. People sometimes think it is Celtic or Latin, but it actually comes from a good Old English adjective meaning 'winding'. The Anglo-Saxon name was *Wendsum* – 'Wend-some', if you like. Our linguistic ancestors probably started calling it that in about AD 500.

There is a river in Kent with a very similar name: the *Wantsum*. The names are so alike because they are actually the same name: rivers do tend, after all, to wind. And we can explain why the two modern names are not exactly the same – the Old English or Anglo-Saxon names were slightly different too: the Kent river was originally called the *Wandsum* rather than the *Wendsum*.

But why was that? Why were they different?

I wondered if this was a regional dialect difference: naturally there were dialects in Anglo-Saxon Britain, just like there are now; and so I made enquiries (this column frequently consults the world's leading linguistic authorities on your behalf).

We have a good idea of the dialect situation in England from about AD 600 onwards. In Kent, they spoke a dialect called, reasonably enough, Kentish. The other major dialects were Northumbrian, which was, rather obviously, spoken north of the River Humber; Mercian, which was found from south of the Humber down to the River Thames; and West Saxon, which was spoken south of the Thames from Sussex to Dorset. (Devon and Somerset were still not English speaking at that time: they still used the Celtic language Cornish.)

Our counties of Norfolk and Suffolk, then, spoke Mercian. The Mercian dialect was subdivided into four sub-dialects: Mercian proper, which was spoken in the West Midlands; Mid-Anglian, in the East Midlands; East Saxon, in Essex; and East Anglian.

The differences between these ancient dialects has given us some modern place-name differences: *Weald* is the West Saxon form of the Old English word for 'forest', while the name of the Lincolnshire *Wolds* is the same word in the Mercian dialect.

We sadly know very little about our Old East Anglian dialects – there are very few records. We can, though, try and draw conclusions about them from the evidence of place-names, including river names; and this is what the experts confirmed when I consulted them about *Wendsum* versus *Wandsum*. The form *wand*, they reckon, actually was a regional element which was found in Kentish and East Saxon dialects but not in East Anglian, where the corresponding form was *wend*. You can see the same correspondence between *en* and *an* in the name of the Essex village *Vange*, which was originally *Fan-ge*. Here *fan* is the same word that we are more familiar with in the form we use for our *fen* wetlands, as for example in the name of *Fenton*, Cambridgeshire.

Modern dialect maps sometimes show examples of this same kind of pattern of distribution today, where Norfolk and Suffolk have one form and Essex and Kent another. For example, in Kent and Essex, it seems, they *gape* at things, while we might sit on the banks of the Wensum and, if a boat comes by, *garp* at it.

## BACKGROUND NOTES

*The Weald is an area which was once covered by dense forest in Sussex, Hampshire, Kent and Surrey. It lies between two parallel ridges of chalk hills, the North Downs and the South Downs.*

*There are ranges of hills called Wolds in Yorkshire and Lincolnshire, as well as Leicestershire and Nottinghamshire; and the Cotswolds are an area of hills in Gloucestershire, Oxfordshire and neighbouring areas of southern England.*

## LINGUISTIC NOTES

- *Wend* and *wind* come from the same common Germanic root, with *wend* originally being the causative of *wind* 'to cause to wind' (on causatives, see 3.7). The word *wander* is also a related form.
- For more information on Anglo-Saxon dialects, see Thomas Toon (1992) "Old English dialects", in Richard Hogg (ed.), *The Cambridge History of the English Language*, vol. 1, *The beginnings to 1066*, Cambridge University Press, chapter 6.
- The <r> in *garp* is unetymological, i.e. there was never an /r/ sound in the word, which is pronounced /ga:p/. Some other dialects have *gawp*. It is not entirely clear whether *gape* and *garp/gawp* are historically related or not.

## 12.4 Great Snoring

Although it is undoubtedly a very fine place, people have been known to wonder exactly what it is that is so great about Great Snoring.

The answer is that it is exactly the same as what is great about Great Walsingham, Great Dunham and Great Witchingham. And that is exactly the same as what is great about Great Britain. *Great* in English village names simply distinguishes these places from nearby villages called Little Walsingham, Little Dunham and Little Witchingham. The name Great Britain similarly serves to distinguish this country from (Little) Brittany, in France.

The distinguishing element is important. Although outsiders may talk about Great Yarmouth, Norfolk people do not do that. For us it is just Yarmouth, because there is no longer a Little Yarmouth, on the other side of the River Yare, to distinguish it from; that got swallowed up by neighbouring Gorleston long ago.

So there is nothing necessarily "great" in an evaluative sense about Great Cressingham, although it does have a very fine church, or about the Great Ouse river. *Great* in these names simply means 'big', which was the older meaning of the word. We can see this from the fact that the Virgin Mary was said to be "great with child". A *greatcoat* is, presumably, bigger than other coats. And a *great tit* is – I am guessing – larger than other birds of the same name.

The word *great* goes back to an ancient West Germanic form *graut*, which meant something like 'big, tall, thick'. The modern word in Dutch and Afrikaans is *groot*, in Low German *grot*, and in German *gross*. In the language which is most closely related to English, West Frisian, which is spoken just across the North Sea from here in the northern Netherlands, the word is *grut*. All these words simply mean 'large, big', and have none of the positively favourable implications associated with English phrases like "We had a great time", or "She's written a great new book."

The fact that *great* no longer necessarily has any connection with size in English can be seen from the fact that it makes perfectly good sense for us to say "That's a great little painting." You could not say that in German.

But in the Norfolk dialect we can still use the word to mean simply 'big', if we want to. A sighting of a bird rather larger than a great tit sitting on the top of a barn might provoke the statement that "There wuz a gret ol' bud up there."

---

## BACKGROUND NOTES

*I have now been assured by ornithologists that great tits are indeed bigger than blue tits, coal tits and other members of that family. In the USA, the birds of the* Paridae *family which are known elsewhere as* tits *are called* chickadees *or* titmice.
*The towns and villages mentioned here are all in Norfolk.*

---

## LINGUISTIC NOTES

- Sociolinguists assume that the American usage of *chickadee* and *titmouse* has come about for reasons of taboo avoidance – see Peter Trudgill (2000) *Sociolinguistics: An Introduction to Language and Society*, London: Penguin, chapter 1.
- I have written "bird" as *bud*, but the actual pronunciation is with vowel /ɐ/, as mentioned in 11. 4.

---

## 12.5 Westlegate: Franks, Normans, Danes

Next time you are walking down Westlegate in Norwich, you might like to reflect on the fact that there is actually nothing very English about this street name. The *gate* part of Westlegate is Scandinavian in origin, and has not got anything to do with gates. We owe this part of the name to the Old Danish language of the Viking incomers who arrived in East Anglia in the 800s and formed a substantial part of the bilingual population of Norwich in the 900s.

*Gate* was the Scandinavian word for 'street', and it still is. There are streets in many Norwegian towns today called Kirkegate, 'Church Street'. Fiskergata in Stockholm is exactly the same name as Fishergate in Norwich – 'Fishermen's Street'. In Norwich we also have Pottergate, Colegate, Cowgate, Mountergate, Finkelgate. In Thetford we have Eastgate, Minstergate, Nunsgate and Redgate.

The *westle* bit is even more interesting. It comes from the mediaeval Middle English word *wastel*, which meant 'finest white flour'. In mediaeval Norwich, there was a part of the market called the Wastelmarket where this special product was sold.

The word itself came into English from the Anglo-Norman French language of the invaders of 1066, like 40 per cent of the rest of our modern English vocabulary; but the French themselves originally got the word *wastel* from the Germanic language of the Franks who had settled in northern France and who gave the country its name.

In the Old French dialect of Paris, unlike in Anglo-Norman, it was usual for the *w* at the beginning of words borrowed from Frankish to become a *g*, as in *guerre* 'war'. In English we have a few pairs of related words that come from Parisian Old French and Anglo-Norman respectively: *guardian–warden, guarantee–warranty*.

So in Old French the word *wastel* became *gastel*. In Modern French, through processes of regular sound change, *gastel* has become *gâteau* 'cake', which originally would have meant a cake made of the highest-quality white flour. And today we have once again borrowed *wastel* into modern English, this time from modern French in the form of *gateau*, meaning a particular type of layered sponge cake containing thick cream or fruit.

I don't know if they serve gateau in the pub on Westlegate these days. I can't imagine anyone in the old days going up to the bar and demanding "a pinta mild 'n'a slice a chocolate gatoo", but maybe they do now – it would certainly be appropriate if so.

The Scandinavian word *gate* is related to our word *gait*, referring to the way people walk. So you can, if you like, think of Westlegate as meaning 'cake-walk'.

## LINGUISTIC NOTES

- The Norwegian word *gate* is pronounced /gaːtə/.
- Germanic /w/ was borrowed into Old Parisian French, which had no /w/, as /gw/. In Normandy, however, where the originally Scandinavian Old French speakers had only recently shifted from speaking Old Danish, the /w/ was retained unchanged. During the mediaeval French period, Parisian /gw/ became /g/, giving us the modern English /g/–/w/ doublets. The /gw/ > /g/ change was paralleled by the change /kw/ to /k/, as in *qui* /ki/ 'who' from earlier Latin *qui* /kwiː/.

*cont.*

- The changes in French which led from *gastel* to *gâteau* can also be seen to have been operative in modern French *château*, from Old French *chastel* 'castle', where the /s/ has been lost and the /l/ vocalised.
- In French orthography, the circumflex accent, as in *â*, is often used where an original consonant, especially an /s/, has been lost. As a result of compensatory lengthening, *â* originally indicated a long vowel as opposed to the short vowel symbolised by *a*, and in some varieties of French this short–long distinction is still maintained. Compensatory lengthening occurs when, as a result of a sound change, a consonant goes missing and a neighbouring vowel is lengthened to "compensate" for this.

J. TRUDGILL

Westlegate

## 12.6 Mystery etymology: the Great Cockey

An interesting item appeared in this newspaper on 23 October 1894. It was a report that some official's attention "had been called to every cockey in Lakenham that smelt badly".

I think it is safe to say that today, 120 years later, very few people in Lakenham, or anywhere else for that matter, would understand what this report meant. What on earth, they would ask, is a cockey?

The clue is the bad smell. By the time that report was published, the word *cockey*, as used in the Norwich area, had come to mean a drain or sewer. The sad truth is that the word had originally been used to refer to the several no doubt rather pleasant watercourses that flowed though mediaeval Norwich; but over the centuries, these had been used more and more for waste and sewage, and they were eventually covered over and often built on.

The Little Cockey was a stream which started in the area of Chapelfield Gardens and flowed across St Giles, along the line of Willow Lane and Ten Bell Lane, across St Benedicts and down into the river.

The best known of the cockeys was the Great Cockey. It started by the top end of Surrey Street and flowed through the All Saints Green area, across Red Lion Street, along the Back of the Inns, down the line of Little London Street, across Bedford Street, through School Lane and across St Andrews. If you go out to the back of the Playhouse on St George's and walk to the edge of the river, you can look across the Wensum and see that there is still an outflow emerging from under the multi-story car park.

At various points in the history of Norwich, the name Cockey Lane was used to refer to the bottom part of London Street, Back of the Inns and Little London Street.

The word *cockey* seems to be purely a Norfolk and Suffolk word – in the *English Dialect Dictionary* there are no reports from anywhere else – but its origins are obscure. The *ey* bit comes from an Anglo-Saxon word for river, which also occurs in the names of the local rivers Waveney and Wissey. But there is much less certainty about the first part of the word. The Swedish expert on Norwich street names, Professor Karl Inge Sandred, tells us that it could be Celtic, Anglo-Saxon or Scandinavian.

But the honest truth is we don't know.

---

**BACKGROUND NOTES**

*Lakenham was formerly a village on the southwestern edge of Norwich, and is now a part of the city.*

*Note that the names* St Benedicts *and* St Andrews *which I have used here conform to the Norwich practice of not using "Street" in the names of streets derived from the saints' names of parish churches (see also 14.13).*

## LINGUISTIC NOTES

– Some of the possible etymologies which Professor Sandred lists for the first part of this name are: Old English *cocc* 'woodcock'; Celtic *kok* 'hollow, water channel'; Old Norse *kók* 'gullet'.

## 12.7 Trunch

There is an old Norfolk rhyme which goes: *Gimingham, Trimingham, Knapton and Trunch, Nurreps and Surrepps, all in a bunch.* "Nurreps" and "Surreps" are the modern local pronunciations of the village names Northrepps and Southrepps – in the Domesday Book of 1086 they are written *Norreppes* and *Sutrepes*.

Five of these six northeastern Norfolk place-names have very straightforward histories. The endings *ingham* 'home of the people of' and *ton* 'enclosure, settlement' are found in very many Norfolk names; and *repps* comes from an Anglo-Saxon word meaning 'strip of woodland'. But Trunch is mysterious.

We do know that the name appeared in a longer form, *Trunchet*, in the Domesday Book. Professor Ekwall, the great Swedish expert on English place-names, thought that it might very well be a Celtic name. If so, its earliest form would have been *Trun-cet*, where the first part has the same Celtic root as Welsh *trwyn* 'promontory, nose', and the second has the same root as Welsh *coed* 'wood'. (Betws-y-Coed in North Wales is 'prayerhouse-in-the-wood'.) *Truncet* 'wood on a promontory' over time became *Trunchet* in the mouths of Old English speakers, and eventually the *et* was lost.

*Coed* is cognate with the English word *heath*. Cognates are words in different languages which come from the same original source: if someone told you that the Dutch word *moeder* 'mother' and English *mother* are cognates, you would not be even slightly surprised. It is much less obvious that *coed* and *heath* come from the same source – but they do.

The source for these two words was *kait*, which in our ancient ancestral Indo-European language meant 'forest, wasteland'. The relationship between them is obscured because Welsh has retained the original "k" sound from *kait* in *coed*, while English *heath* has "h". It was a characteristic of our parent Germanic language that Indo-European *k* sounds changed to *h*. This is why we have *horn* corresponding to Latin *cornu*, French *corne* (which we have borrowed from French in the form of *cornet*) and Welsh *corn*. Similarly, we have *hound* corresponding to Latin *canis* 'dog' (as in *canine*) and Welsh *ci*. And *hundred* is cognate with Latin *centum* and Welsh *cant*. Taking other regular sound changes into consideration, there is no doubting that *coed* and *heath* are related.

Not far down the road from Trunch, near North Walsham, is Witton Heath. There is a strong probability that the *Heath* in Witton Heath and the *ch* in Trunch were originally the same word.

**BACKGROUND NOTES**

*The* Domesday Book *is a record of the results of the massive survey of England and parts of Wales which was carried out on the orders of King William I, "the Conqueror". It was completed in 1086.*

**LINGUISTIC NOTES**

– The change k > h was part of the First Germanic Sound shift, also referred to as Grimm's Law after the German philologist Jacob Grimm. The shift also involved a number of other linked changes, including the two other stop-to-fricative changes p > f and t > θ. These give English *fish* compared to Latin *piscis*, Welsh *pysgod*; and English *three* corresponding to Latin *tres*, Welsh *tri*. Grimm's Law has a very important place in the history of linguistic science in that it represented the first important systematic description of regular sound correspondences between languages, and paved the way for the rigorous analytical study of linguistic change.

## 12.8 Black Shuck

The word *eschew* is not one that everybody uses, but most readers will know that it means 'to deliberately avoid something', as in *to eschew violence*. *Eschew* is one of the many words which were borrowed into English in mediaeval times from Old French, where the word was *eschiver* 'to shun, avoid, do without'. The modern French word is *esquiver*. The Italian equivalent is *schivare*, which may be the source of the etymologically puzzling word *skive*, as in *skiving off school*.

*Eschiver*, though, was originally a word which arrived in France with the Frankish invaders who gave that country its name. The word came from ancient Germanic *skeukhwaz* meaning 'afraid'. Modern German has *scheuen* 'to fear, shrink from' and *scheuchen* 'to scare off'. The German adjective *scheu* 'timid' is also obviously the same as English *shy*, which came down to us from Anglo-Saxon *sceoh*.

There was also a related Anglo-Saxon word *sceucca* or *scucca*, which referred to a being that was to be feared: *scucca* meant 'devil, demon', and was used in Old English to refer to Satan: *Wæs se scucca him betwux*, literally 'Was the devil them between', so 'The devil was amongst them.'

Unlike the adjective *sceoh* which gives us 'shy', this Anglo-Saxon noun does not appear to have any obvious modern counterpart. But here in East Anglia it does. *Scucca* 'devil' is the source of our word *Shuck*, the name of the spectral dog who we know in these parts as Old Shuck or Black Shuck.

Shuck is the demon hound, the black ghost dog with glowing eyes who patrols our marshes and fens and, especially in coastal areas, our country lanes. His apparition is much to be feared because it signifies that some calamity is about to happen, or perhaps has already happened at the spot where you see him. And "if you touch him he bites you to the bone – you will bear his mark to your dying day".

This tradition of a black spectral dog is found in many parts of northern Europe, but the name Shuck is all our own. The *English Dialect Dictionary* found it only in Norfolk, Suffolk and Cambridgeshire.

The demon dog once killed two people in Bungay Church, leaving scorch marks on the door and causing the tower to collapse. It would seem to be a good idea, if you can, to eschew contact with Shuck.

---

**BACKGROUND NOTES**

To skive *means to avoid doing something you are supposed to do.*

*I have taken the quotation about Shuck, "if you touch him . . . ", from* Suffolk Tales and Other Stories *by Lady Eveline Camilla Gurdon, which was originally published in 1897.*

---

## 12.9 Unthank

Visitors to Norwich often comment on the name of that rather important thoroughfare in our city, Unthank Road. The word *Unthank* seems to strike them as being unusual and even amusing. "Why is it called that?", they ask.

Well, it is a very long story, but it is called *Unthank* for a series of very good reasons. Originally, the road was called *Unthank's Road* – this was the nineteenth-century name – because it ran across land owned by the wealthy local Unthank family. When I was younger, I remember hearing older people talk of their memories of a prominent member of the family they called Colonel Unthank. He was born in Heigham, or "Ham" as we say, but the family originally came from the northeast of England. The first Unthank to make an appearance in Norwich was called William. He was born in 1721 in Northumberland; and it is interesting that the well-known contemporary folk-group *The Unthanks*, led by Rachel Unthank, also come from that part of the world.

But why was William named Unthank in the first place? Like many surnames, Unthank was originally a place-name. In mediaeval times, if a man called John moved from a place in Lincolnshire called Huckerby to go elsewhere, he might then be called "John [from] Huckerby" to distinguish him from other Johns. So we can assume that one of William's ancestors had grown up in a place called Unthank and then left it for somewhere else. There are several little villages called Unthank in England which he could have come from: in Leicestershire, Cumbria, Yorkshire and Derbyshire. But the most likely place in his case is one of two hamlets called Unthank in Northumberland, one near Haltwhistle and the other near Alnham.

But why are these villages called Unthank? It is significant that they are all small, and are often referred to as hamlets. In Anglo-Saxon times they went by the term *Unthanc-es*, which meant more or less what it said. People were living there 'un-thank' – without acknowledging that the place belonged to someone else, so 'without consent'.

Every day when I walk into the city along Unthank Road, I can think that this major Norwich road owes its name ultimately to the fact that, a millennium and a half ago, at a spot somewhere in the Old English kingdom of Northumbria, some people, who were certainly far from being as wealthy as Colonel Unthank, started a squat.

---

## BACKGROUND NOTES

*My selection of the place-name and surname Huckerby here was not made entirely at random: one of Norwich City's best, and best-loved, former footballers is called Darren Huckerby (b. 1976).*

---

## LINGUISTIC NOTES

- For more on the origins of English-language surnames, see 4.11.
- The earliest written usage of *squat* in the meaning of 'the illegal occupation of an uninhabited building (especially by a group of homeless people organized for this purpose); the period of such an occupation' is given by the *Oxford English Dictionary* as dating from 1946.

# 13 Accent rules

This section discusses features of our local accents, together with their history, and the ways in which these features have spread from one accent to another. The section stresses that all accents have their own rules and regularities; and that local pronunciations of particular vowels and consonants should not be considered to be "bad" or "ugly" or "wrong": judgements of this type are always social in origin and have no basis in linguistic fact.

## 13.1 In New England

If you look at a map of New England, the region of the northeastern USA which consists of Connecticut, Maine, Massachusetts, New Hampshire, Rhode Island and Vermont, you can see that people from Norfolk and northern Suffolk must have played a big role in the settlement of the area. New England is full of towns with names like Attleboro, Brandon, Burnham, Framingham, Haverhill, Hingham, Lynn, Newmarket, Norfolk, Norwich, Rockland, Thetford, Walpole, Windham, Wolcott and Yarmouth. Some of these names occur more than once: there is a Windham in New York, a Windham in Vermont and a Windham in Connecticut; and there is a Norwich in Connecticut, and another one in Vermont.

Puritanism was a big thing in seventeenth-century East Anglia, and the Pilgrim Fathers included plenty of migrants who would have been *EDP* readers if there had been such a thing at the time. So you would think, then, wouldn't you, that there would be at least a trace of our local Norfolk and Suffolk dialects in the way people speak over there today, even allowing for the fact that nearly 400 years have passed since the arrival of the *Mayflower* in North America?

There are a number of distinctive features in the speech of the people of eastern New England which distinguish them from other Americans. One of these is a pronunciation which American dialectologists call "the New England short *o*". This refers to a short pronunciation of words like *home*, *stone* and *road* which is not found anywhere else in the USA. Americans represent this pronunciation by writing 'hum', 'stun', 'rud'.

Don't you think this sounds rather like something you can hear any day walking around Norwich market? People with truly local accents in our part of the world also pronounce *home*, *stone* and *road* with a short vowel. In the Norfolk accent, *stone* may have the same short *oo* vowel as *stood*, and *comb* the same vowel as in *could*. *Boat* can rhyme with *put*; *coke* can be pronounced the same as *cook*; *whole* often rhymes with *full*; and *toad* may rhyme with *good*. *Suppose* is generally "spoozz" and *only* is "oonny". The short *oo* sound is particularly common in the word *home* – a perfectly normal answer to the question "Where've you been all day?" is "T'oom!" The Hippodrome Theatre in Norwich, which was pulled down in 1964 and replaced with the St Giles multi-storey car park, was always called the Hippadroom. My grandmother called the aerodrome near where she lived "the Droom". And our local poet John Kett, in his lament "The Tawny Owl", uses a typical Norfolk rhyme:

> No more you 'oon't fly up an' down this road,
> No more you 'oon't go in an' out the wood.

The "East Anglian short *o*" is quite old. The Rev. Robert Forby, writing about the Norfolk dialect of the late 1700s, said that the letter *o* "has also in some words the common short sound of the diphthong oo (in foot), or that of the vowel u in pull e.g. bone–stone–whole". The short *o*, then, was already in existence in Norfolk when the first English colonists left for America, and I reckon this pronunciation of *home*, *stone* and *road* crossed the Atlantic to New England, from Norfolk and Suffolk, along with all those place-names. No doubt the sailors on the *Mayflower* called their vessel, in the nautical manner, a ship. But perhaps there were also some Puritan landlubbers from – Wymondham maybe – who spent the nine weeks of their stormy crossing referring to the *Mayflower* as "the boott".

## BACKGROUND NOTES

*The American place-names in the first paragraph are all also found in northern East Anglia, though sometimes with different spellings, such as* Attleborough *rather than* Attleboro, *and* Walcott *rather than* Wolcott. Wymondham *in Norfolk is pronounced as if it was spelt* Windham.

## LINGUISTIC NOTES

– In the dialects of Norfolk and Suffolk, words such as *home, stone, road, boat* are pronounced with the vowel of FOOT: /hʊm, stʊn, rʊd, bʊt/. This does not occur in the case of words like *go, so* because short vowels such as /ʊ/ cannot occur in open syllables, i.e. syllables which do not end in a consonant. (This is a phonotactic fact about English – for the term *phonotactics*, see 8.4.) It does not occur either in words such as *known, towed*, which have a different Middle English source, as explained below in 13.3.

## 13.2 The nineteenth vowel

When I first went to school, we were taught that English has five vowels: *a, e, i, o, u*. This was not very helpful: even if the teacher was just referring to letters, she was forgetting about the *y* in words like *very, tryst* and *rhythm*. But as far as vowel sounds themselves are concerned, English has very many more than five. One of the difficulties of English spelling is caused by the fact that we try and use these six letters to represent more than three times that number of sounds.

In my Norfolk accent, I have nineteen vowels: the sounds in *bid, bed, bad, put, but, pot, bee, bay, buy, boy, lewd, load, low, loud, beard, bird, bard, board*. This is not necessarily the same number that people from outside Norfolk would have – we pronounce *beard* and *bared* the same, other people don't. On the other hand, *load* and *low* have different vowels for us. An old-fashioned posh BBC accent has twenty-one vowels; many Scots have only fourteen.

Even in Norfolk there are differences. I pronounce *are* and *hour* the same; other people pronounce them differently and so have an extra vowel in words like *hour* and *flour*. Older speakers who pronounce *daze* ("dairz") and *days* differently also have an additional vowel.

If you are good at arithmetic, you will have noticed that I said I have nineteen vowels, but my list only has eighteen. The nineteenth vowel, the one I did not give an example for, is the most frequent and most important vowel in our language. There is no obvious single way of writing it. Take *vanilla*. This word has three syllables. The middle one has the same vowel as *bid*. But what about the first and last syllables? This is my nineteenth vowel. We can perhaps write it "uh" – "vuh-nill-uh". Linguists call it *shwa*, from the name of a letter in the Hebrew alphabet.

You can see how frequent it is if you take a perfectly ordinary phrase like *On the ball City – never mind the danger*. This has eleven vowels, but four of them are "uh": the second vowel in *never* and *danger*, and the vowels in the two *the*'s.

In Norfolk we "do different" by using this vowel even more frequently than other people. We pronounce words like *David* and *naked* as "Dayvuhd, naykuhd" rather than "Dayvidd, naykidd". Older dialect speakers say *very* as "verruh" and *money* as "munnuh". We pronounce *Lowestoft* as "Low-stuhff", not "Lowess-tofft". *Have you got any money?* has three shwas: "Ha' yuh got nuh munnuh?"

We are world champions at shwa.

### BACKGROUND NOTES

*"On the ball City – never mind the danger" is the first line of the song sung by Norwich City football club supporters. "On the Ball City" is said to be the oldest football song anywhere in the world; and the abbreviation, OTBC, is a well-known slogan amongst Norwich supporters.*

**LINGUISTIC NOTES**

– *Beard* and *bared* are both pronounced /bɛːd/ in the Norfolk accent (see 13.4). For *load* versus *low*, see 13.3. *Are* versus *our* for those who pronounce them differently is /aː/ versus /ɑː/. In the older dialect, *daze* and *days* are respectively /dɛːz/ and /dæiz/. Some of the pronunciations cited above with shwa [ə] are: *naked* /næikəd/, *very* /vɛrə/, *Lowestoft* /lʌustəf/. *Have you got any money* is [hæjə gɑʔ nə mʌnə]?

## 13.3 Snow joke: when puns don't work

You can tell that some of the editors at the *EDP* do not have local accents. It is easy to see that from the punning headlines they come up with. The newspaper recently ran a nice series of articles on the long, hard winter of 1962–3, with photographs that brought back memories to me of walking to school because buses could not get up Kett's Hill.

One of the pieces had the headline "White-out was snow joke". For most people that is quite amusing, I suppose, but if you have a Norfolk accent, it does not work. It is not a pun. "Was no joke" and "was snow joke" do not sound at all the same, the way I say them. *No* and the *snow* do not rhyme.

For people with real Norfolk accents, there are lots of pairs of words which are not the same even though people elsewhere say them identically. We "do different". We have two different "long o" sounds. Take pairs like *moan–mown*, *nose–knows*, *road–rowed*, *sole–soul*, *Flo–flow*, *doe–dough*, *so–sew*, *toe–tow*. For us, they are different. That is because, originally, all English speakers pronounced them differently; and that is why they are spelt differently: one set with *ow* or *ou*, the other set with *oa* or *o_e*. Modern English spelling is a good representation of mediaeval English pronunciation. That headline would not have been a pun for Shakespeare either.

During the last 400 years, in most of the English-speaking world the distinction between those two vowel sounds has been lost. Not by us, though. We proudly maintain a difference which goes way back into the ancient history of our language.

In my accent, and yours too if you speak like me, we have preserved a difference between two vowels that dates from the very beginning of the English language, 1,500 years ago. I am quite pleased about that. Sadly, nowadays this does not necessarily apply to all of the younger people in Norfolk anymore. Maybe, after you and me and Shakespeare managing to preserve this venerable distinction for many hundreds of years, we are going to be members of one of the last generations to keep it alive.

In the meantime, puns like the Beatles' *Rubber Soul*, and respellings like *Baby Gro* and *donut*, don't work for me. It took me a very long time, as a child, to work out what *IOU* meant. And there is a clothing repair and alteration shop in the city, obviously run by people without local accents, called "Sew Fast". Shakespeare would not have got that either.

## BACKGROUND NOTES

*The county of Norfolk is not at all flat, as some people think. Kett's Hill leads up from the old boundary of the city of Norwich on the River Wensum towards the eastern suburbs of the city. It is well over 100 yards/metres long and has a rather steep gradient of 12 per cent (1 in 8), though it is not nearly as steep as it used to be: some levelling work was carried out in the 1960s to make it easier for buses to get up the hill.*

## LINGUISTIC NOTES

– The two different mediaeval vowels were Middle English ǭ̣̄ and ou, /ɔː/ and /ɔu/. The modern pronunciations in Norwich are approximately /uː/ and /ʌu/: *moan* /muːn/, *mown* /mʌun/. In my speech, *moan* is pronounced the same as *moon*, but it does not rhyme with *rune*, which has a central vowel: /rʉːn/. For details, see Peter Trudgill (2004) "The dialect of East Anglia: phonology", in B. Kortmann & E. Schneider (eds.), *Handbook of Varieties of English*, vol. I, Berlin: Mouton de Gruyter, 163–77.
– Hyperdialectisms (see 9.7) often occur when outsiders attempt to copy the local accent, for instance in the pronunciation of *grow* as */gruː/ rather than the correct /grʌu/.

## 13.4 Hair it is!

In Christchurch in New Zealand, there is a hairdresser's – I hope it is still there, after the terrible earthquake – with a sign outside announcing "Hair It Is!" Here – or should I say hair – in Norfolk, we understand what is going on in this advert. In NZ, words like *here* and *hair*, *beer* and *bare*, *fear* and *fare* are pronounced the same, which is why the hairdresser could come up with this pun.

The *EDP* sub-editors could use puns like this too, but I don't think they do – perhaps they are not from Norfolk – because we do not make a difference between words such as *really* and *rarely*, *dear* and *dare*, *peer* and *pair* either. We used to, just as the Kiwis did; but in the last century and a half or so – it is more recent in New Zealand – we have, as linguists say, merged the two originally different vowels. We have merged them on the vowel of *hair*, so we say "hair and there". The Kiwis have gone the other way and say "here and theer".

There is nothing surprising about two vowels merging; it happens all the time. Pairs of words like *meet* and *meat*, *see* and *sea*, *teem* and *team* used to be pronounced differently – Shakespeare would have done that – which is why they have different spellings. Mergers are not good or bad, they just happen. In this part of the world we have not merged *moan* and *mown* like most English speakers have (see 13.3), but that does not make us better than them. And the fact that we have merged *beer* and *bear*, while they have not, does not make us worse than them either.

This interesting innovation in Norfolk English is one which has also taken place quite independently in New Zealand and other places, such as Newfoundland. There is no surprise about this. The vowels of *here* and *hair* are both rather infrequent, and the difference between them is therefore relatively unimportant. It is very hard to think of a situation where the merger could lead to misunderstanding. If a Kiwi says "I'm going to get my here cut", no one will misunderstand. And if I say "Norwich City are rarely good", you should be able to tell from my tone of voice what I mean.

**BACKGROUND NOTES**

*The* earthquake *I refer to here hit the Christchurch region in February 2011 and caused very significant damage in which 185 people died.*

**LINGUISTIC NOTES**

- A number of vocalic (vowel) mergers are discussed in this book. Mergers are a well-known feature of linguistic change: as we have noted before, a merger is a sound change in which two vowels or consonants collapse into one. The vowel of English *see, meet, teem* used to be, as /eː/, distinct from the vowel of *sea, meat, team*, which was /ɛː/, but now they have become merged as a single vowel /iː/. It might be thought that mergers are hard to account for, because the whole point of a vowel is to be different from all other vowels; but in fact in a language like English, which has a very large number of vowels, the language can work very well with one vowel less. Ancient Greek had twenty-four different vowels. Modern Greek has only five, with the vowel /i/ being derived from as many as seven different Ancient Greek vowels, as the result of mergers.
- In Norfolk, *really* and *rarely* are both pronounced /rɛːliː/.

## 13.5 Norwich rules

All languages have rules – and I do not mean foolish rules invented by self-appointed "experts", like "You must not end a sentence with a preposition." (If someone tells you that, the only correct response is: "Why not?")

What I am referring to are the real linguistic rules that we are all clever enough to acquire as small children without realising it. No one ever told you there was an English rule that adjectives come before nouns – by the time you got to school you knew that already, without knowing you knew it. You had also worked out why the negative of *I will* is *I will not*, but the negative of *I sing* isn't *I sing not*. (To know exactly how this rule works, ask a foreigner who had to learn it in English lessons at school.)

There are pronunciation rules too. Think of how to achieve the true Norwich pronunciation of the name of the local school named after the seventeenth-century Norwich benefactor Mordecai Hewett. The first thing to notice is that you have to omit the "y" sound after the *h* in "hyoo-wit". In Norfolk we pronounce *view* as "voo" and *music* as "moosic" – this is called "yod-dropping" – so you have to say "hoo-wit".

You also have to drop the "h", as city people do. This will give you "oo-wit". But then you have to be sure, too, not to pronounce the second syllable of Hewett like *it*. Unlike Londoners, Norfolk people pronounce *roses* and *Rosa's* the same – "roz-uhz", with the unstressed vowel linguists call *shwa* (see 13.2). So you have to say "oo-wuht", not "oo-witt". *Hewett School* rhymes with *do at school*.

And finally there comes the most important Norwich rule: it's the same rule that sees *Heigham* pronounced "Ham". One Christmas, years ago, when I was working as a temporary postman, I noticed a lot of cards going to the bakery on Unthank Road which were not addressed to *Sewells* but *Searles*. In Norwich these words sound the same. The rule is that if a long "oo" vowel, like in *soon*, comes before an unstressed "uh" vowel – as in *do it* – then they combine to give an "ur" vowel instead. So *do it* and *dirt* are pronounced the same. *Sewer* and *sir* sound the same too. *Chewing* is the same as *churn*; and *pure* is the identical with *purr*. In linguistics we call this rule "smoothing".

So Jake Humphrey, and lots of other good Norwich people, went to the "Urt" School – and by the way, don't forget to pronounce the *t* as a glottal stop.

### BACKGROUND NOTES

*Jake Humphrey (b. 1978), who grew up in the Norwich area, is a television journalist and presenter, best known for covering sporting events.*

## LINGUISTIC NOTES

- I must apologise to North American, Irish, Scottish and other rhotic-accented readers – that is, they actually pronounce an /r/ in words like *car* and *cart* – for writing "Urt" when there is no /r/ in the pronunciation.
- The phonological rules outlined above give the local pronunciation of *Hewett* via the following stages: /hjʉːɪt > hʉːɪt > ʉːɪt > ʉːət > ɜːt > ɜːʔ/. The terms "yod-dropping" and "smoothing" are due to J. C. Wells – see his 1982 book *Accents of English*, Cambridge University Press. *Yod* is another name for the sound [j]. Smoothing refers to the *reduction* of a long vowel or diphthong followed by a [ə] to a long mono-phthong, as in *tower* /taʉə/ > /taː/, *Heigham* /hæiəm/ > /hæːm/. For the full details of East Anglian smoothing, see Peter Trudgill (2014) "The dialect of East Anglia: phonology", in B. Kortmann & E. Schneider (eds.), *Handbook of Varieties of English*, vol. I, Berlin: Mouton de Gruyter, 163–77.

## 13.6 Advanced Norwich

We have already had a number of lessons in this column on how to talk Correct Norwich, for people who are unfortunate enough not to know already. In Lesson 1, we studied the pronunciation of words such as *Hewitt* – "Urt", and *Sewell* – "Searle" (see above, 13.5). There was also a bonus unit on how this rule carries over into more complex words such as *do it*, which should be pronounced, as you will remember, "dirt".

In Correct Norwich Lesson 2, we discussed the important rule which concerns the pronunciation of *here* as *hair*, *beer* as *bare*, *cheer* as *chair* (see 13.4). Most students seemed to pick up on that quite nicely, so we think the class is now ready to move on, in Lesson 3 (Correct Norwich, Advanced), to two closely related but more difficult extensions of that same rule.

The first extension concerns cases where the need to apply the rule is not indicated so obviously in the spelling, since the words involved have no letter *r*. We will begin with a little test. Consider the word *vehicle*. Is your mastery of the rule good enough to work out how to achieve the right pronunciation of this item?

Well done if you got the right answer – which is "vaircle". And what about *leotard*? "Lairtard". And *creosote*? "Crairsoot". Good!

Now let's see if you can perform the operation in reverse. Please identify the following words – the examiners provide clues to help you: "pairnist" (a keyboard instrumentalist); "pairny" (a flower); "Bairtrice" (a woman's name); "K'rairn" (citizen of an Asian country). OK? We hope you didn't find that too disagrairble.

And now, to complete the lesson, we come to those even more difficult situations where the rule has to apply across the boundary between one word and another. This means that *hair* has three possible interpretations. It can mean not just 'hair' and 'here', as we've seen, but also 'he have' – as in *hair gone* (which is another way of saying *he in't hair no more*). Other similar two-word sequences are *be a*, which should be articulated "bair": *Doon't bair nuisance*. And *see her*, as in the question *Are you going to see her?*, which should be said "Are you gawta sair?" (the form "gawta" will be the subject of a later, equally advanced lesson).

We were hoping today that we would be able to get all of you through this advanced part of the course successfully. And now I reckon wair dunnet.

## LINGUISTIC NOTES

– The pronunciations indicated above are *vehicle* [vɛːkʔl̩], *leotard* [lɛːtaːd], *creosote* [krɛːsuːʔ], *pianist* [pɛːnəst], *peony* [pɛːniː], *Beatrice* [bɛːʔrəs], *Korean* [kərɛːn]. *He a' gone*, a reduced form of *he have gone*, is pronounced /hèː gán/. *Don't be a nuisance* is /dɒnʔ bɛː nuːsəns/; *are you going to see her?* is /aː juː gɔːʔə sɛː/; and *we have done it* /wɛː dʌn əʔ/. I must again apologise to readers such as Americans and Scots who have rhotic accents for using spellings such as <air> to represent /ɛː/, but it works for non-rhotic readers, who are the mainstay of the *EDP* readership, and I do not believe there is any other way of doing it using non-phonetic script.

## 13.7 Ugly?

A correspondent has written to the *EDP* asserting that the Norwich pronunciation of the word *twenty* is ugly.

I would like to assert that the Norwich pronunciation of the word *twenty* is not ugly, but I don't think I'll bother. I mean – where would that get us? Beauty is in the eye – or ear – of the beholder. One person's ugly is another person's not-ugly.

But it is really interesting to wonder where that "ugly" judgement comes from. The correspondent obviously has some problem with the vowels and consonants which make up our local rendering of this word, but I can't for the life of me think what it is.

In words like *plenty* and *twenty*, 320 million American and Canadian speakers typically use a pronunciation which merges the *t* with the *n*, to give something like "plenny, twenny". They do the same thing with words like *hunter* and *winter* = "hunner, winner".

In Norwich, the process goes the other way, so that the *n* is merged with the *t*, giving "pletty, twetty". The phrase *didn't he* is subject to the same procedure: *He played very well, ditty?*

Then, in the Norwich accent, after the *n* and the *t* have been merged as *t*, another pronunciation rule clicks in: a *t* between two vowels is pronounced as a glottal stop (see also 8.6), as in *better, city* = "be'er, ci'y". So this rule gives us "ple'y, twe'y, di'y".

These pronunciations are the result of complex, sophisticated, rule-governed articulation habits. But what is it about the pronunciation that could possibly be ugly? The way Norwich people say it, *twenty* rhymes with *jetty*. Is *jetty* an ugly word? Or *petty*? Surely not.

Perhaps it is the glottal stop which is aesthetically displeasing? But that is rather difficult to comprehend, too. The vast majority of people in England and Scotland, not least *EDP* readers, use glottal stops in their everyday pronunciation of English. I would not mind betting that you have a glottal stop before the *l* in the words *atlas* and *Scotland*. If you listen carefully, you will hear that you use one before the *k* in *weeks* as well. Does that sound ugly? Well, as I say, I do not find it so. But if you do, well, you do.

I think we might be the only people in the English-speaking world to pronounce *twenty* as "twe'y". If that is the case, I am rather proud of it. Pi'y not everyone is.

## LINGUISTIC NOTES

– The pronunciations indicated above are *twenty* [twɛʔiː], *didn't he?* [dɪʔiː], *better* [bɛʔə], *city* [sɪʔiː], *atlas* [æʔləs], *Scotland* [skɒʔlənd], *weeks* [wiːʔks].

# 14 Respecting names

There has been considerable in-migration from other parts of England to the Norfolk area in the last few decades. The incomers make for greater diversity; but they also make for less social cohesion, as well as for decreasing amounts of common knowledge about local culture, history and language on the part of the local population. One consequence of this is increasing amounts of ignorance, confusion and disagreement about local place-names. This section is an attempt to make a small contribution to solving this problem.

## 14.1 Changes vs mistakes

Some people tell me they are puzzled about my stance on language change. On the one hand, I am fascinated by current sound changes, like the two *th* sounds merging with *f* and *v* in "fing" and "bovver", and I do not disapprove of them. On the other hand, I am against changes in local place-names like pronouncing Heigham, a part of Norwich, as "High-um" instead of the correct "Hay-um".

My position is easy to explain. The transformation of *th* is a natural, spontaneous sound change. The disappearance of *k* before *n* in all English words like *know* and *Knapton*, which started in the sixteenth century, was a natural sound change. The change in all Anglo-Saxon words like *cu* and *nu* to Modern English *cow* and *now*, which took many centuries, was a natural sound change.

These changes were part of natural linguistic evolution: the sounds of all languages change gradually over time. This mostly happens without anybody noticing, and certainly without anyone intending it; and all instances of a given sound are affected, without exception. Why? Well, languages are just like that.

Sound change is a powerful, inherent, unstoppable feature of human languages. If you could hear Chaucer speaking, you would barely recognise it as English. His version of *When April with its sweet showers* was *Whan that Aprill with his shoures soote*, but it sounded like "Hwan that Ahprill with hiss shoo-ress sawta".

Sound change is part of what gives us different dialects and, ultimately, different languages. If it was not for change, English and German would still be the same language. Even Welsh and Bengali would be the same language: they were 6,000 years ago.

Wrongly changing an individual name from, say, Heigham to "High-um" has got nothing to do with natural sound change. It is simply people guessing from the spelling how an unfamiliar name is pronounced and getting it wrong. When people wrongly say my name as "Trudge-ill", I understand why – the spelling is ambiguous. But when I tell them what the correct pronunciation is, I expect them to use it – it is my name, after all.

Twelve hundred years ago, Heigham was *Heccham*, pronounced "Hetch-ham". Our modern "Hay-um" came about through natural sound changes which occurred gradually over many centuries. Any twenty-first-century change to "High-um" would be the sudden result of conscious but faulty decision-making by people from outside Norwich, encountering this particular name in writing before hearing it, guessing how to say it, and getting it wrong.

But we won't let that happen.

## LINGUISTIC NOTES

- Heigham is correctly pronounced /heɪəm/. In the local dialect, this is often [hæ:m] (see 13.5 on "smoothing").
- Anglo-Saxon *cu, nu* were pronounced /ku:, nu:/.
- In fourteenth-century pronunciation, *Whan that Aprill with his shoures soote*, the first line of the General Prologue to Chaucer's *Canterbury Tales*, was approximately /hwan θat a:prɪl wɪθ hís ʃu:rəs so:tə/.
- "All instances of a given sound are affected, without exception" is a reference to the *Ausnahmslosigkeit der Lautgesetze*, or "the regularity of sound laws" (see 3.2).

## 14.2 Spelling pronunciations: Aylsham and Walsham

Education did not become compulsory in England until 1880, and then only for 5–10-year-olds. Authors like Arnold Bennett and H. G. Wells did not start writing for general mass consumption until about 1900, because it was only then that there were enough people who could read for pleasure; and we did not get to a situation where nearly all adults could read until well into the twentieth century.

It is interesting that this widespread literacy then began having an effect on the English language itself. It was not a very major effect, but from the 1920s onwards it did start having an influence on the way people pronounced certain words. This is because there began to be a rise in what linguists call "spelling pronunciations". Because of the hostile attitude in this country to local ways of speaking, people had been made to feel uneasy about their own natural speech, so if they did not feel entirely sure about how they "ought" to pronounce a particular word, they might change their natural pronunciation to one which seemed more like the spelling, to be on the safe side.

This did not happen with very common words – no one started pronouncing the *g* in *night* – but other words were changed, first by people who were particularly linguistically insecure, and then gradually by everybody else. In 1920, nobody pronounced *handkerchief* like we do today; everyone used to say "hankercha". No one used to pronounce *waistcoat* as "waist-coat"; the normal pronunciation was "weskit". And *forehead* was not "fore-head" but "forrid".

Americans, because of their greater insecurity – after all, a majority of them descend from people who were not English speakers – are even worse at this than we are. They pronounce the *l* in *salmon*. And Irish people say *Anthony* with a "th" sound instead of a "t".

Here in East Anglia we are not immune to spelling pronunciations either. Lots of people now say "Low-ess-toft" when the real pronunciation is "Lowst'ff"; "Norritch" for Norwich instead of "Norridge"; and "Ail-sh'm" for Aylsham, when it should be "Elsh'm" – which is what I have always said, although I must confess that I am wrong too. The proper pronunciation is "Elss'm". The original Old English name was *Ægel's ham*, where *Ægel* was a man's name, and *ham* was the same as the modern word *home*, and meant 'homestead'. So the *s* and the *h* were in different words and were not pronounced "sh". The same is true of North Walsham. My Granny always called it "Wals'm". She was right.

| BACKGROUND NOTES |
|---|
| *Aylsham and North Walsham are both small market towns, 9 miles / 15kms and 15 miles / 24 kms respectively north of Norwich.* |

## LINGUISTIC NOTES

– The spelling pronunciation of place-names is of course by no means confined to Norfolk. It occurs all over England, and is enormously common in the case of those English place-names which have been transferred to the United States: the name of the town of Norfolk in the USA is pronounced /nɔːrfoʊk/ rather than /nɔːfək/, as the name of the English county is pronounced.

## 14.3 Folk etymology: *aspirin, willows* and *Salhouse*

Norfolk was one of the very first places where English was ever spoken, so English-language place-names in Norfolk are very old. And they all tell a story. Some of these stories are not obvious. Weybourne meant 'felon stream': a criminal (the Old

English word, now forgotten, was *wearg*) might be executed there in the stream (or *burn*). Some are more transparent: Blakeney was the 'black isle'. Cley is where the soil was composed of clay. Salthouse is where they used to store salt.

But what about Salhouse? What did they store there? The answer is: nothing. The *house* in Salhouse has nothing to do with a house. The way we spell Salhouse today is due to what linguists call "folk etymology". People have a tendency to try and make sense of words which do not make sense. *Belfry* comes from the Old French word *berfrei* which meant 'watchtower'. This was not known to most English people, who thought of it instead as the place in a tower where the bells were. *Crayfish* comes from Old French *crevis*, but people wanted to make sense of that and, well, it is sort of a fish.

The spelling of Salhouse came about because people no longer understood the original name, which was Sallows. *Sallow* was the ancient name for a kind of willow tree, so Sallows just meant 'place with willow trees'. Salford, now part of Manchester, has the same origin: 'a ford where there are willows'.

The word *sallow* is related to the Latin word *salix*, which is the source of the chemical term *salicylic acid*, which is what aspirins are made of. Aspirin is, or was originally, made from willow bark.

When Sallows no longer meant anything to people, writing the second part of the word as *house* made it seem a bit more transparent. But nowadays something else is happening. Because of the spelling, some people are even beginning to pronounce the name like that too: "Sal-house". That is not the right way to say it: it should be "Sallas". That is what the old people always used to say, even though they had no idea that a thousand years ago it had meant 'the place of the willows'.

If you are inclined to say "Sal-house", you might think of how important aspirin is to us and try to say "Sallas" instead, in honour of our Anglo-Saxon ancestors and their willow trees.

---

**BACKGROUND NOTES**

*Salhouse is a village 6 miles / 10 kms east of Norwich. Weybourne, Blakeney and Salthouse are all on the north Norfolk coast*

---

**LINGUISTIC NOTES**

- A good example of folk etymology in Norwich is the name Tombland (the name is pronounced with the stress on the second syllable) – which was the site of the Anglian-Danish market place in pre-Norman Norwich. *Tombland* comes from Old Danish *tom-land*, where *tom* meant 'empty', as it still does in the modern Scandinavian languages. The *b* in the modern spelling was introduced as a result of the loss of knowledge of what the word *tom* meant and its reinterpretation as having a connection with the well-known English word *tomb*.

Tombland Alley

## 14.4 The BBC Pronunciation Unit

Ever since the 1920s the BBC has had, under various names, a Pronunciation Unit. It has been their job to advise announcers on how to pronounce particular words: new words, foreign words, surnames, place-names. However, they realised early on that members of the general public might also like to receive information of that sort; and in the 1920s and 1930s they published word-lists to help people in this way, in the *Radio Times*, for instance.

More recently they have worked on and produced the authoritative *BBC Pronunciation Dictionary of British Names*, published by Oxford University Press. I have got the second edition: it gives place-names, river names and surnames. It must be useful for foreigners to know that, surprisingly, Thames is pronounced "Temz"; and it tells you that Wymondham (Norfolk) is "Wind'm", and Cholmondeley is "Chumly". They have even got Trudgill in there (with the hard *g*, of course) – so it must be a good book!

I do wonder, though, what has happened to the copy of this important BBC reference work which must surely be on the shelves of the BBC Radio Norfolk studios in the Forum in Norwich. Has anyone there looked at it lately? I really rather doubt it, which is a pity because the dictionary is the result of many years of research, and was specifically designed for BBC broadcasters.

One reason for my doubt is that the dictionary says very clearly, on page 155, that Lowestoft has two syllables: "low", as in *low*; followed by "stofft" or "st'fft" or "st'ff". "Lowst'ff" is the most local pronunciation, but the dictionary also gives the two other choices. What it does not list is a pronunciation with three syllables: "Low-ess-tofft", but we keep hearing this in local traffic reports and sports reports.

The dictionary also tells BBC announcers how to say Sprowston – with the same vowel as in Lowestoft; but have our local BBC presenters looked at page 228 to check up on this? And it also gives Heigham as "Hay-um" (page 116).

It is the official policy of the British Broadcasting Corporation that "for British personal names and titles, the BBC uses the pronunciation adopted by the individual concerned. For British place-names, the BBC follows local educated usage."

So have a look at the dictionary please, together – and if you've lost your Radio Norfolk copy, we'll have a whip round and get you another one.

---

**BACKGROUND NOTES**

*The* Radio Times *is the weekly BBC publication which contains, amongst other things, UK TV and radio listings.*

---

**LINGUISTIC NOTES**

- On the BBC Pronunciation unit, see Jürg Schwyter (2016) *Dictating to the Mob: The History of the BBC Advisory Committee on Spoken English*, Cambridge University Press.

## 14.5 Misinterpretation and Cley-next-the-Sea

Everyone knows that there is a village on the north Norfolk coast called Cley. But does everyone know how to say the name? A reader wrote a letter a little while ago to the *EDP* suggesting that the correct pronunciation is "Clay", and that only posh outsiders say "Cly".

That reader was right.

It is true that the Cley website says "Cly"; and the owners of the "Cley Spy" bird-watching equipment business clearly also think like that. But there is much more evidence in favour of "Clay". Think of the spelling: *obey, grey, prey, they, whey*. This suggests that the owners of the pottery "Made in Cley" are the right-thinking ones

All English place-names meant something to our Anglo-Saxon ancestors. The original Old English name was Clæg, which quite simply meant 'clay'. The village was named 1,500 years ago because of its clayey soil. *Clæg* gives us modern English *clay*, just as Old English *dæg* gives us modern *day*. There are many other place-names in England which come from *clæg*: Claybrooke (Leicestershire), Claydon (Suffolk), Claygate (Surrey), Clayhanger (Cheshire). In every case, the modern pronunciation has "clay", not "cly". Mediaeval documents also show the name as Claya; and I have seen a sixteenth-century map where the name is spelt Clay.

I never heard it called "Cly" until the 1960s, when I noticed this pronunciation from "posh" people, visiting birdwatchers; and I reckon the pronunciation was first introduced in the early 1900s by wildfowlers. When these outsiders first started coming to Norfolk, they heard people saying "Clay" in a Norfolk dialect they were not familiar with. The vowel sound in our accent was very different from what they were used to – think of Her Majesty saying *day* – and they interpreted it as being a long *i* rather than a long *a*. To them, a Norfolk person saying *day* sounded like their own way of saying *die*. They wrongly interpreted "Clay" as "Cly".

The most telling argument for me comes from my family. My uncle was born in Cley in 1911, and quite naturally my grandmother was there at the time. She was born in the 1880s, and came from many generations of North Norfolk stock. She always said "Clay". She was not the sort of person to worry about what was "right", and there was no reason for her to call it "Clay" except that that was what it was called. She called Cley "Clay" because that was what it had always been called, going back countless generations to her Anglo-Saxon forbears.

What my Granny said is good enough for me.

**BACKGROUND NOTES**

*The new pronunciation could have been introduced earlier than I have suggested here: the railways arrived in Sheringham, 8 miles / 13 kms from Cley, in 1877; and in Holt, 5 miles / 9 kms from Cley, in 1883.*

*Some* experts *believe that in the case of Cley, Anglo-Saxon* clæg *is more likely to have referred to mud than to clay.*

**LINGUISTIC NOTES**

- To RP speakers, the Norfolk pronunciation [klæi] would have sounded more like RP [klaɪ] than RP [kleɪ]. Further confusion would have been caused by the fact that most words with RP [eɪ] had Norfolk [ɛː], e.g. *name* [nɛːm], the local dialect having preserved the Middle English distinction between *ai* as in *main* and *ā* as in *mane*.
- The Anglo-Saxon digraph <æ> represented a vowel with a quality around [æ]. In Old English, *clæg* was pronounced [klæɣ] or [klæj].

## 14.6 In-migration and spirited debates

When I was growing up in Norwich in the 1940s and 1950s, the population of Norfolk had remained fairly stable, at around 500,000, for over a century. Then, suddenly, in the 1960s, it started expanding, and by 1970 it had reached 620,000. In 1980 the county's population was 700,000; by 2000 it was 800,000; and now it is climbing towards 900,000.

A large proportion of this increase is due to in-migration: English people moving into Norfolk from elsewhere. This has had one important consequence for Norfolk place-names and their pronunciations: disagreement.

David Clayton, the excellent head of our BBC Radio Norfolk, has been kind enough to discuss with me the "spirited debates" about pronunciations that have been aired on Radio Norfolk. These discussions are all to the good; but they are a sign of the times.

In the 1950s, there were no such debates. There was nothing to debate. Everybody agreed about the pronunciation of place-names. The vast majority of families in Norfolk had lived here for generations, and been exposed to local traditions about names all their lives. There was absolutely nothing to discuss. If any outsider looking for Guist turned up and asked the way to "Gwist", we would just put them right, and that would be that.

When I was at the CNS (the City of Norwich School) in the 1950s, of the 950 boys at the school, 949 pronounced Sprowston with the "low" vowel. The odd one out was a boy who had arrived in Norfolk from Wembley at the age of 12 and delighted in saying it with the "now" vowel just to tease the rest of us.

Some places did have humorous nicknames – like "Hin-doll" for Hindolveston. And some place-names had a formal pronunciation for posh occasions, like "Shering'm", and informal ones for everyday use, like "Sher'n'm". But that was all.

There were a few exceptions, like Hunstanton and Cley, where local pronunciation traditions had been under attack since the railways started bringing holiday-makers to the seaside and wildfowlers to the marshes.

Nowadays, though, there are large numbers of people in Norfolk who were not born here, or were born here to originally non-local families, and who have not been fortunate enough to be exposed to local naming traditions. So the debates that are now going on are about local, traditional, correct pronunciations versus newer, mistaken, spelling-based versions.

I have already explained why Cley is correctly pronounced Clay. Stand by now for spirited debates about Sprowston and Hunstanton.

---

**BACKGROUND NOTES**

Guist *rhymes with* sliced.

---

## 14.7 Sprowston and Old English vowels

Sprowston, just outside Norwich, was called *Sprowestuna* by its Old English-speaking settlers. The name meant 'Sprow's tūn': *Sprow* was a man's name, and *tūn* – pronounced "toon" – meant an enclosure. Sproughton in Suffolk has the same origin – in the 1100s it was written Sproeston – and so does Sproston in Cheshire.

*Tūn* has given us our modern word *town*, as a result of regular sound changes which have occurred over the last millennium. The corresponding German word *Zaun* means 'fence'; and the Dutch version, *tuin*, means 'garden'.

That Anglo-Saxon man's name, *Sprow*, tells linguistic scientists all we need to know to state, categorically, that the modern pronunciation of Sprowston ought to be with the vowel of *low* – not of *now*.

Everybody in Norwich used to know that. When I was a child in the 1940s and 1950s, I never heard anybody pronounce it any other way. Over the last five decades, however, there has been a tendency for some people to use a non-traditional pronunciation with the "now" vowel. Large numbers of people have moved in from outside; they have guessed at the pronunciation from the spelling, and they have guessed wrong.

A thousand years ago, *ow* was the Anglo-Saxon way of representing a diphthong very like the modern vowel in *low* – it has come down into modern Norfolk English almost unchanged. In Old English, 'to grow' was *growan*, 'to flow' was *flowan* and 'to row a boat' was *rowan*.

But words which in modern English have the *now* vowel were not spelt like that at all, because they were pronounced very differently. One of these words was, as just discussed, *tūn* – modern *town*. *Cow* was spelt *cū*, pronounced "koo"; *now* was *nū*, pronounced "noo". If that man's name had been *Sprū*, then the correct pronunciation of Sprowston today would be with the *now* vowel. But it wasn't. And it isn't.

The pronunciation of Sprowston with the *now* sound is wrong. It is a mistake. It is not a surprising mistake because, unlike Old English, modern English spelling is ambiguous. This is not a problem with *ow* words generally, because we learn to say them as children before we can read. But with place-names, it is problematical because they are not part of everyday vocabulary except for locals; so with high in-migration, errors creep in because of spelling ambiguity.

But there is nothing ambiguous about older Norfolk people's desire to have the traditional, centuries-old pronunciations of places in our county respected. We would like to have our place-names back, please.

## LINGUISTIC NOTES

– German <z> as in *Zaun* represents /ts/. This /ts/ corresponds to the /t/ of English and Dutch (and Scandinavian) as a result of the Second Germanic Sound Shift, which took place in southern and central Germany, starting around AD 400. As part of this sound shift, the word-initial plosives /p/ and /t/ became the affricates /pf/ and /ts/.

## 14.8 Hunstanton: twelve hundred years of linguistic change

There are lots of place-names in the *EDP* distribution area which look from the spelling as if they have three or four syllables, but are actually correctly pronounced with only two. The most famous are Costessey ("Cossey"), Happisburgh ("Haze-bruh") and Wymondham ("Wind'm"). But there are many more: Tacolneston ("Tacklest'n") and Lowestoft ("Lowst'ff") are just two of them.

Other Norfolk place-names have lost their two-syllable status in recent times, as people who were not local enough to know the right pronunciation have been increasingly influenced by the spelling. Wiveton has already succumbed – it used to be "Wiff'n". And Letheringsett has now gone to having four syllables – I was going to write "gone back to", but that would not have been correct: within living memory people called it "Larns'tt", but that had descended from the mediaeval three-syllable form "Laringset".

One place that is currently fighting to preserve its two-syllable name, in the face of the current tendency towards longer spelling pronunciations, is our famous Norfolk west-coast resort town Hunstanton. Wikipedia gives its pronunciation as "Hunston", and so does the *Oxford Dictionary of English Place-names*. And they are right.

But other people are getting it wrong and calling it "Hun-STAN-t'n". We can understand why they do that – it is because they have been influenced by the written form. But, happily, lots of Norfolk people are still calling it "Hunst'n", and we understand why they do that too – it's because that's what it's called! There could, after all, be no other reason for pronouncing it in that way.

It is true that, in the distant past, Hunstanton did originally have three syllables. Twelve hundred years ago, it was called *Hunstans-tūn*, meaning 'the homestead of Hunstan'. *Hunstan* was a man's name – it also occurs in Hunstanworth in Durham. But through natural processes of sound change, this three-syllable pronunciation eventually and quite naturally acquired a more reduced form, "Hunst'nt'n", which was later further reduced to "Hunst'n". Even that must have happened long ago, though, since there is an English family name Hunston which derives from the name of the town.

But notice that, even if the three-syllable form had survived naturally into modern times, it would most certainly not have come down to us as "Hun-STAN-ton" – that is a modern mistake. If you did feel inclined to try and preserve the authentic old three-syllable pronunciation, the way you should say it is "HUN-st'n-t'n".

> **BACKGROUND NOTES**
>
> *The surname Hunston may also derive from places called Hunston in Suffolk and Sussex.*

## 14.9 Ipsidge: a terrible lesson

There is a terrible lesson to be learnt by people here in Norfolk from the example of Ipswich. I do not mean from the town itself – it is a fine place, after all. And I do not even mean from the football club, though of course there are things to be said about that. What I mean is that there is a salutary lesson to be learnt from the name of Ipswich itself. The awful truth about Ipswich is that it used to be known as "Ipsidge". That was how the name was pronounced for hundreds of years, until quite recently – perhaps three or four generations ago. Then, outsiders who did not know how to say the name thought they knew better than the locals, and started calling it "Ipp-switch"; and they did that so frequently and for so long and on such a large scale that the locals eventually gave in.

We do not want that to happen to Norwich, do we! There are already several towns in America called "Nor-witch", so we have to be alert.

When Americans say "Lye-cester", we smile benignly and tell them it's "Lester". We should do the same for Norfolk names, and not just with Americans. We now have so many outsiders here who, through no fault of their own, get things wrong. We ought to do them the kindness of putting them right. It might be difficult to smile benignly if they pay no attention because they think they know best. But most incomers actually do want to get things right, and we can help them.

The first thing we can do is to gently point out to people that – this can be an important slogan for us – "there is no itch in Norwich". The right way to say Norwich is so that it rhymes with *porridge*, as in the nursery rhyme "The man in the moon came down too soon . . . ". If you remember, he asked the way to Norwich and burnt his mouth on cold pease-porridge. This "idge" pronunciation is quite normal for "wich" place-names in England. Harwich and Greenwich also end in "idge". And Swanage used to be spelt Swanwich.

## 14.10 Heigham: the role of the media

An article I wrote mentioning the mispronunciation of local place-names seems to have struck a chord, judging from reactions I have received. I suggested that it was one thing to have BBC Radio Norfolk presenters who did not have local accents; but another thing altogether if they did not know, and did not bother to find out, what local streets, suburbs and villages were really called.

I remember it all starting, way back in 1959, when the BBC originally began to broadcast local news on TV. The very first evening, the news bulletin contained an item about Acle. The newsreader, who came from somewhere in the northeast of England, pronounced it "Ackley" instead of "Aykle".

But the problem has worsened recently, as more and more refugees from the Home Counties have moved into Norfolk. They can't be blamed for not knowing how to say things, of course, but it would be nice if they would listen to us and find out – or just ask.

Take Heigham.

Heigham used to be a village just west of the Norwich city wall. The heart of the parish lay on the site of an ancient Anglo-Saxon settlement on the south bank of the River Wensum, north of the Dereham Road, but it eventually stretched as far south as The Avenues and Newmarket Street. It is here that we find Heigham Street, Heigham Watering, Heigham Road, Heigham Grove, Heigham Park and Heigham Park School. And we also have our very own Baroness Hollis of Heigham.

Everyone in Norwich knows that Heigham is pronounced "Hay-um". Or at least everyone used to know that. But some people who have moved into Norfolk recently do not seem to have acquired this knowledge, even though you would think the spelling might at least suggest the possibility: consider *weigh, eight, sleigh, freight, neigh, neighbour, inveigh*. Some of these incomers have even acquired jobs as broadcasters on local radio – Radio Norfolk and Radio Broadland – without taking the elementary precaution of informing themselves about how to pronounce local names.

They call Heigham "High-um".

Some people have suggested that this might actually be the right way of saying it because the name is derived from *high-ham*. But it isn't. As you will know if you have ever cycled up Grapes Hill, there is nothing high about Heigham. It is one of the lowest parts of the city, which was why it was so badly affected in the 1912 floods, as we have recently seen from the old photographs in the *EDP*. The name actually comes Anglo-Saxon *hecc-ham*, where *ham* was the Anglo-Saxon word for 'home, homestead, village' and *hecc* was a sluice – which makes good sense for a settlement by the banks of the Wensum.

When Americans say "Wor-cester", we smile indulgently and tell them it's "Wooster". So we can do the same with Heigham. If you hear someone saying "High-um", please do gently correct them. I know it will be difficult to smile indulgently if they pay no attention because they think they know best, but most incomers do want to get things right. We should try and be protective about our local names because, if we don't, nobody else will.

The truly local pronunciation of Heigham is actually "Ham" or' "'Am". That is our way of saying "Hay-um" – the Norwich accent works like that: *playing* is "plan" and *say it* is "sat".

But as far as broadcasters are concerned, let's just say to them: we do not actually expect you to say "Ham" – it probably would not sound right anyway, unless you have a local accent. But there is nothing difficult about saying "Hay-um", is there? Could you try? Please?

---

## BACKGROUND NOTES

*The Home Counties are the English counties in the area immediately around London: Essex, Kent, Surrey, Berkshire, Buckinghamshire and Hertfordshire. Sussex is also often included in the list.*

*Baroness Hollis of Heigham: Patricia Hollis is a Labour party member of the British House of Lords. She was Lecturer and then Reader at the University of East Anglia from 1967 until 1990.*

## LINGUISTIC NOTES

– For smoothing, as in *playing* pronounced [plæn], see 13.5.

## 14.11 Clay, Lowstof and the £15,000 map

Some months ago, we saw in the *EDP* that a rare first edition set of playing cards was sold at Sotheby's in London for £15,000. This greatly surprised the auctioneers, who were expecting no more than £4,000. The cards were drawn and produced by a famous London cartographer and bookseller called Robert Morden, and published by him in 1676, which was during the reign of King Charles II.

The interesting thing for us was that each of the cards in the pack presented a map of a particular English county. The card which had the map of Norfolk on it was the five of hearts: the *EDP* kindly reproduced a picture of it to accompany their article. One important thing about the playing cards was that, as Sotheby's had announced, for many counties these cards were the first ever maps to actually show any roads. On our map, you can see the Norwich–Cromer road, the Norwich–Thetford road and the Fakenham–Lynn road, among a number of others. The main rivers are also portrayed.

The maps also showed what were, at the time, each county's most important towns, and it is interesting to see what they were in Norfolk – Morden based this aspect of his maps on information received from local informants in each county. Norwich, Lynn, Dereham, Swaffham and Yarmouth are there of course. But Cley, which was a major port at that time, is also shown on the map, and so is Worstead, as an important producer of textiles. Towns just over the border into neighbouring counties are also shown: Wisbech, Brandon, Bungay, Beccles and Lowestoft.

Wisbech is given as *Wisbich* on the map, and Beccles appears as *Beckles*. A number of the other spellings are also very interesting. It is clear that Morden's informants used spellings which represented the way in which the place-names were actually pronounced at the time. Wymondham is spelt *Windham*, which makes very good sense to us; and so does Aylsham as *Alesham*. Worstead is *Wursted*, Lynn is *Lyn* and Diss is *Dis*.

There is also important material here for people who are interested in the correct pronunciation of those local place-names which there has been a certain amount of uncertainty about in recent years. It is good for people who favour our traditional local pronunciations to see that, three and a half centuries ago, Lowestoft was spelt *Lowstof*, and that Cley was spelt *Clay*. That is, of course, how these names should still be pronounced today.

> **BACKGROUND NOTES**
>
> *The locations of the places listed here are given on the map on p. xvii.*
>
> *The village of Worstead was a mediaeval centre for textile production and has given its name to the woollen fabric worsted.*
>
> *On Cley as a port, see the next article, 14.12.*

## 14.12 Nowhere

My grandfather, George Gooch, was born in Wiveton. So was my mother. That is probably why, unlike most children in Norwich, I was brought up with the knowledge that there was something just a little bit mysterious about Wiveton bridge.

Wiveton used to be located on the western edge of what was, until a few centuries ago, the broad estuary of the River Glaven. Clay, as it was spelt in those days, lay across from it on the eastern bank. John Wright, writing in the *Glaven Historian*, the excellent magazine produced by the Blakeney Area Historical Society, tells us that in the old days, tidal sea water reached inland right as far as Glandford Mill. And there were actually two channels of the Glaven between Clay and Wiveton, with something like an island in the middle.

Right up until the early mediaeval period, there was no way to get across the estuary, except at very low tide, until you got as far upstream as Glandford. But then bridges were built. The – very old – bridge we now have in Wiveton, which crossed the western branch of the Glaven, was built in the 1300s, replacing one which had been constructed a few decades earlier. And there also used to be another, wooden, bridge across the eastern branch from Clay.

Being situated on either side of this estuary meant that Wiveton and Clay were, like Blakeney, rather important harbours, which brought the villages considerable wealth. But then in the seventeenth century the embankment which now carries the coast road from Blakeney to Cley was constructed, and the estuary gradually silted up.

There is nothing mysterious about any of this to the historians of the Blakeney area. But there is this one mysterious thing which I came to learn about and ponder in my childhood: there is a special name for the area under Wiveton bridge – for the space between the bottom of the bridge and the water. The name might perhaps have to do with the fact that the Glaven has historically marked the boundary between the parishes of Cley and Wiveton. But nobody really seems to know where the name comes from – please let me know if you do! And, in particular, nobody seems to know why on earth an area under a bridge should have a name at all anyway. Why would it?

But it does. The area under Wiveton bridge is called "Nowhere".

---

**BACKGROUND NOTES**

*For more on the name of Cley/Clay, see above, 14.5.*

*After this article was published in the newspaper, I received a number of helpful comments and suggestions. One was that the parish boundary between Wiveton and Cley was never drawn along the line of the relevant branch of the Glaven. Another was that originally it was the bridge itself which was called "the bridge to nowhere", perhaps because at a certain period it led to nowhere except the island.*

## 14.13 Tuning in to the way we speak

I was about 18 years old before I realised that there was street in Norwich called "Gentlemans Walk". When you have grown up in a city you do not go around looking at street signs, and nobody ever called it anything except "The Walk". That is still pretty true. If you come across the name "Gentleman's Walk", that is either going to be the *EDP* or the *Eastern Evening News* on their best linguistic behaviour, or a newcomer to the city who has not tuned in to the way we speak yet. If you want to sound like a Norwich person – and why wouldn't you? – you can forget the "Gentleman's" bit.

You can also notice that there is something special in Norwich about the names of streets derived from churches and parishes using the word *Saint*. St Stephen's Street is never called that: it is always called just "St Stephens". The same is true of *St Augustiness, St Benedicts, St Andrews, St Georges, St Giles*. The only exceptions I can think of are *St Vedast Street*, which is generally called "Vedast Street", and *St Peters Street*, which everybody calls "in front of the City Hall". This rule does not apply to Roads – you have to say "St Stephens Road" – or Lanes. (But remember that we say the *Faiths* in St Faiths Lane so that it rhymes with "bathes"; this is also true of the villages with this name outside Norwich just to the north of the airport.)

And then of course there's Thorpe Station. This is what people who have not tuned in to us yet refer to as "Norwich station", "the railway station" or, if they're under 40, "the train station" (see 3.6). Until the 1980s, we had to call it Thorpe Station because there were other railway stations in Norwich. City Station was where Barker Street now is. You can see remains of it by the path along the river from the Barn Road – St Crispin's Road roundabout. Victoria Station was where Victoria House is today, by the junction of St Stephens Road and Queens Road: the old railway line is the route of the Lakenham Way footpath. City Station was closed in the 1960s, and Victoria Station in the 1980s, so we don't need the "Thorpe" part of the name any longer. But it has been in use for over 130 years, and we really can't think of any particular reason to change it.

## 14.14 What we call it

We keep hearing these days about a place called Thorpe St Andrew. I wonder where it is. I was born and grew up in a part of Norwich called Thorpe. Strictly speaking, it was not part of Norwich, but we thought of it as if it was. We never said we were going to Norwich; we always just went "down the city". And, strictly speaking, it was not called Thorpe either. Our postal address was Thorpe-next-Norwich. But we always called it Thorpe, and we still do.

There is also another mysterious place we keep hearing about called Great Yarmouth. Well, all right, yes, I am being disingenuous. I know perfectly well that that is the place Norfolk people call Yarmouth. But the *Great* is totally unnecessary. The town used to be called that because in the very old days there was also a Little Yarmouth, on the other side of the river. But that is now part of Gorleston, and so saying Yarmouth is not even slightly confusing (see 12.4).

I was also a bit alarmed recently by a sign I saw in the city pointing the way to Norwich Anglican Cathedral – until I realised that this was simply the structure which has been known to Norwich people for over nine hundred years as the Cathedral. There is also another new place called St John's Roman Catholic Cathedral, but lots of Norwich people will not know what you mean unless you just say the Catholic Church.

On this same theme, some people have actually started saying John Lewis, but most of us, including the people who work in the department store, still call it Bonds. And somebody somewhere decided to try and rechristen Jarrolds as Jarrold, but this has made absolutely no headway at all, and the older and more beautiful part of the shop is still adorned with the real name.

Renaming the City Hall as City Hall, without the *the*, does seem to have had some success, even though this is based on a misunderstanding of American English. When Americans say City Hall, they don't mean the building, they mean the politicians inside it.

But I am afraid there's absolutely no chance that the Norwich and Peterborough Stand will ever catch on at Carrow Road. Norwich City fans are naturally grateful for commercial sponsorship, but it seems unlikely that the boys in the Barclay will ever start chanting "Sing up, the Norwich and Peterborough!" It's the River End, isn't it.

## BACKGROUND NOTES

*The River End is, unsurprisingly, the end of the Carrow Road football ground which is next to the River Wensum. The Barclay Stand is at the opposite end of the ground. The fans in the Barclay Stand, who are rather less sedate than those at the other end, do from time to time chant "Sing up, the River End!" if they think the fans there are not making enough noise.*

Erpingham Gate, Norwich Cathedral

## 14.15 Northwic

You might never have wondered why Norwich is called Norwich, but it is actually an interesting question, not least because the answer is not entirely clear.

The oldest Old English form of the name of our capital city was *North-wic*. The *wic* part was an Anglo-Saxon word meaning 'a dwelling-place, farm, hamlet, village, or town'. It was a word which the Germanic peoples had borrowed very early on from the Romans, from Latin *vicus* 'village, farm-house'. That much is clear.

But what about the *north* part. Why was it called that? North, yes – but north of what? The Swedish place-name expert Professor Eilert Ekwall thought that it might be because Norwich had a northerly position in East Anglia, and specifically because it was north of the other major settlements of Dunwich and Ipswich.

Other scholars, however, including the Swedish scholar who was an expert specifically on Norfolk place-names, Professor Karl Inge Sandred, believe that there is a more local explanation. According to researchers, there were four original Anglo-Saxon settlements on the banks of the River Wensum: these were, many of them think, Westwic, Conesford, Coslany and Northwic.

Westwic was south of the river, in the region where Westwick Street now is. Conesford was to the east of Westwick. The name meant 'King's Ford' – in Old English it was *Cynings-ford*. No one is absolutely sure where the ford was, but it might well have been where Bishop Bridge is now. Coslany was across the river north of Westwic – we still have Coslany Street and Coslany Bridge. And Northwic lay east and north of Coslany. Because of the angle of the river, it was also the northernmost of the settlements, and so it was called 'north' for the same reason that Westwic was called 'west'.

Northwic probably became the largest of the settlements because it was located on the banks of the Wensum at its highest navigable point, and in the area where the two major roads intersected: the north–south road along the route of King Street–Magdalen Street; and the east–west road along the route of St Benedicts–Bishopgate, with the main gathering place being the market on the site of Tombland. Eventually, because of its greater importance, the Northwic name was extended to cover the whole settlement as the four areas expanded and fused into one.

And that, it seems, may well be the true story of why Norwich is called Norwich.

# Postscript

This is the column which was published in the *Eastern Daily Press* on 23 June 2012, in response to an anti-Norfolk dialect column which had been published the previous week. It was to lead to further, shorter contributions on dialect matters which evolved into my weekly column.

It is amazing how often people who do not know anything at all about language still feel free to pontificate about it in public. Language professionals like me – I have been a university teacher of linguistics for forty years – are constantly being surprised by these pontificators – people like Ken Hurst. But Ken's column – where he tells Norfolk people that "the sooner we give up this dialect the better it will be" – is a particularly surprising example.

And not just surprising. Telling Norfolk people how we ought to speak seems like arrogance to me, especially when you start from a position of profound linguistic ignorance. And when I say ignorance, I do mean ignorance. Look at what Ken says: "There's an argument to be had", he reckons, about accent and dialect. No there isn't! Any first-year linguistics student will tell you that accent is about pronunciation, while dialect is about grammar and vocabulary as well as pronunciation. There is nothing to argue about.

And "you see", Ken writes patronisingly, "regional dialects are a bit yesterday". No, they are not. And never will be. Dialects do change through time, but it is not true that "the day of regional dialects is done". Even if you started with a total absence of regionally distinctive speech, dialects would develop – this is happening in Australia right now. Everybody in the world gives away some information about their regional origins as soon as they start speaking. It is true that there is a very small group of people in this country – people educated at Eton and the other public schools, including the ones who are running the country at the moment – who do not betray anything about their origins except that they are from England and upper class, but this is very unusual on a worldwide scale.

Ken also seems to think that "regional speech serves to accentuate narrow economic horizons". You are wrong again, Ken. The European countries where regional dialects are most strongly favoured, nurtured and promoted are Norway, Switzerland and Luxembourg. In Norway, people speak their local dialect all the time, whether they are giving a speech in parliament, lecturing at a university, or commenting on a football match. In German-speaking Switzerland and in

Luxembourg, most people speak their local dialect all the time too – even politicians taking part in *Newsnight*-type discussions on TV. And do you know what the three richest countries in Europe are? Norway, Switzerland and Luxembourg. Luxembourg is the richest country in the world and Norway is second, in terms of per capita GNP. So perhaps what we need in this country is more local dialect, not less – the non-dialect-speaking people who are running things right now do not seem to be making too good a job of it.

Over the last fifty years, we have managed to do quite a lot in the way of removing the bigotry associated with racism, sexism and homophobia from our society. We have not entirely got rid of it. But at least it is no longer respectable in this country to be seen to discriminate against somebody on the grounds of their race, gender or sexual orientation. Sadly, what Ken Hurst illustrates very vividly is the dismal truth that we have made very little progress in getting rid of the bigotry associated with linguicism – yes, that is a real word, just as the prejudices it refers to are only too real.

And in case you think "bigotry" is too strong a word, just look at what Ken has written on the subject of regional dialects in the country's biggest-selling regional morning newspaper. He describes the speech of people here in Norfolk – people like me who he knew were likely to read his column – as "mangled language". He delights in descriptions suggesting that we "jabber". And he says that "thank goodness" he does not have a local accent himself. I think we can assume that, when Ken tells us to get rid of our way of speaking, he reckons we should all speak like him instead – he certainly seems to believe that he knows how English "should be spoken".

Ken also seems to think that getting rid of the local dialect would make our region a more "open-minded", forward-looking place. But Ken himself is a very poor advert for this idea. We have a tradition here in Norwich of being pretty open-minded about most things – we even let people like Ken write in our newspapers. But if I want to go to a place which is even more open-minded and forward-looking, I will go to Norway, where they believe that an open society is characterised by tolerance of other people's ways, including their ways of speaking, and where Ken's column would never have been written because everyone would have found such views ridiculous. What could be more close-minded and backward than denigrating and ridiculing people for the way they speak?

All dialects are equally complex and expressive and valid as ways of speaking. If Ken does not like our dialect, that tells us nothing about our dialect – what it does is tell us about Ken. Happily, Ken is totally without influence over the way future generations of Norfolk people are going to speak. A distinctive way of speaking English in Norfolk is not going to disappear. Don't you worry, together.

# Index